LONGMAN LINGUISTICS LIBRARY

HISTORY OF LINGUISTICS VOLUME I

LONGMAN LINGUISTICS LIBRARY

General editors
R. H. Robins, University of London
Martin Harris, University of Manchester
Geoffrey Horrocks, University of Cambridge

A Short History of Linguistics
Third Edition
R. H. ROBINS

Text and Context
Exploration in the Semantics and Pragmatics of Discourse
TEUN A. VAN DIJK

Introduction to Text Linguistics
ROBERT-ALAIN DE BEAUGRANDE AND WOLFGANG ULRICH DRESSLER

Psycholinguistics
Language, Mind, and World
DANNY D. STEINBERG

Principles of Pragmatics
GEOFFREY N. LEECH

Generative Grammar
GEOFFREY HORROCKS

The English Verb
Second Edition
F. R. PALMER

A History of American English
J. L. DILLARD

English Historical Syntax
Verbal Constructions
DAVID DENISON

Pidgin and Creole Languages
SUZANNE ROMAINE

Historical Linguistics
Problems and Perspectives
EDITED BY C. JONES

Aspects in the English Verb
Process and Result in Language
YISHAI TOBIN

The Meaning of Syntax
A Study in the Adjectives of English
CONNOR FERRIS

General Linguistics
An Introductory Survey
Fourth Edition
R. H. ROBINS

A History of English Phonology
CHARLES JONES

Generative and Non-linear Phonology
JACQUES DURAND

Modality and the English Modals
Second Edition
F. R. PALMER

Semiotics and Linguistics
YISHAI TOBIN

Multilingualism in the British Isles I: the Older Mother Tongues and Europe
EDITED BY SAFDER ALLADINA AND VIV EDWARDS

Multilingualism in the British Isles II: Africa, Asia and the Middle East
EDITED BY SAFDER ALLADINA AND VIV EDWARDS

Dialects of English
Studies in Grammatical Variation
EDITED BY PETER TRUDGILL AND J. K. CHAMBERS

Introduction to Bilingualism
CHARLOTTE HOFFMANN

Verb and Noun Number in English
A functional explanation
WALLIS REID

English in Africa
JOSEF S. SCHMIED

Linguistic Theory
The Discourse of Fundamental Works
ROBERT DE BEAUGRANDE

Aspect in the English Verb
Process and Result in Language
YISHAI TOBIN

History of Linguistics
Volume I: The Eastern Traditions of Linguistics
Volume II: Classical and Medieval Liguistics
GIULIO LEPSCHY

History of Linguistics

Volume I: The Eastern Traditions of Linguistics

edited by Giulio Lepschy

LONGMAN
LONDON AND NEW YORK

Longman Group UK Limited
Longman House, Burnt Mill,
Harlow, Essex CM20 2JE, England
and Associated Companies throughout the world

Published in the United States of America
by Longman Publishing, New York

English translation first published 1994
Chapter 5 translated by Emma Sansone

ISBN 0–582–094–887 CSD
ISBN 0–582–094–895 PPR

British Library Cataloguing-in-Publication Data

A catalogue record for this book is
available from the British Library

Library of Congress Cataloging-in-Publication Data
Storia della linguistica. English.
History of linguistics / edited by Giulio Lepschy.
p. cm.
Includes bibliographical references and index.
Contents: v. 1. The eastern traditions and linguistics — v. 2. Classical and medieval linguistics.
ISBN 0–582–09488–7
1. Linguistics—History. I. Lepschy, Giulio C. II. Title.
P61.S7513 1994
410′.9—dc20 93–31169
CIP

Set by 15M in 10/11 pt Times
Produced by Longman Singapore Publishers (Pte) Ltd.
Printed in Singapore

Contents

Introduction

This work originated in the discussions held by a group of advisors for linguistics of the Italian publishers il Mulino. Examining the areas in which new and useful initiatives could be encouraged, it was thought that a large-scale history of linguistics would meet a widely felt need, and I was asked to elaborate a plan for such a work. The preparation and completion of the project took about ten years, and the work, written by scholars from different countries, began appearing in Italian in 1990. This English edition has been reorganized into four volumes. In this introduction I shall say something about the nature and contents of this work, and its place within the present panorama of linguistic historiography.

What I had in mind was a history of linguistic thought, rather than an account of the development of linguistic science. In other words, for different societies and in different periods, I wanted to have a presentation of the prevailing attitudes towards language: its social, cultural, religious and liturgical functions, the prestige attached to different varieties, the cultivation of a standard, the place of language in education, the elaboration of lexical and grammatical descriptions, the knowledge of foreign idioms, the status of interpreters and translators, and so on.

This implies of course a 'view from within', that is, presenting the linguistic interests and assumptions of individual cultures in their own terms, without trying to transpose and reshape them into the context of our ideas of what the scientific study of language ought to be. The purpose is an understanding of what certain societies thought about language, rather than an assessment of their ideas on a scale of scientific progress.

The problem is familiar to historians of science and the line I am following does not necessarily imply a lack of confidence in the possibility of obtaining reliable findings in linguistic study. Whether 'science' is the most suitable term for what linguistics does, is of course open to debate: see Chomsky (1969, 56) and Graffi (1991b). In any case, the authors of different chapters were also encouraged not to enlarge on methodological problems posed by linguistic historiography but to concentrate instead on the presentation of facts, on the interpretation of texts which they considered relevant and interesting for the periods and cultures they were discussing. But, after obtaining the agreement of my authors concerning the general aims, I left them completely free to organize their chapters as they thought fit, without trying to impose a unifying format, because I thought that differences of perspective and treatment would contribute to highlighting specific features of individual traditions. For instance, the chapters on Indian and Arabic concentrate on the elaboration of grammatical analysis, in both cases an important contribution of these civilizations, whereas the Hebrew chapter places more stress on the theological, mystical and philosophical context of Jewish reflections on language.

The content of the four volumes of the English edition is as follows: Volume I includes the ancient traditions, each of which develops in a manner which is, from a viewpoint both cultural and chronological, largely independent, apart from obvious connections, like those between Arabic and Hebrew thought in the Middle Ages. (The Graeco-Roman tradition, which is the basis of those reflections on language which we present chronologically in Volumes II–IV, appears at the beginning of the second volume.) Chapter 1, by Göran Malmqvist, of Stockholm University, describes the development of Chinese linguistics, analysing the relevant lexicographical and grammatical works, and throwing light on the particular shape imposed on phonological analysis by the logographic nature of Chinese script. Chapter 2, by George Cardona, of the University of Pennsylvania, presents the Indian grammatical tradition, its cultural and religious implications, and particularly the contribution of Pāṇini, illustrating its systematic character and its attention to detail. Chapter 3, supervised by Erica Reiner of the University of Chicago, presents and interprets the documents which bear witness to linguistic interests and knowledge in the civilizations of the ancient near East; the chapter is divided into three sections, devoted to Ancient Egyptian (by Janet Johnson), Sumerian (by Miguel Civil), and Akkadian (by Erica Reiner). Chapter 4, by Raphael Loewe, of the University of London, examines the place of language within the Hebrew tradition, from the Biblical period, through the Talmudists, the mystics, the enlightenment, down to the rebirth of Hebrew as an everyday language, paying particular attention to the philosophical and cultural implications of these trends. Chapter 5, by the late Henri Fleisch, of Saint Joseph University in Beirut, probably the last essay to flow from the pen of this eminent scholar, deals synthetically with the original system of grammatical analysis elaborated by the great Arabic civilization of the Middle Ages.

The following volumes present the main stages of the European tradition, in their chronological succession. They include two chapters each. In Volume II, the first chapter, by Peter Matthews, of Cambridge University, deals with classical linguistics and offers a reading of the main texts of the Graeco-Roman world which elaborate the grammatical categories on which we still base our analysis of language. The second chapter, by Edoardo Vineis, of Bologna University, and (for the philosophy of language) by Alfonso Maierù, of Rome University, presents a detailed discussion of language study from the end of the sixth to the end of the fourteenth century, not limited to the late medieval period which has received most attention in recent years (with particular reference to Modistic philosophy), but extending to the less frequently studied early Middle Ages.

In Volume III, the first chapter, by Mirko Tavoni, of Pisa University, covers the fifteenth and sixteenth centuries, and is completed by two sections, one on *Slavia Romana*, by M. D. Gandolfo, and one on *Slavia Orthodoxa*, by S. Toscano; the bibliography of this chapter takes advantage of the great Renaissance Linguistic Archive set up by M. Tavoni at the Istituto di Studi Rinascimentali in Ferrara. The second chapter, by Raffaele Simone, of Rome University, offers a helpful map of the varied terrain constituted by seventeenth- and eighteenth-century culture, in which many of the roots are found from which the great plant of later comparative linguistics derives its nourishment; R. Simone, who is a professional linguist, keeps in mind the philosophical perspective that is particularly relevant for this period.

In Volume IV, the first chapter, by Anna Morpurgo Davies, of Oxford University, examines the flowering of historical and comparative linguistics in the nineteenth century, stressing in particular some aspects which traditional presentations, focusing on the Neogrammarians, sometimes leave in the shadow, like the interest in typological classifications, and the importance for comparative philology of the newly constituted German university system in the first three decades of the century. The second chapter, by the editor of this work, offers a synthesis of the main developments in twentieth-century linguistics, extending from the progress of comparative studies to linguistic theory, philosophy of language, and the investigation of language use in different areas, from literature to social communication. The Italian edition also includes a chapter on the history of Italian linguistics and dialectology, by Paola Benincà, of Padua University, which has been omitted from the English edition.

Let us briefly look at the present state of linguistic historiography. Over the last three decades there has been a considerable revival of interest in this field. In 1974 Konrad Koerner, a German scholar teaching in Canada, founded the journal *Historiographia Linguistica*, which has become a forum for international discussion on the history of linguistics; in 1978 he was the organizer of the first international congress on the history of linguistics (the meetings continue at three-yearly intervals). There are also several other associations devoted to the history of linguistics, like the Société d'histoire et d'épistémologie des sciences du langage, created in 1978, presided over by S. Auroux, which publishes a Bulletin and the journal *Histoire Épistémologie Langage* (1979–); the Henry Sweet Society for the History of Linguistic Ideas, founded in 1984 on the initiative of Vivian Salmon, which organizes regular meetings and publishes a *Newsletter*; the North American Association for the History of the Language Sciences, founded in 1987. The interest in the history of linguistics over this period is also indicated by the publication of monographs and collections of studies, such as Hymes (1974), Parret (1976), Grotsch (1982), Schmitter (1982), Chevalier and Encrevé (1984), Bynon and Palmer (1986), Formigari and Lo Piparo (1988), and by the two tomes devoted to the historiography of linguistics by Sebeok (1975).

A separate study would be necessary to examine the main available histories of linguistics, from the great works of the nineteenth century devoted to Classical linguistics by Steinthal (1863), to Oriental philology by Benfey (1869), and to Germanic philology by R. von Raumer (1870). Subsequent studies witness the triumph of Neogrammarian comparative philology, from Delbrück (1880) to Meillet (1903) to Pedersen (1924). Since the 1960s numerous historical presentations have been published, from the large and well-informed work by Tagliavini (1963), lacking however in historical perspective and theoretical insight, to the two-volume contribution by Mounin (1967–72), the neat and well-balanced book by Robins (1967), the acute and comprehensive synthesis by Law (1990), the disappointing attempts by Malmberg (1991) and Itkonen (1991). Large-scale works have also started appearing in the last few years, under the direction of Auroux (n.d.) and of Schmitter (1987). There is no space to mention in this context the great many studies devoted, since the 1960s, to individual periods and problems in the history of linguistics, although they often provide the detailed groundwork that makes possible overall synthetic assessments (some titles will be quoted in the list of references).

What is the place of our history of linguistics against this background? To me it seems to be placed in an advantageous position, in the middle ground between the concise, one-author profiles on the one hand, and the extended, multi-authored, multi-volume series on the other. Compared to the former, it has the greater richness of detail, which is made possible by the larger space available and the higher degree of reliability that derives from the authority of contributors who are specialists in the individual areas; compared to the latter, it is more compact and coherent in perspective and basic assumptions, and it can not only be consulted for single questions, or studied in individual sections, but also be read in its entirety.

If I were asked to present a schematic précis of the main features which I see as inspiring this work and characterizing its realization, I would list the following points:

1. A perspective directed towards understanding the past, rather than dealing with present-day concerns. The aim is to reconstruct and illustrate different epochs and traditions within their own context and on the basis of their own values, rather than of their appeal to present-day preoccupations; to highlight their linguistic interests, rather than our own.
2. This is a history of linguistic thought, of interests and attitudes toward language. These may or may not find a place within the elaboration of a 'scientific' study of language (however we may want to define it), but in any case I feel that an account of the preoccupations with linguistic matters in different societies proves to be an interesting and worthwhile object of historical investigation.
3. I have considered it essential, in my choice of authors for individual chapters, that they should be specialists, able to analyse the relevant texts in the original languages, and to present them to a lay readership. I aimed at obtaining not an account of what is known, derived from current literature, but a series of original contributions based on first-hand study of the primary sources.
4. From what precedes it is clear that this work is prevalently concerned with a historical and philological study of ideas, texts from the past, rather than with methodological and theoretical problems posed by historiography. It is an 'extroverted', rather than an 'introverted' history, dealing with the

facts it analyses, rather than with the theoretical and ideological assumptions which lie behind the work of the historian. This obviously does not imply that methodological questions are not a legitimate object of study; but I believe that it is possible to offer useful contributions on the history of linguistics, without dealing in the first instance with the theory of historiography.

5. One of the main linguists of our times, Yakov Malkiel, observed some years ago (Malkiel and Langdon 1969) that to produce good work on the history of linguistics it is not enough to be a linguist: one has also to be a historian, and to fulfil the expectations normally raised by a historical essay. Here, of course, one can only observe that the ability to set some episodes of the history of linguistics within their social and cultural context, is the exception rather than the rule (examples that come to mind are those of Dionisotti (1967a,b, 1972) or Timpanaro (1963, 1965, 1972, 1973)). What I had in mind for this history of linguistics was the more modest aim of providing information about ideas on language, in different periods and societies, which are not easily (and in some cases not at all) accessible elsewhere.

I know from direct experience that linguists feel the need for a work of this kind, and I hope it may also appeal to readers who are interested to know how people, at different times and within different cultural traditions, have looked at one of the most essential and challenging features of our common humanity – that is, language.

G. C. Lepschy

References

AARSLEFF, H. (1982) *From Locke to Saussure. Essays on the Study of Language and Intellectual History*, University of Minnesota Press, Minneapolis.

AMIROVA, T. A., OL'KHOVIKOV, B. A. and ROŽDESTVENSKIJ, JU. V. (1975) *Očerki po istorii lingvistiki*, Nauka, Moskva (German tr. *Abriss der Geschichte der Sprachwissenschaft*, Veb Bibliographisches Institut, Leipzig 1980).

AUROUX, S. (ed.) (n.d.) *Histoire des idées linguistiques. Tome 1: La naissance des métalangages. En Orient et en Occident*, Mardaga, Liège/Bruxelles.

AUROUX, S. (1992) *Histoire des idées linguistiques. Tome 2: Le développement de la grammaire occidentale*, Mardaga, Liège.

BENFEY, T. (1869) *Geschichte der Sprachwissenschaft und orientalischen Philologie in Deutschland, seit dem Anfange des 19. Jahrhunderts mit einem Rückblick auf die früheren Zeiten*, Cotta, München.

BORST, A. (1957–63) *Der Turmbau von Babel. Geschichte der Meinungen über Ursprung und Vielfalt der Sprachen und Völker*, Hiersemann, Stuttgart.

BRINCAT, G. (1986) *La linguistica prestrutturale*, Zanichelli, Bologna.

BYNON, T. and PALMER, F. R. (eds) (1986) *Studies in the History of Western Linguistics. In Honour of R. H. Robins*, Cambridge University Press, Cambridge.

CHEVALIER, J.-C. and ENCREVÉ, P. (eds) (1984) *Vers une histoire sociale de la linguistique* (Langue Française, 63), Larousse, Paris.

CHOMSKY, N. (1966) *Cartesian Linguistics. A Chapter in the History of Rationalist Thought*, Harper and Row, New York.

CHOMSKY, N. (1969) Linguistics and Philosophy, in *Language and Philosophy. A Symposium*, edited by S. Hook, New York University Press, New York, 51–94.

DELBRÜCK, B. (1880) *Einleitung in das Sprachstudium. Ein Beitrag zur Geschichte und Methodik der vergleichenden Sprachforschung*, Breitkopf und Härtel, Leipzig.

DIONISOTTI, C. (1967a) La lingua italiana da Venezia all'Europa. Il Fortunio e la filologia umanistica. Niccolò Liburnio e la letteratura cortigiana, in *Rinascimento europeo e Rinascimento veneziano*, edited by V. Branca, Sansoni, Firenze, 1–46.

DIONISOTTI, C. (1967b) *Geografia e storia della letteratura italiana*, Einaudi, Torino.

DIONISOTTI, C. (1972) *A Year's Work in the Seventies. The Presidential Address of the Modern Humanities Research Association delivered at University College, London, on 7 January 1972*, reprinted from *The Modern Language Review*, Vol. 67, No. 4.

FORMIGARI, L. and LO PIPARO, F. (eds) (1988) *Prospettive di storia della linguistica*, Editori Riuniti, Roma.

GRAFFI, G. (1991a) *La sintassi tra Ottocento e Novencento*, il Mulino, Bologna.

GRAFFI, G. (1991b) Concetti 'ingenui' e concetti 'teorici' in sintassi, *Lingua e Stile*, 26, 347–63.

GROTSCH, K. (1982) *Sprachwissenschaftsgeschichtsschreibung. Ein Beitrag zur Kritik und zur historischen un methodologischen Selbstvergewisserung der Disziplin*, Kümmerle Verlag, Göppingen.

HYMES, D. (ed.) (1974) *Studies in the History of Linguistics*, Indiana University Press, Bloomington.

ITKONEN, E. (1991) *Universal History of Linguistics*, Benjamins, Amsterdam.

KOERNER, K. (1978) *Towards a Historiography of Linguistics. Selected Essays*, Benjamins, Amsterdam.

KOERNER, K. (1989) *Practicing Linguistic Historiography. Selected Essays*, Benjamins, Amsterdam.

LAW, V. (1990) Language and Its Students: the History of Linguistics, in *An Encyclopedia of Language*, edited by N. E. Collinge, Routledge, London/New York, 784–842.

LEPSCHY, G. (ed.) (1990) *Storia della linguistica*, vol. 1 and 2, il Mulino, Bologna.

MALKIEL, Y. and LANGDON, M. (1969) History and Histories of Linguistics, *Romance Philology*, 22, 530–74.

MALMBERG, B. (1991) *Histoire de la linguistique de Sumer à Saussure*, Presses Universitaires de France, Paris.

MEILLET, A. (1903) *Introduction à l'étude comparative des langues indoeuropéennes*, Hachette, Paris (eighth edition, 1937).

MOUNIN, G. (1967—72) *Histoire de la linguistique*, 2 vols, Presses Universitaires de France, Paris.

OL'KHOVIKOV, B. A. (1985) *Teorija jazyka i vid grammatičeskogo opisanija v istorii jazykoznanija. Stanovlenie i evolucija kanona grammatičeskogo opisanija v Evrope*, Nauka, Moskva.

PARRET, H. (ed.) (1976) *History of Linguistic Thought and Contemporary Linguistics*, de Gruyter, Berlin.

PEDERSEN, H. (1924) *Sprogvidenskaben i det Nittende Aarhundrede. Metoder og Resultater*, Gyldendalske Boghandel, København (English tr. *Linguistic Science in the Nineteenth Century*, Harvard University Press, Cambridge, Massachusetts 1931; and with the new title *The Discovery of Language. Linguistic Science in the Nineteenth Century*, Indiana University Press, Bloomington 1962).

RAUMER, R. VON (1870) *Geschichte der germanischen Philologie vorzugsweise in Deutschland*, Oldenbourg, München.

ROBINS, R. H. (1967) *A Short History of Linguistics*, Longman, London (third edition, 1990).

SALMON, V. (1979) *The Study of Language in Seventeenth-Century England*, Benjamins, Amsterdam.

SCHMITTER, P. (1982) *Untersuchungen zur Historiographie der Linguistik. Struktur –Methodik – Theoretische Fundierung*, Narr, Tübingen.

SCHMITTER, P. (ed.) (1987) *Zur Theorie und Methode der Geschichtsschreibung der Linguistik. Analysen und Reflexionen* (Geschichte der Sprachtheorie, 1), Narr, Tübingen.

SEBEOK, T. (ed.) (1975) *Historiography of Linguistics* (Current Trends in Linguistics, 13), Mouton, The Hague.

STEINTHAL, H. (1863) *Geschichte der Sprachwissenschaft bei den Griechen und Römern mit besonderer Rücksicht auf die Logik*, Dümmler, Berlin (second edition, 1890–91).

TAGLIAVINI, C. (1963) *Panorama di storia della linguistica*, Pàtron, Bologna.

TIMPANARO, S. (1963) *La genesi del metodo del Lachmann*, Le Monnier, Firenze (new edition, Liviana, Padova 1985).

TIMPANARO, S. (1965) *Classicismo e illuminismo nell'Ottocento italiano*, Nistri Lischi, Pisa (second, enlarged edition, 1969).

TIMPANARO, S. (1972) Friedrich Schlegel e gli inizi della linguistica indoeuropea in Germania, *Critica Storica*, 9, 72–105.

TIMPANARO, S. (1973) Il contrasto tra i fratelli Schlegel e Franz Bopp sulla struttura e la genesi delle lingue indoeuropee, *Critica Storica*, 10, 53–90.

Acknowledgements

In the preparation of the Italian edition I availed myself of the advice of many friends and colleagues. For Volume I, I should like to thank in particular Zyg Barański, Verina Jones, Anna Morpurgo Davies, Joanna Weinberg (Introduction); Michael Halliday and Michael Loewe (Chapter 1); Anna Morpurgo Davies (Chapter 2); Arnaldo Momigliano (Chapter 3); Ada Rapoport and Joanna Weinberg (Chapter 4); Bernard Lewis (Chapter 5); for Volume II, Tullio De Mauro (Chapter 2); for Volume III: Giuseppe Dell'Agata (Chapter 1), Tullio De Mauro (Chapter 2). I am grateful to Emma Sansone, who has sensitively and helpfully performed the difficult job of translating into English chapters originally in other languages (Volume I, Chapter 5; Volume II, Chapter 2; Volume III, Chapters 1 and 2; Volume IV, Chapter 2). I should also like to thank the series' editors for their advice and comments during the preparation of the English edition. The English version introduces some updatings and improvements on the previous Italian edition. In particular Volume I, Chapter 4 includes a more detailed discussion of Hebrew grammatical ideas. For help and advice concerning the history of Arabic linguistics (Volume I, Chapter 5) I am grateful to Professor E. Ullendorff and Professor A. F. L. Beeston.

Notes on the contributors
(to all four volumes)

George Cardona received a BA from New York University and an MA and PhD in Indo-European Linguistics from Yale University. He has spent several years studying texts of traditional śāstras with paṇḍitas in India (Vadodra, Varanasi, Madras). Since 1960 he has taught at the University of Pennsylvania, first in the Department of South Asian Studies, then (since 1965) in the Department of Linguistics. His major fields of interest and research are ancient Indian grammatical thought, Indo-Aryan, and Indo-Iranian. Among his works are *A Gujarati Reference Grammar* (Philadelphia 1965), *Pāṇini, a Survey of Research* (The Hague 1976; reprinted Delhi 1980), and *Pāṇini's Grammar and its Traditions. Volume 1: Background and Introduction* (Delhi 1988).

Miguel Civil born in Sabadell (Barcelona, Spain), studied Assyriology in Paris (École Pratique des Hautes Études and Collège de France). He worked with Professor S. N. Kramer in Philadelphia for several years and then joined the staff of the Oriental Institute of the University of Chicago. His speciality is Sumerian texts and grammar, with emphasis on lexicography. He is co-editor of *Materials for the Sumerian Lexicon* and member of the editorial board of the *Chicago Assyrian Dictionary*.

Henri Fleisch (1904–85) born in Jonville (France); a Jesuit, he studied in the schools of his Order and in Paris, École de Langues Orientales Vivantes (1934–36) and at the Sorbonne. In 1938 he was appointed Professor of Arabic Philology at the Institut de Lettres Orientales in Beirut, and then Director of the Prehistory Museum, and Scriptor at the Saint-Joseph University. Among his works: *Introduction à l'étude des langues sémitiques* (Paris 1947); *L'Arabe* *classique. Esquisse d'une structure linguistique* (Beirut 1956), *Traité de philologie arabe* (Beirut, vol. 1, 1961, vol. 2, 1979); *Études d'arabe dialectal* (Beirut 1974).

Maria Delfina Gandolfo, born in Rome, graduated in Genoa in Russian Language and Literature, with a thesis on the history of alphabets in the Slavic world. She took an MA and an MPhil at Yale University, and is preparing a PhD dissertation on the orthographic questions in the Slavic tradition.

Janet H. Johnson, born in Everett, Washington, studied at the University of Chicago and is now Professor of Egyptology at the Oriental Institute at that University. Her major philological interests are in Demotic (Egyptian) and the synchronic and diachronic studies of the ancient Egyptian language. She has written *The Demotic Verbal System* (Chicago 1976), *Thus Wrote 'Onchsheshonqy: An Introductory Grammar of Demotic* (Chicago 1986), and numerous articles on the grammar of various stages of Egyptian, including the summary and overview in *Crossroads: Chaos or the Beginning of a New Paradigm*, Papers from the Conference on Egyptian Grammar held in Helsingør, 28–30 May 1986.

Giulio Lepschy, born in Venice, studied at the Universities of Pisa (Scuola Normale Superiore) and Zürich, Oxford, Paris and London. He is Professor in the Department of Italian Studies at the University of Reading, and a Fellow of the British Academy. His research work is mainly on Italian linguistics and dialectology, and on the history of linguistics. Among his publications are: *A Survey of Structural Linguistics* (London 1970); (with Anna Laura Lepschy) *The Italian Language Today* (London 1977); *Saggi di linguistica italiana* (Bologna 1978); *Intorno a Saussure* (Turin 1979); *Sulla linguistica moderna* (Bologna 1989); *Nuovi saggi di linguistica italiana* (Bologna 1989); *La linguistica del Novecento* (Bologna 1992).

Raphael Loewe studied classics at Cambridge before 1939 and semitics (also subsequently in Oxford) after the War. He held teaching posts and fellowships at Leeds, Cambridge, Providence, Rhode Island, and at University College, London, whence he retired from the Goldsmid Chair of Hebrew in 1984. He has concerned himself mainly with the impact of Jewish biblical exegesis and legend on European scholasticism, and with Hebrew poetry in Spain. His publications include: The Medieval History of the Latin Vulgate, in *The Cambridge History of the Bible*, 2 (Cambridge

1969); *The Rylands Haggadah* (London 1988); *Ibn Gabirol* (London 1989).

Alfonso Maierù studied at the University of Rome La Sapienza, where he teaches History of Medieval Philosophy. He has worked mainly on medieval logic (*Terminologia logica della tarda scolastica*, Rome 1972), dealing with some of its problematic aspects (he has written several essays on Trinitarian theology and logic). Since 1978 he has also been working on scholastic institutions and teaching techniques, and on philosophical terminology in Dante.

Göran Malmqvist, Professor of Chinese at the University of Stockholm and a member of the Swedish Academy. He taught Chinese at the School of Oriental and African Studies in London (1953–5); served as Cultural Attaché to the Swedish Embassy in Peking (1956–8) and as reader and subsequently professor in Chinese at the Australian National University in Canberra in 1956–65. He has published in the fields of Chinese dialectology, classical and modern Chinese syntax, Chinese metrics and textual criticism. He has also translated a number of Chinese literary works into Swedish. Among his publications are: The Syntax of Bound Forms in Sich'uanese, *BMFEA* (*Bulletin of the Museum of Far Eastern Antiquities*), 33, 1961, 125–99; Studies in Western Mandarin Phonology, *BMFEA*, 34, 1962, 129–92; *Problems and Methods in Chinese Linguistics* (Canberra 1962); *Han Phonology and Textual Criticism* (Canberra 1963); Studies on the Gongyang and Guuliang Commentaries, I, *BMFEA*, 43, 1971, 67–222; II, *BMFEA*, 47, 1975, 19–69; III, *BMFEA*, 49, 1977, 33–215.

Peter Hugoe Matthews, born near Oswestry in England; graduated University of Cambridge 1957; has taught general linguistics at Bangor, North Wales, at Reading, and, since 1980, at Cambridge, where he is at present Professor of Linguistics and Fellow of St John's College. He is a Fellow of the British Academy. Principal research interests in syntax, morphology and the history of linguistics. His main publications are: *Inflectional Morphology* (Cambridge 1972); *Morphology* (Cambridge 1974); *Generative Grammar and Linguistic Competence* (London 1979); *Syntax* (Cambridge 1981); *Grammatical Theory in the United States from Bloomfield to Chomsky* (Cambridge 1993).

Anna Morpurgo Davies, born in Milan, graduated at the University of Rome before spending a year at Harvard University. She is Professor of Comparative Philology at the University of Oxford, and taught at Yale, Pennsylvania, and other American universities. She is a Fellow of the British Academy. She works on Indo-European comparative grammar (particularly Mycenean, Ancient Greek, ancient Anatolian languages), and on the history of nineteenth century linguistics. She has published *Myceneae Graecitatis Lexicon* (Rome 1963); she has edited with Y. Duhoux, *Linear B: A 1984 Survey* (Louvain 1985), and she has written articles in British, Italian, German, French and American journals.

Erica Reiner, born in Budapest, studied Linguistics and Assyriology at the École Pratique des Hautes Études, Paris, and at the University of Chicago (PhD 1955). She is Professor at the University of Chicago and Editor-in-Charge of the Chicago Assyrian Dictionary. Her major interests are the language and literature of ancient Babylonia and Assyria. Her main publications are: *A Linguistic Analysis of Accadian* (The Hague 1966); *The Elamite Language* (Handbuch der Orientalistik, II-2, Leiden 1969); (with D. Pingree) *Babylonian Planetary Omens*, 1 and 2 (Malibu 1975 and 1981); *Your Thwarts in Pieces, Your Mooring Rope Cut: Poetry from Babylonia and Assyria* (Ann Arbor 1985).

Raffaele Simone, born in Lecce, is Professor of General Linguistics at the University of Rome La Sapienza. He works on the history of linguistics, on Italian linguistics, on theory of grammar and on textual linguistics. Main publications: Introduction to and translation of *Grammatica e Logica di Port-Royal* (Rome 1969); with R. Amacker, Verbi modali in italiano (*Italian Linguistics*, 3, 1977); *Maistock. Il linguaggio spiegato da una bambina* (Florence 1988); *Fondamenti di linguistica* (Bari/Rome 1990); *Il sogno di Saussure* (Bari/Rome 1992).

Mirko Tavoni, born in Modena, studied at the Scuola Normale Superiore of Pisa, taught at the University of Calabria, and is now Associate Professor of the History of the Italian Language at the University of Pisa. He works mainly on the history of Medieval and Renaissance linguistic ideas. Principal publications: *Il discorso linguistico di Bartolomeo Benvoglienti* (Pisa 1975); *Latino, grammatica, volgare. Storia di una questione umanistica* (Padua 1984); *Il Quattrocento*, in the series «Storia della lingua italiana» (Bologna 1992). He is the co-ordinator of the bibliographical project *Renaissance Linguistic Archive* at the Istituto di Studi Rinascimentali in Ferrara.

Silvia Toscano studied at the Universities of Pisa and V. Trnovo;

she is a researcher at the Istituto di Filologia Slava of the University of Pisa. She works mainly on Slavic linguistics. Among her recent works are: *L'«articolo» nel trattato slavo Sulle otto parti del discorso* (Rome 1984); *I «modi verbali» nel trattato slavo Sulle otto parti del discorso* (Rome 1988).

Edoardo Vineis, born at Broni (Pavia), he studied at the University of Pisa (Scuola Normale Superiore). He is Professor of Linguistics at the University of Bologna. He works on Latin linguistics, history of the Italian language, and history of linguistics. Among his publications: *Studio sulla lingua dell'*Itala (Pisa 1974); (with P. Berrettoni) annotated edition of A. Manzoni and G. I. Ascoli, *Scritti sulla questione della lingua* (Turin 1974); Grammatica e filosofia del linguaggio in Alcuino, *Studi e Saggi Linguistici*, 28, 1988, 403–29; Latino, in *Le lingue indoeuropee*, edited by A. Giacalone Ramat and P. Ramat (Bologna 1993, 289–348).

1

Chinese linguistics

Göran Malmqvist

1.1 Introduction*

The Chinese language has traditionally been characterized as a monosyllabic and isolating tone language. This characterization is certainly valid for the earlier stages of the development of the language. In the last thousand years a rapid and far-reaching phonological reduction, accompanied by the development of certain morphological features, such as affixation and compounding, has resulted in the creation of many disyllabic and polysyllabic words. But this development has not reduced the concept of the monosyllabicity of the language to a myth: the overwhelming majority of Chinese morphemes – whether free or bound – are monosyllabic and represented by a unique sign, a written character or logograph.

I shall here devote myself solely to a discussion of the techniques and the results of traditional studies, leaving aside modern studies influenced by trends in Western linguistics. I shall also refrain from discussing the paleographical remains (the oracle bone inscriptions dating back to the Shang period, 1520–1030 BC) which were discovered towards the very end of the last century and the study of which has turned into a highly specialized discipline. Again, I shall refrain from discussing the results of comparative studies within the Sino-Tibetan language family, which since the 1940s have greatly added to our knowledge of both Early Archaic Chinese (roughly the first millennium BC) and Proto-Chinese (the period preceding the earliest literary documents). Traditional language studies recognize the following three stages in the development of the language: Old Chinese (the first half of the first millennium

* See beginning of Notes.

BC), Middle Chinese (the Sui and Tang periods, 581–907 AD) and Old Mandarin (thirteenth and fourteenth centuries AD).

The following periodization of traditional Chinese language studies roughly corresponds with important stages in the development of the language:

1. the period prior to the Qin (–221 BC);
2. the periods of Qin and Han (221 BC–220 AD);
3. the periods of Wei, Jin and Nanbeichao (220–581);
4. the periods of Sui, Tang and Song (581–1279);
5. the periods of Yuan and Ming (1260–1644);
6. the period of Qing (1644–1912) up to the end of the nineteenth century.

The logographic nature of the Chinese script has to a very great extent conditioned traditional Chinese linguistics. The logograph has from earliest times been conceived of as a unit possessing a unique shape, a basic meaning and a particular sound. Traditional Chinese linguistics may therefore be divided into three branches, dealing with the analysis and explanation of logographs, semantic glosses and lexicography, and phonology respectively.

The study of morphology and syntax plays an insignificant role in traditional Chinese linguistics. It is interesting to note that the first systematic *Chinese* grammar of the Chinese language did not appear until 1898 (*Mashi wentong*: the comprehensive grammar of Ma Jianzhong) and that it represents a fairly successful attempt at applying the categories of Latin grammar to the Chinese language. The lack of interest on the part of traditional Chinese linguists in systematic research into the internal structure of words and the functions of words in the sentence is no doubt conditioned by the logographic nature of the script which gives no clue to the internal analysis of the word.

The non-phonetic nature of the script is probably also mainly responsible for the slowly developing awareness of diachronic linguistic change. Also dialectal variation is effectively hidden under the cloak of the logographs. The early ventures into the field of 'dialectology' which will be discussed later were mainly motivated by an interest in semantics.

In traditional China pursuit of learning was considered as an effective tool for the betterment of the self and of society. All branches of learning – and particularly studies in the humanities – had a very strong ideological motivation. The majority of studies in script analysis, semantics and phonology aimed at elucidating ancient texts which issued from the Confucian school and which were revered as classics. The advent of Buddhism in the first century of our era had a strong impact on linguistic, and particularly phonological studies, in connection with the translation of Sanskrit texts into Chinese. On the whole, traditional Chinese linguistics has paid scant attention to vernacular texts which more closely reflected the properties of the spoken language.

Few, if any, of the scholars who engaged in traditional linguistic research were professional linguists. We find here a parallel with the field of creative writing: writers, poets and linguists were scholars who often held high posts in the civil or military administration and who found an outlet for their extensive learning either in creative writing or in research.

The techniques and the terminology employed by traditional Chinese linguists differ widely from those employed in the West. The logographic nature of the script prevented the Chinese phonologists from presenting their results in phonetic transcription. In order to accommodate the reader all modern forms will be given in the official transcription system *pinyin* (sound spelling) which was adopted in 1958. Old Chinese (600 BC) and Middle Chinese (600 AD) forms will be given in the reconstructions (and with the transcriptions) established by the Swedish sinologist Bernhard Karlgren.

1.2 The period prior to the Qin (−221 BC)

Many literary and learned works which later were to be made subjects of philological research were produced during the early, middle and late Zhou (1030–221 BC). To them belong the *Shi* ('The odes'), a collection of songs from early and middle Zhou, the rhymes of which came to play an important role for the reconstruction of the phonology of Old Chinese; the *Shu* ('The documents'), a collection of speeches and statements by kings and statesmen; the *Chunqiu* ('Spring and autumn'), a chronicle of the feudal state of Lu; the *Yi* ('The changes'), a manual in divination; various ritual texts, and the writings of thinkers belonging to the rival schools of Confucianism, Mohism, Taoism, the School of Names, and Legalism, to mention only the most important ones.

Some of the philosophical works from the period of the Warring States (480–221 BC) contain glosses which provide evidence of an interest in semantics. One source from the second century BC[1] mentions that the royal courts of Zhou and Qin in the eighth month of each year dispatched officials travelling in light coaches to various parts of the state for the purpose of collecting information on dialects.

While philology cannot be said to have constituted a special branch of learning prior to the Qin-period, the philosophical writings of the late Chunqiu period (722–480 BC) and the Warring States period (480–221 BC) testify to the interest of thinkers, be they Confucianists, Mohists, Taoists, Dialecticians or Legalists, in such fundamental problems as the relation between name and reality, the distinction between generic and particular appellations, and the nature and function of attribution. The most original and brilliant contributions to this discussion were made by the Confucian philosopher Xun Zi (fl. in the mid third century BC). One of the chapters in the book which bears his name is entitled 'Zheng ming' ('On rectifying names'). In it Xun Zi expounds on the arbitrary relation between the signifier and the signified:

> Names have no intrinsic appropriateness. One agrees to use a certain name and issues an order to that effect, and if the agreement is abided by and becomes a matter of custom, then the name may be said to be appropriate, but if people do not abide by the agreement, then the name ceases to be appropriate. Names have no intrinsic reality. One agrees to use a certain name and issues an order that it shall be applied to a certain reality, and if the agreement is abided by and becomes a matter of custom, then it may be said to be a real name. There are, however, names which are intrinsically good. Names which are clear, simple, and not at odds with the thing they designate, may be said to be good names.[2]

1.3 The periods of Qin and Han (221 BC–220 AD)

The ruler of the state of Qin, who in 221 BC succeeded in uniting all of China under his power, was a pragmatic despot who had little patience with the conservative literati of the Confucian school. In an attempt to silence their opposition to his anti-intellectual policies he decreed that all books in the empire should be burned. In order to stamp out the script variants which had been created in the various feudal states he ordered his prime minister Li Si to create a uniform script standard, known as 'the small seal script'. After the collapse of the Qin empire in 207 BC Confucian scholars busied themselves with gathering and editing what remained of the literature of the past. The Qin auto-da-fé gave rise to an unprecedented scholarly activity and to a branch of learning which was termed *xiaoxue*, philology. This term had been coined already before the Han, but then referred to the 'School of lesser learning' which sons of noble families entered at the age of eight and where they studied the script and fixed text curricula until they were fifteen and were transferred to the 'School of higher learning' (*daxue*). Fragments of texts studied in these schools, such as the *Cang Xie pian* ('The treatise of Cang Xie') attributed to Li Si, have been preserved to our time.

Three works, *Erya*, *Fangyan* and *Shuo wen jie zi*, played a dominating role in the philology of the Han period and they have continued to retain the interest of scholars up to modern times.

Erya is the earliest Chinese lexicographical work. The question of the origin and the date of the work has not as yet received a satisfactory answer. What we do know is that *Erya* in the first century AD was considered as an authoritative guide to the language of the classics and that by Tang times it had become part of the Confucian canon. Guo Pu (276–324), who wrote a commentary on the *Erya*, states in his preface that the work is of pre-Han origin. The consensus of learned opinion is that the *Erya* dates from the third century BC.

The work may be best described as a compendium of semantic glosses on the classics and other pre-Qin texts, some of which date from the late Warring States period. The title of the book consists of a verb-object expression which may be translated as 'approaching what is elegant and correct usage'. The current *Erya* text, which is probably more or less identical with the Han version, is made up of nineteen chapters. Each chapter carries a title, containing the word *shi*, 'to explain', followed by a noun signifying the material treated in the chapter. The first three chapters differ from the rest of the work in that they provide glosses on verbs, adjectives, adverbs, a few grammatical particles and reduplicative expressions of a descriptive nature. The remaining sixteen chapters contain glosses on kinship terms; architectural terms; utensils and tools, and verbs related to these items; musical instruments; astronomical, calendrical and meteorological terms; geographical and geological terms; hills; mountains; rivers and streams, and items related to rivers; grasses, herbs and vegetables; trees and bushes; insects, spiders and reptiles; fish and other aquatic creatures; wildfowl; wild animals, and domestic animals and poultry.

It is quite clear that the *Erya* was not meant to serve as a dictionary, but as a compendium of direct glosses to passages in ancient texts. Many of these passages have been identified by painstaking and cumulative research by generations of philologists.

The favourite formulae of the *Erya* are $a, b, c, d = f$ ('the words a, b, c, and d mean f') and $a = b$ ('the word a means b'). The gloss is always a word the meaning of which would be easily understood by the reader. Occasionally we find that a word serving as gloss is itself glossed by another word, as in the example '*Liu* ('to flow') means *tan* ('to extend'); *tan* ('to extend') means *yan* ('to continue')'.

In some instances the *Erya* describes, rather than glosses: 'The *zong* tree has needles like a fir and a trunk like a cypress'; 'What has feet is referred to as an insect; what has no feet is referred to as a reptile'. We sometimes find that the text places the modern term in initial position, as in '*Ni liu er shang* ('to travel upstream') is called *suohui*'; '*Shun liu er xia* ('to travel downstream') is called *suoyou*'.

Fangyan ('Dialects'), China's earliest work on dialect vocabulary, has been attributed to Yang Xiong (53 BC–18 AD), a learned philosopher and poet. In the preface to his work *Fengsu tong yi* ('A comprehensive account of customs and mores') Ying Shao (second century AD) refers to a few dialect compilations of the early Han period and states that Yang Xiong liked these works, that he checked their content with people of all walks of life and spent 27 years adding to the material. Yang Xiong was well qualified for his task. At the age of 40 he moved from Chengdu in Sichuan to the capital Chang'an, where he spent the rest of his life. He must therefore have been well versed both in the local dialect of Chengdu and in the *koine* of the capital, where he must have had ample opportunities to meet people from all parts of the country. Having written extensive glosses on the *Cang Xie pian* he must also have had an expert knowledge of ancient logographs.

The current version of the *Fangyan* contains 658 entries, divided into 13 chapters. The contents of the various chapters are not clearly differentiated. Some chapters (1, 2, 3, 6, 7, 10) deal mainly with words (verbs, adjectives and nouns), while those remaining deal with clothing (4), utensils, furniture and farming implements (5), wild and domestic animals, wild birds and poultry (8), wagons, boats and weapons (9), and insects (11). The first eleven chapters contain a wealth of dialect information. The final two chapters differ greatly from the rest in that they mainly contain glosses of the *Erya* type and lack dialect information.

The favourite formula of the *Fangyan* is that of the *Erya* (*a, b, and c = d*) followed by attributions of the glossed words to individual dialects or larger dialect regions. All forms are referred to by their logographs and no indication of the pronunciation is given. Large dialect areas are indicated with reference to topographical features such as the Hangu pass in northern Henan (*Guan*), the Yellow River (*He*), the Yangzi river (*Jiang*), Mount Hua in present Shaanxi (*Shan*): 'The area west of the pass' (*Zi Guan er xi*), 'The area north of the Yangzi River' (*Zi Jiang er bei*), and so on. Smaller dialect regions are designated by the rivers which flow through them and by the name of the former feudal state which occupied the region. The most frequently occurring dialect regions are Qin (present Shaanxi), Jin (present Shanxi), Yan (present

Hebei), Qi and Lu (present Shandong), Chu (north of the mid range of the Yangzi River), Wu (present Zhejiang) and Yue (present Fujian-Guangdong).

The terms *tongyu*, *tongming* and *fanyu* (common expression) designate words which are used all over China and belong to the common language. Sometimes the same terms designate words which are used within a large dialect area. All words which are used to gloss dialect words quite clearly belong to the common language. The 32 words which are used as glosses in the first chapter with very few exceptions belong to the common language of contemporary China.

While the common language of the late Chunqiu and Warring States period (722–221 BC) probably was based on the dialect spoken in the state of Jin (Shanxi), the common language of the Han period was based mainly on the dialect of Qin (Shaanxi). It is very likely that these dialects by the time of Yang Xiong had merged so as to constitute a large *koine* dialect and that the vocabulary of this *koine* during the course of Han slowly spread over the whole of northern China and also penetrated into the southern dialects.

The *Fangyan* uses the term *zhuanyu* (phonetic variant) to designate dialectal phonetic variants of forms obtaining in the common language of the time. Since these variants are designated by logographs the phonetic reality behind the *zhuanyu* was, and of course still is, effectively hidden. Many dialectal expressions which in the *Fangyan* are represented by strange logographs have been identified in the dialects and the common language of present-day China, but written with different graphs.

A comparative study of the *Erya* and the *Fangyan* reveals that many of the words which the former text treats as synonyms in fact are dialectal variations of one and the same form.

Guo Pu, the commentator of the *Erya*, also wrote a commentary on the *Fangyan*. Using vocabulary from the common language of his own time (275–323 BC), Guo Pu gives a great many examples which serve to elucidate Yang Xiong's glosses. It is particularly interesting to note that he often uses compound expressions where Yang Xiong uses monosyllabic words. He also notes that some of Yang Xiong's dialectal synonyms in fact are phonetic variants.

The *Shuo wen jie zi* ('Explanations of simple graphs and analyses of compound graphs'), which was completed in 121 AD (a few years before the Greek Sophist and grammarian Julius Pollux of Naucratis completed his *Onomasticon*), has ever since served as a model for dictionary compilers in China. The dictionary treats 9431 logographs and 1279 variants. In his postface to the work the author Xu Shen (58–147 AD) discusses his views on the nature and the history of the logographs and the structural principles on which they are built. He recognizes the following six types of graph: (1) pictographs (drawings of the objects denoted by the graphs); (2) ideographs (depictions of abstract notions); (3) compound ideographs (combinations of pictographs or ideographs); (4) phonetic compounds (combinations of a 'classifier', indicating the semantic sphere of the graph, and a 'phonetic', serving to indicate the sound); (5) loan characters (characters borrowed to serve for semantically unrelated homophones), and (6) derivative graphs (graphs which Xu Shen considered semantically related and which exhibit minor graphic variations).[3]

Of the 9431 graphs treated in the dictionary no less than 7697 are phonetic compounds. The next largest category are the compound ideographs (1167), followed by pictographs (364) and ideographs (125).

Each graph is listed and defined under one of 540 classifiers which forms the whole or part of the graph. In addition Xu Shen provides one or more of the following items of information: (1) an attribution of the graph to one of the six types; (2) analysis of the graph into classifier and phonetic, where applicable; (3) a quotation from the classics illustrating the use of the graph; (4) ancient forms of the graph; (5) variant forms of the graph, and (6) a sound gloss, which normally follows the pattern *x du ruo y*, 'the graph x is read as the graph y'.

The *Shuo wen jie zi* is an important milestone in the stuggle between the Old Text School and the New Text School which raged throughout the Han period and which was revived in the eighteenth century. The adherents of the Old Text School based themselves on the classics written in the old script antedating the script reform of the Qin period, while the adherents of their rivals based themselves on the classics which had been written down in the official script of the Han period (*lishu*, 'clerk script'), a modified version of the 'small seal', the official script of the Qin. Xu Shen's monumental work signals the victory of the Old Text School over their opponents.

Since the second century AD the *Shuo wen* has been studied and revered by a great many scholars. The rise of textual criticism in the Qing period gave an important impetus to the study of the work. It is interesting to note that the *Shuo wen* has proved an indispensable tool for the study of the great wealth of paleographical material (oracle bone inscriptions, bronze inscriptions and other epigraphs), which has come to light in this century and to which Xu Shen himself therefore lacked access.

Mention must also be made of the work *Shi ming* ('Explaining names'), compiled by Liu Xi about 200 AD. The *Shi ming* is a dictionary containing more than 1500 items arranged under twenty-seven headings, such as Heaven, Earth, Body Parts, Kinship, Food and Drink, Boats, and Mourning Rites. The favourite formula of the work is *a* = *b*, in which *b* is a homophone or near homophone meant to serve both as a sound gloss and as an indicator of a semantic connection between the two words. The supposed semantic connection is often extremely tenuous, as shown by the following example: '*Zu* (Old Chinese *tsi̯uk* 'foot') is *xu* (Old Chinese *dzi̯uk* 'to continue'). This means that it is the continuation of the leg.'

The *Shi ming* is important in that its sound glosses throw light on the phonological structure of the late Han period.

1.4 The periods of Wei, Jin and Nanbeichao (220–581)

This period is of great importance in the history of traditional Chinese linguistics, and particularly phonology. Buddhism, which was introduced in the first century of our era, and large-scale and ever increasing endeavours to translate Sanskrit and Pali texts into Chinese brought a new awareness of the uniqueness of the structure of the Chinese language. During a large portion of this period China was split into North and South. The political disunion was paralleled by cultural flourishing. New prosodic techniques were developed, both in prose and poetry, in which the tonal properties of the language played an important part.

Each monosyllabic morpheme of the common language of today is, when stressed, accompanied by one of four tones, which may be described as falling, rising, both falling and rising, and neither falling nor rising (level). There are strong reasons to believe that the tones of earlier stages of the Chinese language were characterized by similar features. (The question concerning the *origin* of the tones has aroused little interest among traditional Chinese linguists. Western research in recent decades has shown that the tones in all probability developed from the presence of voiced and unvoiced phonation types in the earliest history of the language.)

Shen Yue (441–513) was the first to identify the tones and to prescribe rules for their role in the metrics of poetry. For metrical purposes the tones were divided into two categories (level and non-level). The rules, which were further developed by generations of poets, required a well-balanced antithetical arrangement of level and non-level tones within the verse and the stanza.

The new interest in linguistic matters gave rise to a sophisticated technique for specifying the pronunciation of monosyllabic morphemes. This technique, which is called *fanqie* (reverse-cutting), was used already at the end of the Han period, but was further developed by commentators of classical texts and compilers of rhyme dictionaries. It is generally assumed that the technique of *fanqie* 'spellings' was the result of contact with learned Buddhist scholars from India.

A Chinese syllable is made up of an *initial*, a *final* and a *tone*. In the rhyme dictionaries which began to appear in this period all morphemes were arranged under their respective tone and rhyme. Disregarding the tonal categories, a similar arrangement of English morphemes would classify *ban*, *pan*, *fan*, *man*, *can*, *van* and *tan* under the rhyme *an*. But there is not necessarily a one-to-one correspondence between *final* and *rhyme*. Just as in English *tin* and *twin*, *kite* and *quite*, and *court* and *quart* are considered perfect rhymes, authors of rhyme dictionaries did not always take account of the presence of certain palatal and velar semi-vowels in their rhyme classification. Such distinctions are revealed, however, by the *fanqie* spellings. Translated into English this method can be described in the following way: the English morpheme *man* begins with the same sound as *mat* and ends in the same sound as *can*. These two morphemes – *mat* and *can* – can therefore be used to spell the pronunciation of *man*. In the same way, *kite* may be spelled by *can* and *might*, but *quite* by *cool* and *white*. The introduction of *fanqie* spelling played an enormously important role for the subsequent development of Chinese phonology and lexicography. Without resort to this ingenious method of spelling Chinese phonologists would not have achieved their spectacular results with regard to the categorization of the phonological entities of Middle Chinese.

Also lexicography made rapid strides in the period between Han and Sui. The largest dictionary of its time was the *Yupian* ('Writing slips of jade'), which was compiled in the years 547–549 and treated 16,917 graphs. Its author, Gu Yewang (519–581), modelled his work on the *Shuo wen jie zi*, but adduced a great many more text examples and also indicated the pronunciation with the aid of *fanqie* spellings. Only a fraction of the original work has been preserved to our times. The *fanqie* spellings of the *Yupian* have survived in a Song edition of the *Shuo wen jie zi*.

In the early part of the period Zhang Yi, who served as Doctor of the Imperial Academy in the years 227–237, compiled a greatly expanded and modernized version of the *Erya*, which he entitled *Guangya* ('The augmented *Erya*'). The topical arrangement of the 2345 entries follows exactly that of the *Erya*. The work is an important guide to the development of the vocabulary in the 4–500 years which separate the two dictionaries.

1.5 The periods of Sui, Tang and Song (581–1279)

The earliest extensive work to make full use of *fanqie* spelling is the *Jingdian shi wen* ('Explaining graphs in the canonical texts'), compiled by Lu Deming (556–627). This compilation, which was completed in 583, contains glosses and explanations of words found in eleven texts of the Confucian school, the Taoist works *Dao de jing* and the *Zhuang Zi*, and the *Erya*. In his preface, the author writes as follows:

> Phonetic glosses differ with the times. Learned writers of the past often failed to follow the pronunciations indicated by the glosses, and the readings of the commentators themselves are not always mutually consistent. In this compilation I have deliberated somewhat over these matters. Such pronunciations as are often found in literary works and are synchronically consistent, and therefore generally accepted, have been placed in the initial position. In the case of graphs with variant readings, which may be correlated to differences in meaning, or in the case of graphs with more than one reading which have been variously glossed by different commentators, I have taken down all available information and in each instance given the name of the author of the relevant gloss in order to facilitate the reader's discrimination. Expressions such as *huo yin* ('sometimes pronounced as') and *yi yin* ('according to one source pronounced as') indicate that these forms are of recent origin and lack textual evidence.

The material presented in the *Jingdian shi wen* has great relevance for our understanding of the phonological structure of the language of the late sixth century.

One of the most important works in the history of Chinese phonology, the rhyme dictionay *Qieyun* ('Reverse-cutting rhymes'), was published in the year 601. In his preface the author, Lu Fayan, tells how eight of his friends used to gather in his home in the beginning of the Kaihuang reign (581–600):

> In the evenings, after having enjoyed our wine, our discussions always turned to phonology. Differences obtain between the pronunciations of the past and the present, and different principles of selection are followed by the various authors. In the [southern] regions of Wu and Chu the pronunciation is at times too light and shallow. In [the northern regions of] Yan and Zhao it is often too heavy and muted . . . And so we discussed the right and the wrong of South and North, and the prevailing and the obsolete of past and present. Wishing to present

> a more refined and precise standard we discarded all that was ill-defined and lacked precision . . . A knowledge of phonology is necessary for any literary undertaking . . . And so, choosing from the various rhyme books and other lexica, old and new, and basing myself on my earlier notes, I organized the material into the *Qieyun*, in five volumes, analysing minutiae and making fine distinctions. It is not that I have been the sole judge in these matters. I have merely related the opinions of my worthy colleagues.

The original *Qieyun* was lost at an early stage. Two augmented editions of the eighth century were also lost. A ninth century calligraphic copy of one of these editions (of 706 AD) was found in 1947. The *fanqie* spellings of the other edition (of 751 AD) were incorporated in a Song edition of the *Shuo wen jie zi*. The work which has played the most important part in traditional Chinese phonology is an augmented edition of the *Qieyun*, the *Guangyun*, published in the year 1008.

Rhyme dictionaries of the *Qieyun* type divide the words into four tonal categories: *ping*, *shang*, *qu* and *ru*. The tones of the first three categories may have been level, rising, and falling, respectively. Words belonging to the *ru* category were at the time characterized by the presence of final *-p*, *-t* or *-k*. (Since these forms are in complementary distribution with words of the *qu* category ending in *-m*, *-n* and *-ng*, the *ru* category could be eliminated in a phonemic treatment.) Since the *ping* (level) tone category contains more words than any of the other three categories it has been divided into two volumes. Within each tonal category the words are divided into rhyme categories. The *Guangyun* comprises 206 rhymes, of which 57 belong to the *ping*, 55 to the *shang*, 60 to the *qu*, and 34 to the *ru* category.

Within each rhyme the words are arranged in groups of homophones. The first word within each group is spelled by the *fanqie* method. The spelling is followed by a figure indicating the number of words within the homophonous group.

Lu Fayan's group of friends included Yan Zhitui (531–591), a descendant of a scholar-official family. Like many other men of his status Yan Zhitui wrote a 'family instruction', a moral and ethical guide for his children and descendants. The *Yanshi jiaxun* ('Family instructions for the Yan clan') was completed in 589. In it he treats a number of important topics, such as 'Teaching children', 'Brothers', 'Remarriage', 'Family management', 'Customs and manners', 'Reputation and reality', 'A warning against becoming warriors', 'Evidence on writing', and, of course, 'Phonology'. Discussing erroneous pronunciations, Yan Zhitui admonishes his children in the following words: 'My sons and daughters, even during your childhood your speech was seriously drilled and corrected. Any single mispronounced character was considered my own fault, and I dared not name any actions, words or objects without consulting books. You know it well.'[4]

Buddhist studies flourished in the Tang period, when many learned scholars engaged in the translation and elucidation of Buddhist texts. The greatest translator was the monk Xuanzang (596–664), who went on a pilgrimage to India in 629. Upon his return to the capital Chang'an in 645 he organized and led a tremendous translation project, through which no less than 75 basic Buddhist texts were rendered into Chinese.

Taking Lu Deming's work *Jingdian shi wen* as his model one of Xuanzang's assistants, the monk Xuanying, compiled the work *Yiqiejing yinyi* ('Glosses on Buddhist texts'), which appeared in 650, exactly 50 years after the completion of the *Qieyun*. While Xuanying's work employs other spelling graphs than those used in the *Qieyun*, there is a close agreement between the phonological categories of the two works. Xuanying does not refer to the *Qieyun* and it is unlikely that his own work was based on it. The close agreement between the two works therefore seems to indicate that they were based on the same dialect. The phonological affinities found in the two works also speak against the hypothesis that the *Qieyun* system represents an artificial construct, incorporating a great many diachronic and synchronic variants. Xuanying's work had a purely practical purpose, that of elucidating the pronunciation of words in the translated Buddhist texts. There is no reason to believe that the author would base himself on a standard which did not represent the living speech of his time.

Another work with the same title as Xuanying's was published in 810. Its author, the monk Huilin, who spent nearly twenty years compiling his work, mentions explicitly that he based himself on the *Qinyin*, that is the dialect of the capital Chang'an, which by this time undoubtedly had become a *koine*. Huilin's work shows that certain important sound changes, which for hundreds of years were left unrecognized by other phonological works, had started to occur already in the early ninth century. One example of this is the change from the *shang* tone to the *qu* tone in syllables beginning with voiced fricatives and affricates, and aspirated voiced stops.

One further point must be raised in connection with Huilin's work. The phonological system of the *Qieyun* comprises three nasal initial consonants, *m-*, *n-* and *ng-*, which in the pre-Tang and early Tang period were employed to transcribe the nasal consonants of Sanskrit. From the end of the seventh century the same initials were employed to transcribe Sanskrit unaspirated and voiced stops (*b*-, *d*-, and *g*-). The phonetic reality underlying this change of transcription standard was obviously a partial denasalization of the Chinese nasals: *mu* had turned into *mbu*, *nu* into *ndu*, and so on. Such denasalization is evidenced in literary pronunciations in the Min (Fujian) dialects, which represent relics of the standard dialect of the Tang period, carried south by refugees from the north. This feature is quite widely spread in the present-day dialects of Shaanxi, eastern Gansu and Sichuan.

The language of the Song period was far removed from that of the *Qieyun* standard. This meant that Song users of the *Qieyun* experienced difficulty in finding the rhyme of the word the definition of which they were seeking in the dictionary. In order to remedy this situation phonological tables were devised, which at a glance show the position of any distinctive syllable in the language of the time, and its relation to the phonological system of the *Qieyun*. The most important and best known of these rhyme tables is entitled *Qieyun zhizhangtu* which may be freely rendered as 'The *Qieyun* made easy'. Traditionally this work has been attributed to the Song historian Sima Guang (1019–1086). This attribution is definitely wrong. Modern scholars suggest a considerably later date of publication than the year 1067 which is traditionally given.

The work consists of a complete tabulation of all distinctive syllables in the language, arranged in 20 tables. Within each table the graphs are located on a coordinate system. A set of 36 initial consonants is placed on the longitudinal axis, which reads from right to left. Rhymes are graded on the vertical axis on the left-hand side of the table. Such *Qieyun/Guangyun* rhymes as were no longer distinctive in the Song language occupy the same grade on the vertical axis. Within each table the words are divided into tonal categories. Words belonging to the *ru* category, and which therefore ended in *-p*, *-t* and *-k*, are correlated both with words ending in the corresponding nasal consonants *-m*, *-n*, and *-ng* and with words with open syllables: *kâng/kâk* (table 13); *kuo/kuk* (table 3), and *kâ/kât* (table 11). Within each tonal category there is a further split into four *deng* (divisions). These divisions denote differences in vowel quality (back and velarized vowels are placed in division I, while fronted vowels are placed in division II). Divisions III and IV have been interpreted as signalling the presence of a consonantal palatal glide and a vocalic palatal glide respectively. (The question whether words placed in division IV contained a vocalic palatal glide is a moot point.)

The 36 initials which appear in these tables have been attributed to the Buddhist monk Shouwen, who lived at the end of the Tang period. A fragment of a Tang manuscript, which has been discovered in modern times, contains only 30 initials and the list must therefore have been subsequently revised.

According to Joseph Needham the rhyme tables 'merit more attention than they have received from historians of mathematics, for precise tabulation was surely one of the roots of coordinate geometry'.[5]

In the early thirteenth century the 206 rhymes of the *Guangyun* were reduced to 106, in order to make the system conform with the rhyming practices of the poets of late Tang and Song. In the Qing period this set of rhymes was used as a classification system in several major lexica.

Philologists of the period between Han and Tang had realized that the rhymes of the *Shijing* ('The book of odes'), dating from the first half of the first millennium before our era, failed to rhyme in the language of their own times. In order to remedy this lack of agreement they introduced the notion of *xieyun*, 'harmonizing rhymes'. Confronted with the rhyming pair *nan* 'south' (Old Chinese *nəm*, Middle Chinese *nam*) and *yin* (Old Chinese and Middle Chinese *ʔiəm*) one fifth-century commentator suggested the reading *niəm* for the first word. The notion of harmonizing rhymes was adhered to during the Tang and the Song.

The first scholar to make a systematic study of the *Shijing* rhymes was Wu Yu (1100–54). He divided the 206 rhymes of the *Guangyun* into nine classes which he considered valid for the *Shijing*. There are a great many inconsistencies in his classification and his work is of only historical interest.

1.6 The periods of Yuan and Ming (1260–1644)

The Mongol rulers who held power in China during the Yuan dynasty had little regard for traditional Chinese scholarship. The time-honoured civil service examinations were temporarily discontinued and most Chinese literati were barred from an official career. The Mongol language, for which Kublai Khan's Tibetan advisor Phagsba (died 1279) had devised a versatile script based on the Tibetan alphabet, became the official language, accompanied in a subordinate role, by a vernacular form of written Chinese. The decline of classical scholarship and the break with the cultural heritage were no doubt partly responsible for the rapid rise of the opera-theatre and this, in turn had a tremendous impact on the direction of phonological studies. The major phonological work of the Yuan period is the *Zhongyuan yinyun* ('Sounds and rhymes of the Central Plain'), completed in 1324. Of the author Zhou Deqing

(1277–1365) we only know that he was a native of Jiangxi, south of the Yangzi River, and that, besides compiling this phonological handbook, he wrote a number of songs (*qu*). The prosodies and the rhymes of the *qu*, which flourished in the thirteenth and fourteenth centuries, were based on the living language of the time (Old Mandarin). The Northern *qu* (*beiqu*) closely reflected the language of North China, and particularly the dialect of the area around the capital Dadu (the present Peking). These songs, which could be used either alone and off-stage, or linked together to form ballad suites, or interspersed with dialogue to form plays, soon became very popular and spread to other areas with diverging dialects. The *Zhongyuan yinyun* was meant to serve as a guide to writers of *qu*. The work is divided into two parts: a list of graphs organized into homophone groups, and a discussion of the techniques of *qu* writing, with illustrative examples.

The *Zhongyuan yinyun* comprises 5865 entries, divided into 19 rhyme groups. Within each group the words are divided into the four tonal categories of Old Mandarin, *ying ping*, *yang ping*, *shang*, and *qu*. The tonal categories of Old Mandarin (thirteenth–fourteenth centuries AD) differ from those of Middle Chinese (early seventh century AD) in the following respects: Old Chinese (sixth century BC) *ping* has split into two categories, depending on the absence or presence of voice in the initial consonant. The Middle Chinese *ru* tone which accompanied syllables ending in *-p*, *-t*, and *-k* was no longer distinctive in the rhyming of *qu*. Words which formerly belonged to the *ru* category have been transferred to non-*ru* groups of words with non-consonantal endings, where they are kept together as separate entities.

Within each tone group the words are arranged in groups of homophones amounting to a total of 1627 groups. Apart from these divisions of the words into rhymes, tones and homophone groups, the *Zhongyuan yinyun* provides no information on pronunciation. Modern reconstructions of the phonological system of Old Mandarin, which have been achieved with the aid of internal evidence and external evidence provided by Middle Chinese and Modern Mandarin, show a very close agreement between Old and Modern Mandarin. The main differences between the two stages are the lack of palatal initial consonants, and the retention of the final consonant *-m* in Old Mandarin. Considerable differences also obtain with regard to the distribution of former *ru* tone words in Old and Modern Mandarin.

The *Hongwu zhengyun* ('The correct rhymes of the Hongwu reign'), which was published in 1375, shows a considerably more complex phonological structure than the *Zhongyuan yinyun*. The main differences between the two works are that the *Hongwu zhengyun* retains the four tonal categories of Middle Chinese; that it establishes 32 rhyme classes, of which 10 belong to the *ru* tone category, and that it has no less than 31 initial consonants, which comprise voiced stops, affricates and fricatives. These initial consonants had disappeared in the northern dialects prior to the publication of the *Zhongyuan yinyun*. The discrepancy between the two works probably results from the fact that the compilers of the *Hongwu zhengyun* were natives of southern China. They apparently also felt less free than Zhou Deqing to deviate from established norms of phonological description.

In the Yuan period we find the first attempt at a systematic study of grammar. In the year 1324 Lu Yiwei completed his work *Yuzhu* ('Grammatical particles'). The work contains 66 entries and discusses the functions of 135 particles. The author notes that some particles may appear in both sentence-initial and sentence-final position and attempts to define the differing functions which accompany the change of position.

He also tries to define the differing semantic connotations of one and the same particle in different contexts. He occasionally makes comparison between particles used in the classical language and particles employed in the vernacular of his time.

In this period some advances were made in the field of Old Chinese phonology. Chen Di (1541–1617) wrote the *Maoshi guyin kao* ('An investigation of the rhymes in the *Shijing*') and an essay on the rhyming in the *Chuci* ('Songs of the Chu'), an anthology of poetry from the period of the Warring States. He was the first scholar entirely to break with the notion of *xieyun*, 'harmonizing rhymes'. Chen Di showed awareness of the processes of diachronic change, and of dialectal differences and their influence on sound change.

1.7 The period of Qing (1644–1912) up to the end of the nineteenth century

During the 250 years of this period spectacular advances were made in all branches of linguistics and philology, which had a very great impact on the development of textual criticism. The greatest scholar of the early Qing period, Gu Yanwu (1613–82), had achieved a considerable reputation for learning already before the capital Peking was taken by the Manchus in 1644. To Gu Yanwu the subjective and empty speculation of the Neo-Confucian thinkers of the Ming, who had shied away from research on practical subjects, was one of the causes of the fall of the dynasty. Being himself interested in a great variety of subjects, such as economics, geography, government, military defence, literature, history and philology he successfully advocated a new approach to research, characterized by inductive methods and applicability.

The study of Old Chinese phonology was mainly based on two sources: the rhymes in the ancient anthology *Shijing* ('The book of odes') and the phonetic indications obtaining in the script (the phonetic compounds).

Throughout the period the identification of the rhyme sequences in the *Shijing* became more and more precise and the number of rhyme categories increased accordingly. Gu Yanwu wrote five books on Old Chinese phonology, of which he himself considered the *Shi benyin* ('The original sounds of the odes') as the most important one. He discarded the concept of *xieyun*, 'harmonizing rhymes', considering that the rhyming of the *Shijing* was loose, and established 10 rhyme classes. He also offered the opinion that words with the tones *ping*, *shang* and *qu* often rhymed together, while words with the *ru* tone were mostly kept apart as a special category.

In his *Guyun biaozhun* ('The standards of Old Chinese phonology') Jiang Yong (1681–1762) criticized Gu Yanwu for failing to take into account the evidence of the modern dialects. Himself an expert phonetician Jiang Yong sometimes used modern dialects, and especially his own Zhejiang dialect, as evidence for his classification of the old rhymes. Jiang Yong agreed with Gu Yanwu as to the existence of four tones in Old Chinese, but argued that the tones were not always accounted for in the rhyming. Jiang Yong's rhyme classification was further refined by his disciple Dai Zhen (1724–1777), one of the greatest thinkers in eighteenth century China.

A major breakthrough in research in the phonology of Old Chinese was achieved when Duan Yucai (1735–1815) discovered the important principle that graphs which contain the same phonetic element belong to the same rhyme category of the *Shijing*. This would imply that the rhymes of the *Shijing* and the principle underlying the construction of phonetic compounds (combinations of a classifying element and a phonetic element) represent homogeneous linguistic material. While Duan Yucai's principle is of the greatest importance we find that it is not valid in all instances: the graphs *nan* (Old Chinese *nân*), 'difficult', and *nuo* (Old Chinese *nâr*), 'to expel demons and noxious influences', share the same phonetic but belong to different rhyme classes.[6] The same is true of the graphs *yu* (Old Chinese *ngi̯u*), 'monkey' and *yong* (Old Chinese *ngi̯ung*), 'great'.[7] We therefore have to assume that phonetic compounds sometimes reflect an earlier phonological stage and that significant changes have taken place between the appearance of the phonetic compounds and the *Shijing* period.

Wang Niansun (1744–1832) wrote a number of important works on Old Chinese phonology, some of which have not as yet been published. His categorization of the *Shijing* rhymes was published by his son, Wang Yinzhi (1766–1834), in his *Jingyi shu wen* ('Account of what I have heard [from my father] concerning the interpretation of the classics').

Jiang Yougao (?–1851) continued the work of Wang Niansun. His classification of the *Shijing* rhymes has served as the basis of all subsequent phonological research. Jiang Yougao also investigated the rhymed portions obtaining in a number of prose works of the pre-Qin period.

The two sources for research into Old Chinese phonology, the rhymes and the phonetic compounds, are of unequal value: the rhymes can of course only be used for the reconstruction of the finals of the syllables, while the phonetic compounds may be used also for the reconstruction of initials. The first scholar to pay attention to the Old Chinese initial consonants was Qian Daxin (1727–86). Noting that the *Qieyun* initials *duan* (a voiceless and unaspirated dental stop) and *zhi* (a voiceless and unaspirated palatal stop) frequently occur in syllables belonging to the same phonetic series, that is in a series of graphs sharing one phonetic, and that dental and palatal stops alternate in graphic variants in ancient texts and in different *fanqie* spellings, Qian Daxin proposed that Old Chinese lacked palatal initials. He also correctly assumed that Old Chinese lacked labiodental initial consonants.

While using some of the rhyme categories of the *Qieyun/Guangyun* as labels for their classification of the *Shijing* rhymes the scholars engaged in research on Old Chinese phonology were rarely interested in the phonology of Middle Chinese. The major contribution to this branch of study was made by Chen Li (1810–82), author of the *Qieyun kao* ('Investigation of the *Qieyun*'). Chen Li made a systematic study of the 452 graphs used to 'spell' the initial categories and the 1200 graphs used to spell the finals of the *Qieyun/Guangyun*. He applied an ingenious method involving three direct and one indirect criteria in order to deduce, from these unsystematized spelling graphs, the initial and final categories of the *Qieyun* language. His direct criteria are as follows: (1) the graphs A and B are both 'spelled' by the graph C. Therefore A, B and C have the same initial category; (2) the graphs A and B 'spell' one another. Therefore A and B have the same initial category; (3) A is 'spelled' by B; B is 'spelled' by C. Therefore A, B and C have the same initial category.

Chen Li explains his indirect criterion as follows:

> Identity of initial category is established on the basis of contacts between the first *fanqie* spellers [i.e. contacts of the types described sub (1), (2) and (3) above]. But there are instances of identical categories where such contracts cannot be established, on account of the fact that *fanqie* graphs are paired together and employed to spell one another. The four graphs *duo*, *de*, *du* and *dang* belong to the same initial category, but since *duo* is used to spell *de* and vice versa, and since *du* is used to spell *dang* and vice versa, no contact can be established between all four graphs. However, when we examine the *Guangyun fanqie* spellings found in cross-references to words which have two pronunciations, we are bound to conclude that the two *fanqie* graphs, which spell the initials of the two forms which have the same initial, belong to the same initial category. For example, under the rhyme *dong* (*ping*-tone) we find the graph *dong* (to freeze) with the two spellings *de-hong* and *du-gong* (the latter a *qu*-tone word). Under the corresponding *qu*-tone rhyme song we find the same graph, with the spelling *duo-gong*. Since the spellings *du-gong* and *duo-gong* refer to the same pronunciation, the two graphs *du* and *duo* in fact belong to the same initial category.

Using this method Chen Li established 40 initial categories for Middle Chinese. It should be pointed out, however, that he failed to carry out his strict principles in practice. If we apply only his first three criteria we arrive at 47 initial categories. If we base ourselves on his indirect criterion we would end up with 33 distinctive initial categories. This far too low number results from the fact that the *Qieyun*/*Guangyun* contains a number of variant readings, which may reflect dialect variation, archaisms or borrowings from earlier rhyme books and that therefore Chen Li's indirect criterion is not always applicable.

The rapid advances in phonological studies in the eighteenth and nineteenth centuries stimulated a renewed interest in the *Shuo wen jie zi*. No fewer than eighteen major studies were devoted to the textual criticism and elucidation of the *Shuo wen*. The most important works are the *Shuo wen jie zi zhu* ('Commentary on the *Shuo wen*') by Duan Yucai, the *Shuo wen yizheng* ('Textual corroborations of the *Shuo wen*') by Gui Fu (1733–1802), the *Shuo wen tongxun dingsheng* ('Phonological arrangement of the glosses in the *Shuo wen*') by Zhu Junsheng (1788–1858), and the *Shuo wen shi li* ('On the structural principles of the graphs in the *Shuo wen*') by Wang Yun (1784–1854).

Duan Yucai's study comprises both a careful collation of the various editions of the *Shuo wen* and elucidations of the definitions of the meanings of graphs. He takes particular care distinguishing the basic meaning and derived meanings of the graphs. Gui Fu adduces a great many text examples which corroborate the definitions given in the *Shuo wen*. Zhu Junsheng radically changes the original format of the *Shuo wen* and rearranges both the original graphs and later additions into 18 rhyme categories and proceeds to define meanings on the basis of mainly phonological criteria. He particularly emphasizes the function of loan graphs. Wang Yun attempts to establish a number of sub-classes of the six types of graphs discussed in the *Shuo wen*.

Three major dictionaries were produced during the reign of Kangxi (1661–1722), the *Peiwen yunfu*, the *Pianzi leibian* and the *Kangxi zidian*.

The *Peiwen yunfu* ('The treasury of rhymes and phrases') was compiled under Imperial auspices by a committee of scholars headed by Zhang Yushu (1642–1711) and published in 1711. Compound expressions (words and phrases) are classified under their *final* characters which are arranged under 106 rhymes. There are no definitions, but a wealth of illustrative examples are provided, chosen from the traditional four branches of literature, the classics, the histories, the philosophers and *belles-lettres*.

The *Pianzi leibian* ('Topical compilation of two-character phrases'), also compiled by Imperial command, was published in 1726. The work is divided into 13 sections (Heaven and Earth, Seasons, Mountains and Rivers, Housing, Precious Objects, Numbers, Directions, Colours, Utensils, Grasses and Trees, Birds and Animals, Insects and Fishes, and Human Affairs). In each section, the two-character expressions are listed according to the rhyme of the *first* character. The *Peiwen yunfu* and the *Pianzi leibian* complement one another and are both indispensable for the location of literary and historical allusions.

The *Kangxi zidian* ('The Kangxi dictionary'), which was compiled by a committee of scholars and completed in 1716, treats 47,035 graphs and 1995 variants. In order to comply with the emperor's command that the work be completed in five years the compilers incorporated material from two dictionaries of the early seventeenth century. One of these, the *Zihui* ('Compilation of graphs'), published 1615, supplied a set of 214 classifiers or radicals, under which all graphs are arranged. Under each radical graphs are listed according to the number of pencil strokes required to write that part of the graph which does not constitute the radical. For each graph the dictionary provides eventual variant forms, *fanqie* spellings from early rhyme books and the modern pronunciation indicated by a homophone graph. Definitions of meaning are introduced by references to entries in the *Shuo wen* and the *Yupian* and illustrated by quotes from the classics, the histories, the philosophers and *belles-lettres.* Even though the hasty compilation of the work has resulted in a great many errors, the *Kangxi zidian* still serves as an indispensable tool for sinologists.

A major philological tool is the *Jingji zuangu* ('Explanations of graphs in the classical literature'), compiled by a board of scholars under the guidance of Ruan Yuan (1754–1849), a great philologist and expert on textural criticism. The dictionary, which is arranged according to the system of 106 rhymes, includes the entire vocabulary of the classics and their commentaries, histories, important philosophic writings and polite literature written before the middle of the Tang period.

Grammatical studies in the Qing period were mainly concerned with the elucidation of the functions of 'empty words', a category which in traditional Chinese linguistics comprises interjections, adverbs, prepositions, conjunctions, various substitute forms, sentence suffixes, modal particles, etc. The two main works in this field are the *Zhuzi bian lüe* ('Compendium of grammatical particles') by Liu Qi and the *Jingzhuan shi ci* ('Explanations of words in the classics and the commentaries') by Wang Yinzhi (1766–1834). Liu Qi's work, which appeared in 1711, treats 476 grammatical particles and defines their functions in texts ranging from the pre-Qin period and up to the Yuan dynasty. Wang Yinzhi's compilation, the preface of which is dated 1798, treats 167 grammatical particles and other 'empty words', used in classical texts and commentaries of the pre-Qin period. In the regrettable absence of a comprehensive grammar of the classical Chinese language these two works still fulfil important functions.

The combined efforts of the great Qing philologists and linguists paved the way for the flourishing of textual criticism which stands out as the most important branch of humanistic learning in the Qing period.

Notes

* The transcription of Chinese is in pinyin. The letters used have the following values (IPA symbols in square brackets): Pinyin initials: *b* [b̥], *p* [pʰ], *m* [m], *f* [f]; *d* [d̥], *t* [tʰ], *n* [n], *l* [l]; *z* [d̥z̥], *c* [tsʰ], *s* [s]; *zh* [d̥ʐ̥], *ch* [tʂʰ], *sh* [ʂ], *r* [ʐ]; *j* [d̥ʑ̊], *q* [tɕʰ], *x* [ɕ]; *g* [g̊], *k* [kʰ], *h* [x]; Pinyin finals: *i* [i] (after the initials *z, c, s* the vowel *i* is realized as a vocalized [z̩]; after the initials *zh, ch, sh, r* the vowel *i* is realized as a vocalized [ʐ̩]), *a* [ɑ], *e* [ɤ̂], *o* [ɔ], *ai* [ai], *ei* [ei], *ao* [ɑʊ], *ou* [ou], *an* [an], *en* [ən], *ang* [ɑŋ], *eng* [ʌŋ], *ong* [ʊŋ], *er* [əʴ]; *ia* [iɑ], *ie* [iɛ], *iao* [iɑʊ], *iu* [iu] (with tones 1 or 2), [iou] (with tones 3 or 4), for the tones see p. 9, *ian* [iɛn], *in* [in], *iang* [iɑŋ],

ing [iŋ], *iong* [iʊŋ]; *u* [u], *ua* [uɑ], *uo* [uɔ], *uai* [uai], *ui* [ui] (with tones 1 or 2), [uei] (with tones 3 or 4), *uan* [uan], *un* [un], *uang* [uɑŋ], *ueng* [uʌŋ]; *ü* (after the initials *j*, *q*, *x* pinyin omits the trema above the vowel *ü*) [y], *üe* [yɛ], *üan* [yan], *ün* [yn].

1. *Fengsu tongyi* ('A comprehensive account of customs and mores'), by Ying Shao (second century BC).
2. *Hsün Tzu* (Xun Zi) (1963) *Basic Writings*, trans. by B. Watson, Columbia University Press, New York and London, 144.
3. Examples of the six types of graphs in the *Shuo wen jie zi* in their ancient and modern form:

Pictographs		日	'sun'
		月	'moon'
		子	'child'
Ideographs	一	一	'one'
	三	三	'three'
Compound ideographs		明	'bright'
Phonetic compounds		江	'The Yangzi river'
		河	'The Yellow river'

In these graphs the common left-hand element is a classifier signifying 'water'. The right-hand element in the first graph reads *gong* (Old Chinese *kung*) and serves to indicate the pronunciation of the graph in which it is included, which was Old Chinese *kŭng*, modern *jiang*. The phonetic in the second graph is *ke* (Old Chinese *k'â*), approximating the pronunciation of the graph in which it is included, *he* (Old Chinese *g'a*).

Loan characters		來	'wheat'.
used to denote the homophone verb 'to come'.			
Derivative graphs		考	'high age'
		老	'old'

4. Teng, Ssu-Yü (1968) *Family Instructions for the Yen Clan (Yen-shih chia-hsün) by Yen Chih-t'ui. An Annotated Translation with Introduction* (Monographies du T'oung Pao, 4), E. J. Brill, Leiden.
5. Joseph Needham (1961) *Science and Civilisation in China, Vol. 1*, Cambridge University Press, Cambridge, 34.
6. 難 nan; 儺 nuo.
7. 禺 yu; 顒 yong.

Bibliography

BODMAN, N. C. (1954) *A Linguistic Study of the Shih Ming* (Harvard-Yenching Institute Studies, II), Harvard University Press, Cambridge, Mass.

COBLIN, W. S. (1972) An Introductory Study of Textual and Linguistic Problems in Erh-ya (PhD Thesis, University of Washington), University Microfilms, Ann Arbor, Michigan.

KARLGREN, B. (1940) Grammata Serica, *Bulletin of the Museum of Far Eastern Antiquities*, 12, 1–471.

KARLGREN, B. (1954) Compendium of Phonetics in Ancient and Archaic Chinese, *Bulletin of the Museum of Far Eastern Antiquities*, 26, 211–367.

LO, CH'ANG-P'EI (1944) Indian Influence on the Study of Chinese Phonology, *Sino-Indian Studies*, 1, 115–27.

STIMSON, H. (1962) Phonology of the Chung-yüan yin-yün, *Tsinghua Journal of Chinese Studies, New Series*, 3, 114–59.

TENG, SSU-YÜ and BIGGERSTAFF, K. (1950) *An Annotated Bibliography of Selected Chinese Reference Works*, Harvard University Press, Cambridge, Mass.

THERN, K. L. (1966) *Postface of the Shuo-wen Chieh-tzu, the First Comprehensive Chinese Dictionary* (Wisconsin China Series, 1), Department of East Asian Languages and Literature, University of Wisconsin.

2

Indian linguistics

George Cardona

2.1 Introduction*

Ancient and medieval Indian scholars produced works of linguistic interest concerning Sanskrit, the high language (*saṁskṛtā vāk* 'refined, ritually pure speech') accepted by an early Indo-Aryan élite as the most correct speech form, and related Middle Indic vernaculars (called *prākṛta*), as well as Dravidian languages. In the following, I shall concentrate on the works that deal with Sanskrit. I shall consider in particular some of the major concerns of Indian grammarians – principally within the Pāṇinian traditions – and others with respect to topics of linguistic importance. These are justifiably considered the most original and important contributions early Indian scholars have made to the study of language, and Pāṇini is generally acknowledged as a grammarian of the first rank.

2.1.1 Linguistic work connected with the Vedas

Early Indian thought concerning language was intimately connected with the sacred texts called the Vedas, India's most ancient literary documents. From early on these were associated with six ancillaries (*vedāṅga* [nom. pl. nt. *vedāṅgāni*], 'limbs of the Veda') intended to help in the proper maintenance and application of these texts. Three of the vedāṅgas concern areas that in modern times would come within the purview of linguistics: śikṣā ('phonetics'), vyākaraṇa ('grammar'), and nirukta ('etymology'). Works in the first area deal with the production of sounds and their proper pronunciation for various recitational traditions. Such phonetic matters are treated also in works called *prātiśākhya*. In addition, these deal in great detail with the relations between continuously recited versions

* See beginning of Notes.

(*saṁhitāpāṭhāḥ*) of Vedas and the analysed texts (*padapāṭhāḥ*) associated with them. The procedures for positing the various padapāṭhas show that the authors of these analysed texts followed definite principles whereby divisions were made at particular places – not only between syntactic words and members of compounds but also at certain morph boundaries within syntactic words – and particular words were left unanalysed. Moreover, padapāṭhas came to be viewed as the sources from which saṁhitāpāṭhas were derived, so that phonological rules of derivation, together with phonological classifications, came under consideration. Vyākaraṇa serves to account for the relations among components of sentences (*vākyāni* 'utterances') through derivational systems. Nirukta concerns itself with the etymological explanation (*nirvacanam*) of particular words in Vedic texts.

2.1.2 Pāṇini and his successors

The culmination of early linguistic thought in India is represented in the grammar, called the Aṣṭādhyāyī ('group of eight chapters'), of the renowned grammarian Pāṇini, who cannot reasonably be considered to have lived later than the early fourth century BC. Pāṇini's work not only surpassed and eclipsed works of earlier grammarians, upon whose work he drew, but also became the object of intense scrutiny. The earliest author whose discussions are available is Kātyāyana (c. third century BC), who takes up problematic issues concerning particular rules (*sūtra*, nom. pl. *sūtrāṇi*) in his vārttikas (see note 1), and Patañjali (mid-second century BC), whose Mahābhāṣya ('great commentary') not only incorporates Kātyāyana's vārttikas – which are paraphrased and discussed – but also includes independent considerations of certain problems. Traditionally, vārttikas are viewed as intended to consider what is said, what is left unsaid, and what is possibly wrongly said in sūtras.[1]

There can be no reasonable doubt that commentatorial works on Pāṇini's grammar were produced before Kātyāyana, and commentaries continued to be produced later, right up to the present day. These commentaries differ among themselves not only as concerns particular interpretations accepted and defended but also in the way they organize the source text. Some follow the order of the sūtras as found in the Aṣṭādhyāyī. The most famous and widely used commentary of this type is the Kāśikāvṛtti (c. seventh century AD) of Jayāditya and Vāmana, which is based on a conflated version of the Aṣṭādhyāyī, including additions and modifications suggested in vārttikas of Kātyāyana and accepted earlier by Candragomin in his own grammar, the Cāndravyākaraṇa. Some commentaries, on the other hand, reorder the sūtras of the Aṣṭādhyāyī into thematic groups: rules concerning terminology (*saṁjñāsūtrāṇi*), metarules (*paribhāṣāsūtrāṇi*), sandhi rules, sūtras that apply in the derivation of nominal forms, and so on. The most widely used text of this kind is the Siddhāntakaumudī of Bhaṭṭojidīkṣita (sixteenth century).

2.1.3 Non-Pāṇinian works

Although grammatical works associated with Pāṇini are justly the most well known, there are other grammatical treatises and commentaries. One such grammar, Candragomin's, is renowned not only because it reflects modifications in Pāṇini's statements but also because, according to tradition, Candragomin is considered to have revived the study of Pāṇinian grammar after this had ceased to be handed down traditionally from teacher to pupil. Other well-known grammars are the Kātantra and a whole series of works by Jainas, among them the Jainendravyākaraṇa and Hemacandra's Siddhahemaśabdānuśāsana. Some of these works, such as the Kātantra, are methodologically interesting in that they revived procedures found in prātiśākhya descriptions but abandoned by Pāṇini and other grammarians.

The discussions found in commentatorial works are not restricted to circles of grammarians alone – whether of the Pāṇinian 'school' or within any of the various non-Pāṇinian traditions – but extend to thinkers in areas such as the exegesis of ritual texts (*mīmāṁsā*), poetics, different schools of logic, and others, including Buddhist thinkers. It is not without reason that Patañjali says that grammar is the principal one among the six vedāṅgas (*pradhānaṁ ca ṣaṭsv aṅgeṣu vyākaraṇam*: Abhyankar I.1, line 19).

2.2 Early work on phonetics and phonology

2.2.1 Speech production

Early prātiśākhya texts such as the Ṛgvedaprātiśākhya and the Taittirīyaprātiśākhya deal with the relations between padapāṭha and saṁhitāpāṭha and also include descriptions of speech production which show considerable sophistication. Attention is paid not only to places (*sthānāni*) where particular sounds are produced but also to the types of articulation involved – whether full occlusion (*spṛṣṭam*), slight occlusion (*duspṛṣṭam*), and so on – as well as to how the air stream is modified as it is emitted. Different varieties of air stream emitted, dependent on the status of the glottis, are also distinguished and associated with distinct groups of sounds.

A brief summary of the major points made in the Taittirīyaprātiśākhya concerning speech production and phonologically distinct sets of sounds will serve to illustrate.[2] Three varieties of air stream are recognized, depending on whether the glottis (*kaṇṭha*) is close (*saṁvṛte kaṇṭhe*), open (*vivṛte* [*kaṇṭhe*]) or midway (*madhye*) between these states; these are respectively called *nāda*, *śvāsa*, and *hakāra*.[3] They are the basic matter (*prakṛti*) of articulated sounds (*varṇaprakṛtayaḥ*): nāda for vowels (*svara*) and voiced consonants (*ghoṣavat*), hakāra for *h* and voiced aspirated stops (*caturtha*), śvāsa for voiceless consonants (*aghoṣa*).[4] The same work also distinguishes between the gestures made in producing vowels and consonants at places of production (*sthāna*). In producing vowels, a speaker brings an active articulator (*karaṇam*) into proximity (*upasaṁharati*) with a place of production (*sthānam*); for producing other sounds, one brings an articulator into contact (*sparśayati* 'causes to touch') at a place of production.[5] For example, in producing sounds of the group *c ch j jh ñ* (*cavarge*), one lets the blade of the tongue (*jihvāmadhyena* 'middle of the tongue') make contact at the palate (*tālau*), but for producing *i*- vowels and *e* one brings the tongue blade (*jihvāmadhyam*) into proximity with the palate.[6]

2.2.2 Phonological classifications and operations

A distinction is made between phonetics and phonology. Terms like *svara*, 'vowel', *vyañjana*, 'consonant', *ghoṣavat*, 'voiced consonant', *aghoṣa*, 'voiceless consonant' are used with reference to members of phonological classes, so that in treatises which observe the distinction strictly *ghoṣavat* is not used of vowels, although these are obviously voiced. The phonological classes in question are pertinent to phonological rules of conversion, of the type $a \rightarrow b$, whereby forms in saṁhitāpāṭhas are derived from forms in padapāṭhas. For example, the saṁhitāpāṭha of Ṛgveda 8.100.10a: *yád vā́g vádanty avicetanā́ni*, 2.18.4b: *ā́ catúrbhir ā́ ṣaḍbhír hūyámānaḥ* contain *yád*, 'when', before *vā́g* (nom. sg.) 'speech', which is followed by *vádanty* 'uttering' (nom. sg. fem. agreeing with *vā́g*), and *ṣaḍ*- 'six' before the instrumental plural ending *-bhir*. The corresponding passages of the padapāṭha are: *yát/vā́k/vádantī/ avi-cetanā́ni/*, *ā́/catúḥ-bhiḥ/ā́/ṣaḍ-bhíḥ/hūyámānaḥ*, with pauses not only between syntactically separate words such as *yát* and *vāk* but also between the ending *bhiḥ* and preceding stems. A rule of the Ṛgvedaprātiśākhya[7] provides that voiceless unaspirated stops (*prathamāḥ*) change to corresponding (*svān* 'own') voiced unaspirated stops (*tṛtīyān*) if they are followed by voiced consonants (*ghoṣavatparāḥ*): *yát vā́k* → *yád vā́k*, *vā́k vádantī* → *vā́g vádantī*, *ṣaṭ-bhíḥ* → *ṣaḍbhíḥ*. Similarly, a rule of the Taittirīyaprātiśākhya[8] provides that a voiceless unaspirated stop (*prathamaḥ*) changes to a voiced unaspirated stop (*tṛtīyam*) of the same class (*savargīyam*) if it is followed by a vowel or a voiced consonant (*svara-ghoṣavatparaḥ*).

2.2.3 Criteria for recognizing separate constituents in padapāṭhas

As noted earlier, the continuously recited text of a Veda is generally treated as derived from a corresponding analysed text. The Ṛgveda-prātiśākhya[9] explicitly states that the continuous recitation in close junction (*saṁhitā*) has for its source the separately recited padas (*padaprakṛtiḥ*) of the padapāṭha, and it goes on to say that the former (*sā*) is derived from the latter through bringing pada-final sounds (*padāntān*) into contact with the initial sounds of padas (*padādibhiḥ*) without any interval (*kālāvyavāyena*).[10] As I have also pointed out, the padas which the padapāṭha recognizes as separate units are not only syntactic words, including clitics, but also endings such as *-bhiḥ* and stems that precede them.

Such divisions are based on phonological criteria. Thus, one has final *-o* instead of *-aḥ* before such endings (e.g. *támobhiḥ*: *támaḥ* [nom.-acc. sg.] 'darkness'), just as *-o* is found instead of *-aḥ* at a full word boundary where a voiced consonant follows; and *-n*-stems such as *rā́jan-* 'king' have forms without *-n-* not only at full word boundaries (nom. sg. *rā́jā*) but also before an ending like *-bhiḥ* (instr. pl. *rā́jabhiḥ*). Accordingly, composers of padapāṭhas (*padakā-rāḥ*) such as Śākalya, who composed the padapāṭha to the Ṛgveda, treat such endings as preceded by a pada boundary. On similar grounds, certain derivational affixes are also treated as preceded by a pada boundary under the appropriate circumstances. For example, *gó-mat* 'rich in cattle' (acc. sg. masc. *gó-mantam*) is split as shown, but the suffix of *ū́rjasvantaḥ* (nom. pl. masc.) 'full of strength' is not so split: if *-vantaḥ* were preceded by a pada boundary, one should have *-o* instead of *-as* before *-v-*. Again, corresponding to *vṛṣāyáte* 'acts like a bull' of the saṁhitāpāṭha, the padapāṭha has *vṛṣa-yáte*, recognizing that a derivate with the denominative suffix *-yá-* corresponds to a syntactic complex that includes a nominative form of the stem *vṛṣan-*: *vṛṣāyáte* = *vṛ́ṣā íva ā́carati*.

Of course, components of compounds are split, for comparable reasons; e.g. *prajā́-patiḥ*. In addition, padakāras split items into two component padas at most, and in doing so they recognize a hierarchy. Thus, *pra-jā́* 'creature, progeny', *prajā́-vat* 'rich in progeny', *prajā́-patiḥ*. 'Prajāpati', *prajā́pati-gṛhītayā* 'seized by Prajāpati' (instr. sg. fem.) are split as shown.

Moreover, the authors of padapāṭhas show evidence of letting semantic considerations also influence their analysis. For example, although *ṛtvíj-* 'ritual officiant, priest' is obviously divisible into *ṛtu-* 'appropriate time, season' and *ij*, an agent noun derived from *yaj* 'venerate, perform a sacrificial rite', the components of forms such as *ṛtvíjam* (acc. sg.) are not separated by pause in the padapāṭha. This reflects a possible ambiguity in the precise phrase to which the compound is considered to correspond and the fact that *ṛtvíj-* came to have a meaning ('priest') not associated with a fixed etymological segmentation. In its commentary on Pāṇini 3.2.59, where *ṛtvíj-* is given as a ready-made derivate with a zero-affix ***kvin*** (= *v* with markers *k*, *i*, *n*; see section 2.4.1) the Kāśikāvṛtti gives different paraphrases of the compound, including ones such that this corresponds to phrases in which *yajati* 'performs a rite, venerates' is construed with a locative (*ṛtau yajati* ' . . . at the appropriate time, season') or an accusative (*ṛtuṁ yajati*); it also notes that this is used as a term with a fixed meaning not necessarily associated with its etymological analysis. Again, corresponding to *duṣṭáraḥ* of Ṛgveda 3.24.1, the padapāṭha has *dustáraḥ* instead of *duḥtáraḥ*. The same verse occurs in the Yajurveda, as Vājasaneyisaṁhitā 9.37. The padapāṭha corresponding to this shows that *duṣṭárah* is a compound by giving *duṣṭáraḥ dustára iti dustáraḥ*, but it does not separate the pre-verb from the following verbal derivative by means of a pause, so that it does not give *duḥ-táraḥ*. In the Vājasaneyiprātiśākhya,[11] moreover, *duṣṭáraḥ* is given as one of a series of compounds in which there is no separate pronunciation (*nāvagrahaḥ*) of components divided by pause, and commentators explain that this reflects a possible ambiguity concerning the derivation of the verbal noun, from different verbs *tṝ*. Centuries earlier than these commentators, Bhartṛhari, in the autocommentary on verse 2.13 of his Vākyapadīya, remarks that *dustáraḥ* is given in the padapāṭha without pause between components because the second element of the compound could derive from either of two verbs.[12]

The authors of padapāṭhas thus clearly followed certain principles in setting up their analysed texts. They were also clearly aware of grammatical derivations and phonological processes.[13] One of these padakāras, moreover, antedates Pāṇini, who refers to Śākalya, the author of the padapāṭha associated with the Ṛgvedasaṁhitā (see section 2.4.3).

2.3 Etymology

2.3.1 Introduction

Vedic texts, especially Brāhmaṇas and Āraṇyakas, abound in etymological explanations meant to demonstrate the essential properties on account of which entities are called by the names they bear. For example, *puruṣa* ('man') used in the sense of 'life breath' (*prāṇaḥ*) is explained as follows: The life breath resides (*śete* 'lies') in the body (*puri*), so that, being so (*puriśayaṁ santam* [acc. sg.]), it is referred to (*ācakṣate* '[the gods] call') *puruṣa*, in an oblique manner (*parokṣeṇa* 'beyond direct observation'); for the gods (*devāḥ*) are fond of what is not directly observable (*parokṣapriyā iva*) and dislike what is obvious (*pratyakṣadviṣaḥ*).[14]

2.3.2 Yāska's Nirukta

Etymology came to be used as a tool in Vedic exegesis. An early collection of words subject to such analysis is the Nighaṇṭu (nom. pl. *nighaṇṭavaḥ*), which Yāska took as a basis for etymological discussions in his work called Nirukta. In this work, Yāska also explains the status of nirukta relative to grammar (*vyākaraṇa*) and the procedures to be followed in giving etymological explanations. He remarks that without this (*idam antareṇa*) etymological science there is no proper understanding of the meanings to be understood in Vedic mantras (*mantreṣv arthapraptyayo na vidyate*).[15] Moreover, one who does not comprehend the meaning (*artham apratiyataḥ* [gen. sg.]) of a given item cannot have an absolute understanding of the proper accent and grammatical formation of the term in question (*nātyantaṁ svarasaṁskāroddeśaḥ*), since these are dependent on the meanings of terms; for example, a derivate may be accented in two different manners, depending on its meaning. Hence, this science of etymology, which is the abode of other sciences (*vidyāsthānam*), is a complement to grammar (*vyākaraṇasya kārtsnyam*) while it also serves its own purpose (*svārthasādhakaṁ ca*).[16]

2.3.3 Grammar presupposed in Nirukta

Clearly, Yāska assumes that etymological explanation presupposes grammar. Thus, for example, he recognizes four classes comparable to what Westerners call parts of speech: nominal forms (*nāman*), verb forms (*ākhyāta*), preverbs (*upasarga*), and particles (*nipāta*). Yāska goes on to note what are said to be the distinctive characteristics of nominal and verbal forms. A verb form (*ākhyātam*) has an activity as its principal meaning (*bhāvapradhānam*), but nominal forms (*nāmāni*) have substantial beings as their principal meanings (*sattvapradhānāni*). Moreover, he remarks, in cases where both nominals and verbals signify actions, one uses a verb form to signify (*ākhyātenācaṣṭe* 'expresses with a verb form') an act in sequence, in progress (*pūrvāparībhūtaṁ bhāvam*), as when one says *vrajati*, 'is going', *pacati*, 'is cooking'; and nominal forms like the action nouns *vrajyā*, 'going', *paktiḥ*, 'cooking' are used to signify an action as a being, an embodied entity (*mūrtaṁ sattvabhūtaṁ sattvanāmabhiḥ*) encompassing an act from beginning to end (*upakramaprabhṛty apavargaparyantaṁ*), but not viewed as sequential.[17]

2.3.4 Views of etymologists and grammarians contrasted

Yāska contrasts the views of etymologists and grammarians: The convention of etymologists is that all substantives (*nāmāni* 'nominals') arise from verbs (*nāmāny ākhyātajāni*), and this is accepted also by the grammarian Śākaṭāyana; but other grammarians hold that not all substantives derive from verbs (*na sarvāṇīti*), and this view is accepted by the etymologist Gārgya.[18] Adherents of these opposing views also present arguments. Two of the arguments given against the position that all substantives derive from verbs are as follows.

Any entity that carried out the action (*yaḥ kaśca tat karma kuryāt*) which serves as a basis for something being designated by a particular substantive derived from a verb denoting that action would be referred to by that term (*sarvaṁ tat sattvam tathācakṣīran*); for example, if a horse is called *aśva* because it covers a distance on a path (*adhvānam aśnute*), anything that performs the action denoted by the verb *aśnute* should equally be called *aśva*, but this is not so.[19] In addition, things would be referred to by means of derivates with the formations which are appropriate, according to grammatical rules of derivation, to their being derived from the verbs in question and such as would be immediately understood; accordingly, instead of using *puruṣa* one would refer to the entity in question by means of the derivate *puriśaya*,[20] and instead of *aśva* one would use *aṣṭṛ*-, a derivate in which *aś*, 'reach', is followed by the general agentive suffix *tṛ*.[21]

2.3.5 The etymologists' stand maintained

Adherents of the etymologists' position defend their stand. The first objection noted is met with an appeal to general usage: we see (*paśyāmaḥ*) that of many people who perform the same act (*samānakarmaṇām*), some receive a particular appellation (*nāmadheyapratilambham ekeṣām*) by which they are specifically referred to but others do not (*naikeṣām*); for example, *takṣan*-'carpenter' is used only of some people who hew, not of any one who engages in this act.[22] Against the second objection, etymologists argue that there are indeed other instances of derivates with primary suffixes (*kṛtaḥ*) that have restricted usage (*alpaprayogāḥ*)[23] and whose meanings are nevertheless clearly understood.

Yāska stands firmly by the etymologists' tenet: it is fine to follow the derivations of grammarians in the case of words like *kartā* (nom. sg. of *kar-tṛ-* 'one who does, makes, an agent'), for which accent and derivational formation (*svarasaṁskārau*) in terms of bases and affixes are clearly capable (*samarthau*) of association with the meanings, being linked harmoniously with a modification of a verb (*vikāreṇānvitau*). Even if such obvious derivation is not available, however, one should explain words in terms of acts signified by verbs, and in no instance should one not give such an etymological explanation (*na tv eva na nirbrūyāt*), giving priority always to the meanings (*arthanityaḥ*) of terms being explained.[24]

2.3.6 Yāska and Pāṇini

Although Yāska does indeed presuppose grammatical descriptions, the available evidence is not sufficient to determine whether he preceded or succeeded Pāṇini. From the point of view of methodology, however, this is not a crucial issue, since such early works as Śākalya's padapāṭha to the Ṛgveda already give clear evidence of sophistication regarding grammatical analysis.

2.4 Pāṇini

2.4.1 Introduction

The culmination of early phonological and grammatical work in ancient India is to be seen in the work of India's most outstanding and famous grammarian of all time, Pāṇini. He follows earlier traditions in that he describes Sanskrit by means of a derivational system wherein final utterances are obtained by performing operations on posited strings (see section 2.4.4.2). Pāṇini also adopts a typical grammarian's stance with respect to the etymological controversy (see section 2.3.4): he does indeed provide for the derivation of such obviously analysable items as *kar-tṛ-* (← *kṛ-tṛ*) 'one who makes, does, an agent', *pāc-aka-*, 'cook' (← *pac-aka*), *kṛ-ta-*, 'made, done', *kar-aṇa-* (← *kṛ-ana*) 'means of making, doing, instrument'; and he also accepts the derivation of nominals such as *jāgṛ-vi-*, 'vigilant one, king', for which he does not explicitly set down rules for introducing affixes, but he does not insist on deriving substantives like *go-* or *puruṣa-* from verbs.[25]

2.4.2 The Aṣṭādhayāyī and its ancillaries

The core of Pāṇini's work is a set of nearly 4000 sūtras distributed among eight chapters, the Aṣṭādhyāyī, each chapter (*adhyāya*) of which is subdivided into four quarter-chapters (*pāda*). The Aṣṭādhyāyī proper is accompanied by three ancillary texts.

First, there is Pāṇini's catalogue of sounds (*akṣarasamāmnāya*), which is divided into 14 groups of sounds in an order corresponding to the way in which Paṇini formulates phonological rules. Each of the 14 groups is closed by a marker (called *it*: shown here in bold face): *a i u* ***ṇ****, ṛ ḷ* ***k****, e o* ***ń****, ai au* ***c****, h y v r* ***ṭ****, l* ***ṇ****, ñ m ṅ ṇ n* ***m****, jh bh* ***ñ****, gh ḍh dh* ***ṣ****, j b g ḍ d* ***ś****, kh ph ch ṭh th c ṭ t* ***v****, k p* ***y****, ś ṣ s* ***r****, h* ***l***. Such markers serve to form abbreviatory terms referring to groups of elements: a term **iM**, consisting of an item **i** and a final marker **M**, refers to **i** and all subsequent items of a list up to the marker; for example, ***ac*** refers to the sounds from *a* through *ai*, that is, to all the vowels; ***hal*** signifies consonants; ***aś*** designates voiced segments; ***ik*** denotes *i u ṛ l*; ***yaṇ*** designates the corresponding semivowels *y v r l*; ***jaś*** refers to voiced unaspirated non-nasal stops.

The sūtra text is also accompanied by a catalogue of verbs (*dhātupāṭha*), in which verbal bases, starting with *bhū*, 'be, become', are distributed among ten classes, depending on the operations appropriate to these classes: verbs of the first class have present and imperfect stems with a low-pitched (*anudātta*) suffix *a* that conditions guṇa substitution in the base (e.g. *bháv-a-ti* 'is' ← *bhū-a-ti*); those of the second class have corresponding stems without a suffix before endings (e.g. *át-ti* 'eats' ← *ád-ti*); verbs with reduplicated present and imperfect forms are included in the third set (e.g. *juhóti* 'offers oblations' ← *hú-ti*); bases of the fourth set form radically accented presents and imperfects with a suffix *-ya-* (e.g. *dī́v-ya-ti* 'gambles' ← *dív-ya-ti*); the next group consists of verbs whose present and imperfect stems have the suffix *-nu-/-no-* (e.g. *sunóti, sunuté* 'presses juice out of . . .' ← *su-nu-ti, su-nu-ta*); verbs in the sixth class have corresponding stems with high-pitched (*udātta*) *-á-* that does not condition guṇa substitution (e.g. *tud-á-ti* 'shoves, goads, wounds'); the seventh class contains bases whose present and imperfect stems have an infix *-na-/-n-* (e.g. *ruṇáddhi* 'obstructs' ← *rúdh-ti, rundhánti* (3rd pl. pres.) ← *runadh-ánti* ← *rudh-ánti*); bases of the eighth class have corresponding forms with *-u-/-o-* (e.g. *tan-ó-ti* [← *tan-ú-ti*], *tan-u-té* 'stretches' ← *tan-té, kar-ó-ti, kur-u-té* 'makes, does' ← *kṛ-ú-ti, kṛ-u-té*). Verbs of the ninth class take an affix *-nā-/nī* (e.g. *krī-ṇā́-ti* [← *krī-nā́-ti* ← *krī-ti*], *krī-ṇī-té* [← *krī-nī-tá krī-na*] 'buys'). Verbs in the tenth class take a suffix -*i-/-e-* that is followed by low-pitched *-a-* in present and imperfect forms (e.g. *cor-áy-a-ti* 'steals' ← *cur-í-a-ti*).

Finally, the appendix called gaṇapāṭha consists of groups of items which are pertinent to particular operations and are recited along with the rules in which these operations are provided.

2.4.3 The language described

Pāṇini describes not only the language current at his time in his native area – traditionally said to be Śalātura in the north-west of the Indian subcontinent – but also characteristics of other dialects, including features particular to archaic dialects reflected in Vedic texts. In addition, Pāṇini refers to other grammarians, some by name. For example, he notes that according to Śākalya, *-o* of a vocative singular form is *pragṛhya* – that is, exempt from contextual phonological modification – when it is followed by *iti* that does not belong to the original Vedic text.[26] This reflects the practice which Śākalya follows in his padapāṭha to the Ṛgveda. In order to show that *-o* of a vocative singular form such as *vāyo* 'Vāyu' is exempt from prevocalic alternation, in accordance with usage of his own dialect, Śākalya puts the citation particle *iti* after the form: *vāyo íti* instead of *vāyav íti*.

2.4.4 Pāṇini's derivational system

2.4.4.1 The units of the system

Pāṇini describes Sanskrit by means of a derivational system. This involves in the first instance introducing affixes after bases under meaning conditions: an affix A occurs with base B if meaning M is to be signified.[27] Initial strings of the type (1a)–(2a) are thus set up, and operations then apply to such strings to arrive at strings such as (1b)–(2b), which are actually used in communication. The fundamental units of this derivational system are bases, stems (*aṅga*),[28] affixes (*pratyaya*),[29] and padas.

A syntactic pada is an item that terminates in a nominal or verbal ending (*suptiṅantam*).[30] Pāṇini also recognizes, as did padakāras before him, morphological padas, with pada boundaries between stems and certain endings; e.g. the stem *támas-* of *tamas-bhis* is classed as a pada,[31] so that the operations apply which allow deriving *támobhis*, with *-o-* before the ending *bhis*.

A stem is either simple or complex. For example, *kṛ-a* (→ *cakāra* [3sg. pfct. act.]) is a pada with a simple stem, the verbal base *kṛ* 'do, make', followed by the verb ending ***ṇal*** (= *a* with markers *ṇ*, *l*); *go-s* (→ *gaus* [nom. sg.]) is a pada in which the simple nominal stem *go-* 'cow, ox' is followed by the nominal ending ***su*** (= *s* with marker *u*). On the other hand the pada *bhū-a-ti* (→ *bhavati*) contains two stems: the verbal base *bhū* is a simple stem with respect to the affix *-a-*, and *bhū-a-* is a complex stem with respect to the ending *ti*; *kar-tṛ-ī-ā* (→ *kartryā* [instr. sg.]) is a pada with complex stems that include the agent affix ***tṛc*** (= *tṛ* with marker *c*) and the feminine suffix ***ṅīp***. (= *ī* with markers *ṅ*, *p*).

Bases, both verbal and nominal, are either primitive or derived. A primitive verbal base is a root such as *bhū*, and a primitive nominal base is one such as *go*, not derived with an affix. Derived verbal bases are either deverbative or denominative. For example, causatives such as *kṛ-i* (→ *kār-i*: 3sg. pres. *kārayati* [act.], *kārayate* [mid.]) 'have . . . do, make' and desideratives such as *kṛ-sa* (→ *cikīrṣa*: *cikīrṣati, cikīrṣate*) 'wish to do, make' are deverbative verbal bases, formed from primitive verbs through suffixation; a verb like *vṛṣa-ya* (3sg. pres. *vṛṣāyate*) 'act like a bull' is denominative, formed by adding an affix to a nominal pada (*vṛṣan-s-ya*), the ending of which is deleted in the course of derivation: *vṛṣan-s-ya* → *vṛṣan-ya* → *vṛṣa-ya* → *vṛṣā-ya*. Derived nominal bases are also either deverbative or denominative. For example, derivates such as *kṛ-tṛ* (→ *kar-tṛ*: nom. sg. masc. *kartā* 'one who makes, does, an agent'), *kāri-itṛ* (→ *kāray-itṛ*: *kārayitā*) 'one who has someone do something' are deverbative, formed by adding the suffix *tṛ* to verbs. Denominative derived nominal bases are either compounds – such as *upāgni,* 'near the fire', *tatpuruṣa*, 'his servant', *bahuvrīhi*, 'someone who has much rice', *mātāpitṛ* (nom. du. *mātāpitarau*) 'mother and father' – or derivates with affixes called *taddhita*, such as *aupagava* (← *upagu-as-a*, with the affix *a* following a pada containing the genitive ending ***ṅas***) 'descendant of Upagu' or *tatra* (← *tad-i-tra*, with the affix ***tral*** after a pada with the locative ending ***ṅi***) 'there, in that . . .'. Derived bases enter into the same derivational procedures as do primitive bases.

2.4.4.2 The derivational procedure

The derivational procedure which Pāṇini operates with can be illustrated briefly by means of the following sentences:

(1b) *devadatta odanaṁ pacati* 'Devadatta is cooking rice'.
(2b) *devadattenaudanaḥ pacyate* 'Rice is being cooked by D'.

These are derived from the initial strings

(1a) *devadatta-s odana-am pac-L*
(2a) *devadatta-ā odana-s pac-L*

in which the verb *pac* 'cook' is followed by an abstract L-affix – here ***laṭ***, with the markers *a*, *ṭ* – and the nominal bases *devadatta*, 'Devadatta', *odana*, 'cooked rice' are followed by the endings ***su***, *am*, ***ṭā***, ***su***.

Pāṇini takes certain aspects of meaning into consideration from the very beginning of a derivation. Thus, any L-affix is introduced to signify an agent (*kartṛ* [loc. sg. *kartari*]) or an object (*karman* [*karmaṇi*]) as in (1a) and (2a) respectively.[32] Particular L-affixes are introduced under more specific conditions of time reference and modality; for example, ***laṭ*** is introduced if an act is referred to current, present time (*vartamāna*). An ending of the second triplet of nominal endings (*dvitīyā*), such as the accusative singular ending *am*, is introduced after a nominal if an object is to be signified; an ending of the third triplet, such as *ṭā* (instr. sg.), is introduced if an instrument or agent is to be signified. Moreover, sentences such as (1) and (2) are related in Pāṇini's system by making them alternative expressions of the same syntactic-semantic relations and subordinating the expression of agent and object by nominal affixes to their expression by verbal ones. Thus, the object-signifier *am* follows *odana* in (1a), where ***laṭ*** is introduced to signify an agent; the agentive ending *ṭā* does not follow *devadatta* in this string. In (2a), on the other hand, ***laṭ*** is introduced to signify an object, so that the agentive ending *ṭā* does follow *devadatta*, but here *odana* does not take an object-signifying ending.

Operations apply to initial strings like (1a), (2a) in order to arrive at final strings such as (1b), (2b). The principal operations with which Pāṇini operates in this respect are replacing one unit with another, introducing affixes, and adding augments to given items. For example, an L-affix like ***laṭ*** is subject to replacement by a verb ending: by ***tip*** in deriving (1b), by *ta* in deriving (2b); moreover, since the ending *ta* derives from an L-affix marked with *ṭ*, its *-a* is replaced by *e*. One thus gets *pac-ti*, *pac-te*, which are subject to additional affixations: ***śap*** is introduced after *pac* followed by the agentive ending *ti*, and *-ya**k**-* is introduced after *pac* followed by the object-signifying ending *te*. Nominal endings also are subject to substitution in particular contexts; thus, *ṭā* is replaced by *ina* after a stem in *-a*: *devadatta-ā* → *devadatta-ina*.

Phonological substitution rules apply within padas across affix boundaries as well as across pada boundaries. For example, the *-a* of *devadatta-* and the *i-* of the ending *ina* are replaced by the single sound *-e-*: *devadatta-ina* → *devadattena*; the *-a* of *odana-* and the *a-* of the ending *am* are both replaced by the stem-final vowel (*odana-am* → *odanam*; similarly: *agni-am* → *agnim* 'fire'); the *-a* of *devadattena* and the *o-* of *odana-s* are both replaced by *-au-*. The other substitutions that apply to derive (1b) and (2b) all concern pada-final sounds: *-s* → *-r* → *-o* (*devadatta-s o-* → . . . *devadatta o-*), *-m* → *-ṁ* (*odanam p-* → *odanaṁ p-*, with the nasal offglide called *anusvāra* [*ṁ*]), *-s* → *r* → *-ḥ* (*odanas p-* → . . . *odanaḥ p-*, with the voiceless spirant *-ḥ*, called *visarjanīya*).

Denominative derived bases are formed from elements in strings such as (1a)–(2a). For example, *tatpuruṣa* can derive from *tad-as-puruṣa-s*, with two constituent padas: *tad-as* with the genitive singular ending ***ṅas*** and *puruṣa-s* with the nominative singular ending ***su***.

Once these are bracketed to form a compound (*samāsa*), the endings contained in the derived base are dropped: *tad-as-puruṣa-s* → *tad-puruṣa* (→ *tatpuruṣa*). Since such a compound alternates with a syntactic string, however, this composition is optional, so that *tad-as puruṣa-s* also serves to derive the string *tasya puruṣah*.

2.4.5 The scope of the grammar and differences from predecessors

As I have already noted, Pāṇini's procedure continues a tradition of deriving actual utterances from posited strings, a tradition which goes back at least to the earliest padakāras. Pāṇini's grammar is intended to account for an entire language system, not merely for a particular corpus of text, such as the saṁhitā-pāṭha of a particular Vedic tradition. Accordingly, the Aṣṭādhyāyī deals not only with phonological rules but with a wider range of rules, covering grammar, including syntactic rules. Also in accordance with this wider scope, Pāṇini differs from his predecessors with respect to the sorts of operations performed on elements. In prātiśākhya systems such as those of the Ṛgveda- and Taittirīyaprātiśākhya, the norm is to formulate phonological changes (*vikāra*, 'modification') whereby given sounds found in the pada-pāṭha change to other sounds to give the saṁhitā-pāṭha (see section 2.2.2). Instead of following this procedure, Pāṇini operates with rules of substitution, whereby a given element subject to replacement (*sthānin*) is replaced by a specified substitute (*ādeśa*). This applies not only to individual sounds in phonological contexts but also to higher units, such as bases and affixes; for example, one of the operations involved in deriving *bhavitum* (inf.) 'be', corresponding to the verb *as* used in finite forms like *asti* (3 sg. pres.) 'is' consists in substituting *bhū* for *as*, and the derivation of a form like *devadattena* involves replacing the instrumental affix *ṭā*, found in forms like *vācā*, 'speech, voice', with *ina*.

In addition, Pāṇini presupposes a knowledge of phonetics, so that he can define sets of homogeneous (*savarṇa*) sounds in terms of their places of production and the articulatory efforts within the oral cavity involved in producing them,[33] but without explaining such matters of phonetics, which are treated as being outside the purview of his grammar.

2.4.6 Decision procedures, relations among rules and operations

2.4.6.1 Introduction

Pāṇini's grammar reflects general guiding principles, which Pāṇinīyas such as Kātyāyana and Patañjali explicitly mention and discuss. Although Pāṇini himself does not overtly state them, it is clear from his rules that he did indeed operate with these principles.

2.4.6.2 General rules and related exceptions

The major principle governing how rules are formulated and apply lies at the very core of any grammar that aims at generalization and concerns intrinsic relations among rules in terms of their domains: a general rule (*utsarga*), formulated with respect to a broad domain, takes effect in the domain which remains after any exceptions (*apavāda*) have captured their subdomains of the general domain. For example, there is a general rule of semi-vowel replacement,[34] whereby any *i- u- ṛ-* or *ḷ*-vowel is replaced by the corresponding semi-vowel (*y v r l*) before any vowel; an exception to this[35] provides that *i-* and *u-* vowels of verbal bases, verb stems with the suffix *-śnu-*, and the nominal stem *bhrū*, 'brow' (*śnudhātubhruvām*) are replaced by *-iy*, *-uv* (*iyaṅuvaṅau*) before vowels (*aci*) of affixes, as in *āpnuvanti* (← *āpnu-anti*), 'they reach, obtain'. This exception blocks the application of the general rule of semi-vowel replacement, so that a special rule[36] is required to account for *yanti*, 'they go' (← *i-anti*).

2.4.6.3 Bracketing

Another principle concerns bracketing. Consider, for example, the string *ayaja-i indra-am*, from which one should derive *ayaja indram*, 'I venerated Indra': *ayaja-i* → *ayaje*, *ayaje i-* → *ayajay i-* → *ayaja i-*. Now, there is a rule whereby two contiguous homogeneous vowels are both replaced by a single long vowel.[37] If this were to apply in *ayaja-i indra-am*, one would derive **ayajendram*: *ayaja-ii-* → *ayajaī-* → *ayaje-*. However, this is not allowed: the internally conditioned (*antaraṅga*) operation that applies within the single pada *ayaja-i* takes effect before the externally conditioned (*bahiraṅga*) operation that depends on a sound of a following pada.

2.4.6.4 Operations that apply necessarily

Still another principle is illustrated by the derivation of *kṣiyáti*, 'dwells' from *kṣi-a-ti*, a pada with two stems: *kṣi-* with respect to *-a-* and *kṣi-a* with respect to *ti*. The affix *-a-* is introduced after *kṣi* when this is followed by the agentive ending *ti*. This ending also conditions the substitution of a guṇa vowel *e* for stem-final *-i*, as in *éti* 'goes' (← *i-ti*) and for a penultimate short vowel *i*, as in *vetti* 'knows' (← *vid-ti*). Now, given *kṣi-ti*, it would be possible for such guṇa substitution to apply or for an affix *-a-* which is excluded from conditioning guṇa replacement to be introduced. Whether the former operation applies or not, the latter can apply, but if *-a-* is introduced guṇa replacement cannot take place. Of the two operations in question, then, the introduction of *-a-* is one that necessarily takes effect (*nitya*), in contrast to guṇa replacement, which does not necessarily take place (*anitya*) here. The necessary operation takes precedence, so that one gets *kṣi-á-ti*. At this stage, *-a-* does not condition guṇa replacement on its stem. Nor can *-ti* now determine the same substitution for the penultimate sound *i* of its stem *kṣi-a-*, by virtue of the bracketing principle noted: the internally conditioned operation of substituting *-iy* for *-i* takes precedence.

2.4.6.5 Extrinsic ordering

There are instances where such principles of organization cannot determine the proper results, so that Pāṇini must then resort to extrinsic rule ordering. The last three pādas of the final chapter in the Aṣṭādhyāyī are thus ordered, so that a rule of this section is suspended (*asiddha*) with respect to rules of the rest of the grammar, and each rule of this section is suspended with respect to a preceding rule in the same section. The rules in question concern relatively late phonological replacements.

In addition, a set of rules in the section headed by Aṣṭādhyāyī 1.4.1: *ā kaḍārād ekā saṁjñā* is also crucially ordered. 1.4.1 provides that only one class name (*ekā saṁjñā*) of those assigned by the rules in question may apply to any given entity at once. In this section, moreover, a particular metarule is in effect, whereby in case of conflict (*vipratiṣedhe*), the operation stated later (*paraṁ kāryam*) takes precedence.[38] This is needed both for instances of disjunct classes and for other particular operations concerning affixes. Consider, for example, the sentences:

(3) *asinā chinatti* '. . . is cutting (*chinatti*) with a sword/axe'
(4) *sādhv asiś chinatti* 'the sword/axe (*asiḥ*) cuts well (*sādhu*)'.

The word *asinā* of (3) contains the instrumental singular ending *-nā*, signifying an instrument.[39] A sword or axe is used as a means of cutting something, so that it is classed as an instrument (*karaṇa*) with respect to this action.[40] In (4), on the other hand, a sword or axe is spoken of as an agent, a participant in cutting that functions independently (*svatantraḥ*).[41] Of course, even if a sword or axe is spoken of as in (4), the fact remains that it differs from agents like Devadatta or any other being capable of volition. That is, the sword which is spoken of as cutting must be wielded by someone, so that, if it is to be classed as kartṛ (see note 41), one has also to let it be eligible for being simultaneously classed as an instrument. For purposes of grammatical derivation, however, only one such classification is now allowed, the one provided for by the later rule

1.4.54 (note 41), so that classification as kartṛ blocks classification as karaṇa.[42]

The sentences

(5) *tvaṁ gacchasi* 'You are going'
(6) *ahaṁ gacchāmi* 'I am going'
(7) *tvaṁ cāhaṁ ca gacchāvaḥ* 'You and I are going'

involve the selection of triplets of verb endings called *madhyama* and *uttama* – corresponding respectively to what are called second- and first-person endings in Western terminology – to replace L-affixes (see section 2.4.4.2). A sūtra provides that madhyama endings are selected if the L-affix in question is coreferential (*samānādhikaraṇe*) with a potentially co-occurring (*sthāniny api*) form of the second-person pronoun *yuṣmad*, and a subsequent rule provides for selecting uttama endings if the L-affix in question is coreferential with a potentially co-occurring form of the first-person pronoun *asmad*.[43] These rules apply to select the endings *-sip*, *-mip* of *gacchasi*, *gacchāmi* in (5) and (6). They come into conflict, however, in instances such as (7). By the metarule whereby what is provided for in a later rule takes precedence over a previous rule, the uttama ending *vas* is alone selected for (7), so that one does not allow also an unacceptable sentence with the form *gacchathaḥ* (2nd pers. dual).

2.5 Pāṇini and later commentators

2.5.1 Introduction

Pāṇini's work had a profound and lasting effect on later scholars of India, who subjected the Aṣṭādhyāyī to a scrutiny which has few parallels for acuteness of observation and argumentation. In particular, Kātyāyana and Patañjali, both of whom must have had at least a quasi-native command of Sanskrit, could contrast what rules of the grammar would allow and what was desirable in terms of actually observed usage.

2.5.2 Usage as the prime guide in description

This emphasis on being guided by usage is neatly encapsulated in Patañjali's statement (Abhyankar I.366, lines 12–13) that speech is the grammarian's authority for judgement: *sabdapramāṇakā vayam/yac chabda āha tad asmākaṁ pramāṇam*, 'We (*vayam*) have speech as our authoritative means of knowledge (*śabdapramāṇakāḥ*); what speech says (*yac chabda āha*) is our authoritative means of knowing (*tad asmākaṁ pramāṇam*).[44] This statement is made in connection with something said about utterances like

(8) *ayaṁ daṇḍo harānena* 'Here is a stick; carry . . . with it'

In his fifth vārttika on Aṣṭādhyāyī 2.1.1,[45] Kātyāyana remarks that, if a particular position is adopted, one must provide for disallowing verb forms without high-pitched vowels in particular utterances, and Patañjali gives (8) as an example: a Pāṇinian rule[46] lets a finite verb form (*tiṅ* '[a pada] that terminates in a verb ending') have all low-pitched vowels (*anudāttaṁ sarvam*) if it follows a non-verbal form (*atiṅaḥ* 'after [a pada] that has an ending other than a verb ending'). The verb form *hára* (2sg. imper.) of (8) meets these conditions, but it should nevertheless have a high-pitched vowel, as shown. Accordingly, Kātyāyana proposes a negation (*pratiṣedhaḥ*) to the accentual rule in question. This is disallowed if the verb form in question follows a term that refers to a participant that is distinct (*nānākārakāt*) from the one involved in the action denoted by that verb. Now, an interlocutor argues that (8) is not a proper example. Not only are *hara* and *daṇḍah* linked semantically in that the stick referred to is the one with which one is supposed to carry something, there is only one participant (*kāraka*) involved here, namely the stick – referred to by *daṇḍaḥ* and by the anaphoric instrumental singular *anena* – so that the condition of involving distinct participants is not met; one attaches something to the very same stick with which one is to carry that thing (*tenaivāsajya hriyate*). The following answer is given to this: we do not say that the thing to be carried is attached to something distinct from that by means of which it is carried (*nāpi brūmo 'nyenāsajya hriyata iti*). On the contrary, we have speech for our authority, and in this instance, speech conveys being (*sattām āha*): one understands *asti*, 'is', upon hearing *ayaṁ daṇḍaḥ*. The stick in question is first agent (*sa daṇḍaḥ kartā bhūtvā* 'That stick, after being an agent . . .'); then, when a syntactic link is made with another speech form – the verb of *hara* – it becomes an instrument (*anyena śabdenābhisambadhyamānaḥ karaṇaṁ sampadyate* 'becomes an instrument when it is connected with another word').

2.5.3 Major differences between Pāṇinian grammarians and Naiyāyikas

Considering that the stick (*daṇḍaḥ*) of (8) (section 2.5.2) or the car (*rathaḥ* 'chariot') of

(9) *ratho grāmaṁ gacchati*, 'The car is going to the village'

is an agent involves a notion of agency that does not require volition. In this respect, Pāṇinian grammarians differ radically from other thinkers, in particular from certain logicians of the Nyāya school, who insist that a proper agent is one capable of volitional effort (*kṛti, yatna*).

Now, Pāṇini simply says that a participant which, relative to other participants in a given action, functions as the independent one (*svatantraḥ*) is called *kartṛ* ('agent', see note 41). He does not specify just what qualifies a participant to be independent. Bhartṛhari does consider reasons for which an agent is said to have the property of being independent (*svātantryaṁ kartur ucyate*). These are as follows: the participant in question enters into play (*śaktilābhāt* 'because it obtains its capacity of being a participant') before any other participant (*prāg anyataḥ*) in an act; accordingly, it makes other participants subordinate to it (*nyagbhāvāpādanāt*); it causes other participants to cease playing roles in an action (*pravṛttānāṁ nivarttanāt*), since their entry into play is dependent on it (*tadadhīnapravṛttitvāt*); it is not substituted for (*adṛṣṭatvāt pratinidheḥ*);[47] even if there is no other participant, there is an agent (*praviveke ca darśanāt*).[48]

Bhartṛhari goes on, however, to say that the restriction (*niyamaḥ*) such that a participant must be qualified by the properties (*dharmaiḥ*) mentioned (*dharmair abhyuditaiḥ ... niyamaḥ*) applies in relation to speech (*śabde*), not to things (*vastuni* [loc. sg.] 'thing') in the external world (*śabde ... na tu vastuni*): if someone wishes to speak (*vivakṣāyām*) of something as having the properties of an agent (*kartur dharmavivakṣāyām*), then one understands an agent (*kartā pratīyate* 'an agent is understood') from the speech form used (*śabdāt kartā pratīyate*).[49] Nor is this position one adopted by Pāṇinian commentators alone. Pāṇini himself explicitly provides for classifications in a manner that allows deriving sentences like (4) (see section 2.4.6.5). He also envisions that the sunlight (*ātapaḥ*) spoken of in a sentence like

(10) *śoṣayate vrīhīn ātapaḥ* 'sunlight dries out rice'

is as much an agent as is the person named Yajñadatta spoken of in

(11) *yajñadatta āsayati devadattam* 'Yajñadatta has Devadatta sit'

For, in a sūtra which provides for affixes of the parasmaipada class, including active endings such as *-ti* in examples like (11), Pāṇini says that such affixes follow a causative verb derived from a non-causative that is intransitive (*aṇāv akarmakāt*) and has a sentient being for agent (*cittavatkartṛkāt*).[50] If a participant to be classed as agent were assumed necessarily to be a sentient being capable of volition, it would be otiose to specify *cittavatkartṛkāt* in this sūtra.

Naiyāyikas, on the other hand, do insist that one deal not only with speech but also have one's analysis of this speech accord with a reality of the world as we experience it, so that they do maintain that true agents are necessarily sentient beings capable of volition. Thus, a sentence like (1b) (see section 2.4.4.2) *devadatta odanaṁ pacati* is paraphrased by

(12) *odananiṣṭhaviklittyanukūlakṛtimān devadattaḥ.*

Both are considered to speak of an individual named Devadatta, of whom it is predicated that he is the locus of a volitional effort (*kṛtimān*) which leads to (*anukūla*) softening (*viklitti*), which is a result of cooking, in rice (*odananiṣṭha* 'situated in cooked rice'). A sentence like

(13) *devadatto grāmaṁ gacchati* 'Devadatta is going to the village'

is comparably paraphrased:

(14) *grāmasaṁyogānukūlagamanānukūlakṛtimān devadattaḥ* 'Devadatta is the locus of a conscious effort leading to going (*gamanānukūla*) which leads to conjunction with a village (*grāmasaṁyogānukūla*)'

A sentence such as (9) above *ratho grāmaṁ gacchati*, is considered to convey something different. The chariot spoken of is the locus of a movement initiated by some other entity. In accordance with this, two distinct meanings are attributed to L-affixes that are replaced by endings in such sentences. The primary meaning of any L-affix is considered to be the conscious effort on the part of an agent to carry out an act. For sentences like (9), on the other hand, an L-affix is considered to have a secondary meaning: it signifies that the car in question is a locus of movement.

Although they accepted verbal transmission as a valid means of obtaining correct knowledge, Naiyāyikas did not compose grammars of their own. Instead, they generally accepted Pāṇini's grammar as a model of description. On the other hand, they could not accept all the views held by Pāṇinīyas, so that they subjected sūtras of the Aṣṭādhyāyī to interpretations that accorded with their own analyses. For example, the term *kartari* in Aṣṭādhyāyī 3.4.69 (see note 32) is not interpreted as a noun form signifying an agent but as a form denoting the property agency (*kartṛtva*); since the property which characterizes a true agent is conscious effort (*kṛti*), then, this sūtra is considered to provide that an L-affix follows a verb when such effort is to be signified.[51]

2.5.4 Pāṇini and Mīmāṁsakas

Mīmāṁsakas, scholars who dealt with the interpretation of Vedic texts connected with rituals, also interacted with grammarians. In one respect, mīmāṁsā is in fact complementary to grammar. As can be seen from the foregoing, a grammar like Pāṇini's is essentially a sentence grammar: it accounts for the structure of sentences, including complex sentences, through a derivational system, but it does not deal in any detail with larger discourses. On the other hand, mīmāṁsā has for one of its tasks to relate different statements of ritual texts in manners that let them harmonize and serve towards the appropriate performance of rituals. Accordingly, mīmāṁsā is known as the *vākyaśāstra* ('utterance śāstra').

Mīmāṁsakas also developed particular views concerning the interpretation of sentences and how their components are related. For example, a Mīmāṁsaka of the Bhāṭṭa school gives a particular paraphrase to a sentence such as

(15) *svargakāmo yajeta* 'One who desires heaven should have a rite performed'

namely:

(16) *svargakāmo yāgena svargaṁ bhāvayet* 'One who desires heaven should bring heaven about through a sacrificial rite'

A sacrificial rite is viewed as the instrument of bringing about a result, and a verb ending is considered to signify the act of bringing something into being (*bhāvanā*). Sentences like (1b), which are not directly linked to ritual practice, are given comparable interpretations: *devadattaḥ pākenaudanaṁ bhāvayati*, 'Devadatta brings softened rice into being through cooking.' And the principal meaning of both kinds of sentences is considered to be the act of bringing into being (*bhāvanā*). Since they did not compose grammars of their own, moreover, Mīmāṁsakas also resorted to reinterpretation of Pāṇinian sūtras in order to account for their analyses (see note 51).

2.5.5 Later Pāṇinīyas' refutations of suggested interpretations

The interpretations given to Pāṇinian sūtras by scholars such as Naiyāyikas and Bhāṭṭa Mīmāmsakas of course provoked reactions from more strict Pāṇinīyas, and the arguments continued back and forth for centuries, with each generation taking into account objections posed and solutions suggested by predecessors. The last major scholar to deal with all such issues in the Pāṇinian tradition is Nāgeśabhāṭṭa (late seventeenth century), author of the Vaiyākaraṇasiddhāntamañjūṣā ('Jewel chest of final views of grammarians') and its more widely known companion, the Vaiyākaraṇasiddhāntalaghumañjūṣā ('Small chest . . .').

2.6 Interest in dialects

2.6.1 Various dialects recognized

From very early on, Indian scholars showed an interest in the varieties of speech used in different areas known to them. One of the earliest and most famous passages concerning this occurs in Yāska's Nirukta, where he notes that in some areas verbal bases (*prakṛtayaḥ*) are used (*bhāṣyante* 'are spoken') while in other areas nominal derivates (*vikṛtayah* 'modifications') of these bases are used; for example, the verb *śav* (*śavatiḥ*) 'go' (*gatikarmā*) is used only in the area of Kamboja – within what is modern Afghanistan – and among the Āryas a derivate of this verb is used: *śava* ('corpse'); in the east, *dā* is used in the meaning 'cut' (*dātir lavanārthe*), but northerners use only the derivate *dātra* 'sickle'.[52]

In the same vein, during a discussion in the introductory section of the Mahābhāṣya, Patañjali remarks that the verb *śav,* 'go', is used (*bhāṣitaḥ* 'spoken') only in Kamboja (*kambojeṣv eva bhāṣito bhavati*), while Āryas use only a derivate of this with reference to a corpse, and that *dā,* 'cut', is used in the east, while northerners use the derivate *dātra.* He also notes that different verbs meaning 'go' occur in various areas; *hamm* (*hammatiḥ*) in Surāṣṭra, *ramh* in the east and midlands, but Āryas use only *gam.*[53]

2.6.2 Āryas and their region

Both Yāska and Patañjali speak of usages particular to Āryas (see section 2.6.1). In fact, the Āryas were conscious of themselves as a cultural and linguistic group opposed to non-Āryas, and this awareness stems from Indo-Iranian times.[54] Within the subcontinent of India, moreover, there was an area called Āryāvartta, 'abode of the Ārya'. The specific confines of this area differed through time, but whatever its particular geographical characteristics, one distinctive characteristic remained constant: this was the area where proper practices of Ārya Brāhmaṇas were observed. One of the practices which characterized the group of Brāhmaṇas residing in Āryāvartta referred to as *śiṣṭa*, 'élite', is their use of correct speech forms (*śabda*, *sādhuśabda*). Indeed, grammar (*vyākaraṇa*) is viewed as a means of setting correct speech apart from incorrect speech forms (*apaśabda*, *asādhuśabda*), viewed as corruptions (*apabhraṁśa*),[55] and one of the purposes of studying grammar is to avoid speaking like barbarians (*mleccha*).[56] Thus, a grammar like Pāṇini's was traditionally viewed as an instrument allowing one to discriminate between correct and incorrect speech, although within the domain of the former, no further levels of acceptability are strictly defined.

2.6.3 Sanskrit and vernaculars

One could take an extreme position regarding the use of Sanskrit and vernacular forms. Thus, according to Bhartṛhari, some maintained that a vernacular term (*āsādhuḥ* 'incorrect speech form') like *gāvī*, *goṇī*, *gotā*, *gopotalikā*, 'cow', did not directly signify; instead, it signified through inference (*anumānena vācakaḥ*), in that a person knowing Sanskrit would, upon hearing such a term, infer the use of the corresponding Sanskrit term, *gauḥ*, which he would link directly with the meaning in question.[57] Of course, this extreme position was found desirable only by some (*kaiścid iṣyate*). Nor could one claim that any hearer who heard a word like *gāvī* necessarily could link it with a corresponding Sanskrit word, since not all speakers of vernaculars knew Sanskrit. Indeed, as all Pāṇinīyas have recognized, so far as conveying what one wished to say in every day life, it did not matter whether one used correct speech forms or 'corruptions' of these: a Sanskrit term like *gauḥ* and vernacular terms such as *gāvī* equally referred to cows. In the context of ritual performance, of course, something more comes into play. The mantras uttered in the course of a rite must be uttered properly if the desired effect is to come about, so that a true restriction applies here, such that merit (*dharma*) accrues only to one who uses speech correctly.

Through an understandable development, then, the use of correct speech forms itself came to be treated as a means to acquire merit, thus distinguishing correct and incorrect speech with respect to a moral efficacy if not in respect of signifying.[58] This view goes back at least to Kātyāyana, who explicitly remarks that the grammar serves to establish a restriction for the sake of merit (*śāstreṇa dharmaniyamaḥ*) and that the use of correct speech forms preceded by a knowledge of grammar leads to felicity (*śāstrapūrvake prayoge'bhyudayaḥ*). Indeed, Patañjali cites a traditional passage saying that a single correct speech form precisely known in accordance with what grammar teaches and uses properly is a wish-granting cow in heaven.[59] In addition, speech was early on hypostasized and given an ultimate divine status, so that among the purposes for studying grammar which Patañjali gives is this: grammar should be studied in order to attain unity with the great deity that is speech.[60]

2.7 Development of a philosophy of language

2.7.1 Introduction

Ideas expressed in the Mahābhāṣya must have become objects of prolonged consideration by grammarians proper and adherents of other schools in the last century of the pre-Christian era and the early centuries of the present era. For in his Vākyapadīya Bhartṛhari – who certainly lived no later than the fifth century – gives evidence of a true ferment of ideas and arguments concerning language, its analysis, and how these are treated from various epistemological and ontological viewpoints.

2.7.2 Bhartṛhari's system

Bhartṛhari himself has a fully thought-out system, based on ideas already found in earlier works, principally the Mahābhāṣya, but elaborated and confronted with ideas of other scholars. To begin with, Bhartṛhari espouses a strong epistemological viewpoint: there is no knowledge (*na so'sti pratyayaḥ*) in the realm of worldly intercourse (*loke*) that is not accompanied by speech (*yaḥ śabdānugamād ṛte*); all knowledge is as though pierced through with speech (*anuviddham iva jñānam*) and appears only through speech (*sarvaṁ śabdena bhāsate*).[61]

Bhartṛhari also has a definite general theory of language and how this relates to grammar. The basic characteristic of Bhartṛhari's view of language is the essential unity of higher units, utterances (*vākyāni*) and their meanings (*arthāḥ*). An utterance, viewed as it is used by speakers in real-life situations, is an atomic unit, and the meaning associated with such an utterance is equally atomic (*akhaṇḍa* 'without parts'). Hence, Bhartṛhari can say explicitly: 'There are no sounds (*varṇā na vidyante*) in a word (*pade*), as there are also no actual parts (*avayavā na ca*) in sounds (*varṇeṣu*); there is no absolute division at all (*atyantaṁ pravibhāgo na kaścana*) of words (*padānām*) from the utterance (*vākyāt*)'.[62] Of course, analysis does take place, and this is not restricted to grammarians alone; everyone who learns a language performs some sort of analysis.[63] And it would be impossible to describe a language like Sanskrit without recognizing such units as words, bases and affixes. Accordingly, Bhartṛhari does recognize such sub-sentential units. Nevertheless, he maintains that this analysis is intended essentially for grammatical discourse.[64] Ultimately, a speech form like (1b) or *pacati* is an unanalysable unit, and its meaning is also an unanalysable unit.[65] A grammatical analysis and a grammar based on it serve only as a means, a path upon which one first goes, though it is actually false (*asatye vartmani sthitvā* 'after staying on the false path'), and which one leaves in quest of the truth (*tataḥ satyaṁ samīhate* 'then one strives for the true').[66]

2.7.3 The ultimate in Bhartṛhari's system

The true thing for which one strives, moreover, is none other than the ultimate being, *brahman*. In this system of thought, however, the beginningless and endless (*anādinidhanam*) brahman, which evolves as all things we speak of (*vivartate'rthabhāvena*) and from which the entire development of the world as we experience it proceeds (*prakriyā jagato yataḥ*), has the property of being speech (*śabdatattvam*).[67] This obviously is linked with what was said earlier in the Mahābhāṣya (see section 2.6.3) about grammar being studied in order to attain unity with the god that is speech, and the Vakyapadīya exlicitly elaborates on this theme. As in one stream of throught tracing its soures to Upaniṣadic statements there is an ultimate being with which one's self (*ātman*) is identical and ultimate release from the cycle of being is attained when one realizes this identity, so in Bhartṛhari's view is the self of one who uses (*prayoktuḥ*) speech none other than this self, situated within (*antar avasthitam*); but it is now a self that is speech (*śabdam*), spoken of as the great bull, union with which is said to be desired.[68]

2.7.4 Kinds of speech and grammar as a means to salvation

In accordance with this theme, Bhartṛhari speaks of grammar as a means of purifying speech. According to him, there are three major levels of speech (*vāc*): the scattered sound that people perceive in every day life (*vaikharī vāk*); the 'middle speech' (*madhyamā vāk*) or interior speech, that is not actually uttered but is in speakers' and hearers' minds a potential utterance; and 'seeing speech' (*paśyantī vāk*), which lacks any sequentiality. This last has a variety, the ultimate (*parā*), in which the distinction among languages and between signifier and signified is transcended.[69]

Also in accordance with his predecessors, Bhartṛhari maintains that the correct use of speech in harmony with what grammar says concerning its structure serves to purify this speech, and this is a means of attaining the ultimate self.[70] In this connection,

Bhartṛhari speaks of a *śabdapūrvayoga*, 'yoga preceded by speech', and says that as a consequence of using correct speech (*sādhuśabdaprayogāt*), one achieves a state where one has manifested in oneself a particular merit (*abhivyaktadharmaviśeṣaḥ*); one thus acquires unity with the great self that is speech and suppresses the senses (*mahāntaṁ śabdātmānam abhibhavan vaikaraṇyaṁ prāpnoti*).[71] In this manner, grammar, which is the treatment that rids speech of its impurities (*vāṅmalānāṁ cikitsitam*), is treated as the way (*dvāram* 'door') to ultimate release (*apavargasya*).[72]

2.7.5 Grammar incorporated in traditional philosophical systems

In view of Bhartṛhari's development of ideas put forth in earlier works such as the Mahābhāṣya and of his elaborate discussions of positions other than his own, it is not surprising that the fourteenth-century compendium of philosophical views compiled by Mādhava-Sāyaṇa, the Sarvadarśanasaṁgraha, includes among these systems the pāṇinidarśana.

2.8 Summary

In this brief consideration of linguistics in ancient and medieval India, I have concentrated on the major figures in the history of Sanskrit grammar. I have left aside scholars who composed grammars of Pāli and various Middle Indic dialects (*prākṛta*), and I have not considered what is to be found in the works of grammarians of Dravidian languages. What has been said nevertheless suffices, I think, to illustrate the richness of thought on language to be found among early Indian scholars and their accomplishments. In contrast with linguistics as it developed in the Graeco-Roman Western traditions, grammar in ancient India evolved independently of logic, with which it came to interact. Moreover, again in contrast with early Western grammatical thought, from earliest times Indian grammarians conceived of a grammar as a set of interrelated rules that served to describe usage through a derivational procedure. This required their considering details of how rules could be related to each other and how particular aspects of semantics are linked with linguistic expressions. Consequently, we see that certain aspects of language and of rules were known and discussed in India long before scholars elsewhere gained a clear understanding of the points at issue. For example, Pāṇini had a clear notion of the difference between the use and mention of terms. Indeed, he formulated a sūtra establishing a usage convention which is the reverse of what obtains in common usage: a term (*svaṁ rūpam* 'own form') other than a technical term of grammar (*aśabdasaṁjñā*) is understood as self-referring (*śabdasya* [*saṁjñā*] '[name] for the term').[73] Pāṇini was also aware of a distinction comparable to the one between sentential and nominal negation: stating that an operation O does not apply (*na bhavati* 'does not occur') with respect to A is distinct from saying that O applies to something other than A.[74] Further, his way of deriving utterances required him to consider that particular aspects of semantics must be called into play with respect to grammatical categories and operations, while others do not.[75] And, of course, the manner in which rules of the Aṣṭādhyāyī are related to each other reflects a sophistication with respect to principles that govern grammatical systems which can hardly be paralleled, even in modern times. Aspects of language, both formal and semantic, continued to attract the attention of Indian scholars within grammar and other areas of thought, century after century, with the result that India possesses possibly the richest and most sophisticated traditions of linguistic thinking anywhere in the world.

A great deal of research has been done in this field,[76] but I do not exaggerate by saying that an enormous amount of serious thinking remains to be done, in order to understand more fully what Pāṇini and his followers accomplished, to compare this with what was done by Pāṇini's predecessors – on the basis of evidence available in early works such as the Ṛgveda- and Taittirīyaprātiśākhya – and to place these accomplishments in the framework of the history of linguistics in general. It is also to be hoped that some of the insights gained through a study of Pāṇini might be applied in modern considerations of languages, especially as concerns the connection between syntax and morphology.

Notes

Transliteration. I have used the scheme of transliteration that is standard among Sanskritists. The approximate IPA equivalents are as follows: a [ə], ā [ɑ], i [i], ī [iː], u [u], ū [uː], ṛ [ərə] (modern pronunciation is usually [ri] in the north-central part of India), ḷ [ələ] (modern pronunciation is usually [lri], [li] in the north-central part of India), e [e], ai [əy/ɑy], o [o], au [əw/ɑw], k [k], kh [kʰ], g [g], gh [gʰ], ṅ [ŋ], c [c], ch [cʰ], j [ɟ], jh [ɟʰ], ñ [ɲ], ṭ [ʈ], ṭh [ʈʰ], ḍ [ɖ], ḍh [ɖʰ], ṇ [ɳ], t [t], th [tʰ], d [d], dh [dʰ], n [n], p [p], ph [pʰ], b[b], bh [bʰ], m [m], y [j], r [r/ɽ] (some ancient phonetic texts describe this as alveolar, others as retroflex), l [l], v [v], ś [ç], ṣ [ʂ] (modern pronunciation generally does not distinguish between the palatal and retroflex spirants; the usual pronunciation of both closely approximates [ʃ]), s [s], h [ɦ], ḥ [h] (ancient phonetic texts describe this sound (called *visarjanīya*), which replaces *-r* or *-s*, as voiceless and produced in the throat or at the point of production of the preceding vowel; in modern pronunciations, it can be voiced and is generally followed by an echo vowel with the same features as the vowel that precedes), ṁ: a nasal offglide (called *anusvāra*) following a vowel; for example aṁ = [ə$^{\tilde{ə}}$] (this accords with what ancient phonetic texts say. Modern realizations of ṃ vary according to phonological contexts and languages; they include a nasalized bilabial [w̃], [ŋ], a nasal homorganic with a following consonant, and nasalization of a preceding vowel).

1. *uktānuktaduruktānāṁ cintā yatra pravartate/taṁ granthaṁ vārttikaṁ prāhur vārttikajñā manīṣiṇaḥ//* 'Learned men who know vārttikas declare that a vārttika work is one in which thinking (*cintā*) is carried out (*pravartate* 'proceeds, comes into play') concerning what is said, what is unsaid, and what is badly said (*uktānuktaduruktānām*)'.
2. For additional details and references to comparable texts, see recently Cardona (1986). My presentation of materials here is necessarily simplified to some extent.
3. Taittirīyaprātiśākhya 2.4–6: *saṁvṛte kaṇṭhe nādaḥ kriyate, vivṛte śvāsaḥ, madhye hakāraḥ*, 'When the glottis is close, it is made into nāda; if open, into śvāsa; if midway, into hakāra.' What is converted (*kriyate* 'is made') into nāda and so on is actually said to be a primitive sound (*śabdaḥ*) produced as a result of the movement of breath.
4. Taittirīyaprātiśākhya 2.7–10: *tā varṇaprakṛtayaḥ, nādo'nupradānaṁ svaraghoṣavatsu, hakāro hacaturtheṣu, aghoṣeṣu śvāsaḥ*, 'These are the original stuff of articulated sounds. Nāda is the original emitted material in vowels and voiced consonants, hakāra in *h* and voiced aspirated stops, śvāsa in voiceless consonants.'
5. Taittirīyaprātiśākhya 2.31–34: *svarāṇāṁ yatropasaṁhāras tat sthānam, yad upasaṁharati tat karaṇam, anyeṣāṁ tu yatra sparśanaṁ tat sthānam, yena sparśayati tat karaṇam*, 'For vowels, the place of production is where approximation is made; what one brings into proximity is the active articulator. For other sounds, the place of production is where contact takes place, and the active articulator is the one which causes to make contact.'
6. Taittirīyaprātiśākhya 2.36: *tālau jihvāmadhyena cavarge*, 'In (producing) the *c*-group, one (causes) the middle of the tongue (to make contact) at the palate.' 2.22–23: *tālau jihvāmadhyam ivarṇe, ekāre ca*, 'In (producing) *i*-vowels and *e*, one (brings) the middle of the tongue (into proximity) at the palate.'
7. 4.2: *ghoṣavatparāḥ prathamās tṛtīyān svān*, 'Voiceless unaspirated stops followed by voiced consonants change to voiced unaspirated stops of their own sets.' Stops (*sparśāḥ*) are arranged in five sets of five: *k kh g gh ṅ, c ch j jh ñ, ṭ ṭh ḍ ḍh ṇ, t th d dh n, p ph b bh m*. The sounds in each quintuplet are referred to as *prathama*, 'first', *dvitīya*, 'second', *tṛtīya*, 'third', *caturtha*, 'fourth', and *uttama*, 'last'.
8. 8.3: *tṛtīyaṁ svaraghoṣavatparaḥ* (*savargīyam* 2, *prathamaḥ* 1), 'A voiceless unaspirated stop followed by a vowel or a voiced consonant changes to the voiced unaspirated stop of its own group.'

9. 2.1: *saṁhitā padaprakṛtiḥ*, 'The saṁhitā has the padas as its origin.'
10. Ṛgvedaprātiśākhya 2.2: *padāntān padādibhiḥ sandadhad eti yat sā kālāvyavāyena*, 'It (the saṁhitā) is the one that proceeds putting pada-finals together with pada-initials, without any intervening time.'
11. 5.41: *duṣṭaro viṣṭaro viṣṭapo viṣṭambho viṣṭambhanīm* (*nāvagrahaḥ* 24), This sūtra simply lists five complex padas whose components are not pronounced separated by pause. In his commentary on Vājasaneyiprātiśākhya 5.1, Uvaṭa tells us what avagraha is: separately pronouncing two padas (*dvayoḥ padayoḥ pṛthaggrahaṇam avagrahaḥ*).
12. Subramania Iyer (1983, 198): . . . *dustara ity api tarates tṛṇāter vā*, '. . . *dustara* (also has a component that derives) from (the verb whose present is) *tarati* or *tṛṇāti*.'
13. Questions concerning principles followed by authors of padapāṭhas are discussed in Varma 150–79, Jha.
14. Gopathabrāhmaṇa 1.1.39: *prāṇa eṣa sa puri śete/puriśayaṁ santaṁ prāṇaṁ puruṣa ity ācakṣate parokṣeṇa/parokṣapriyā iva hi devā bhavanti pratyakṣadviṣaḥ*.
15. Nirukta 1.15 (Sarup 37): *athāpīdam antareṇa mantreṣv arthapratyayo na vidyate*.
16. Nirukta 1.15 (Sarup 37): *artham apratiyato nātyantaṁ svarasaṁskāroddeśas tad idaṁ vidyāsthānaṁ vyākaraṇasya kārtsnyaṁ svārthasādhakaṁ ca*.
17. Nirukta 1.1 (Sarup 27–8): *tad yāny catvāri padajātāni nāmākhyāte copasarganipātāś ca tānīmāni bhavanti/tatraitan nāmākhyātayor lakṣaṇaṁ pradiśanti/bhāvapradhānam ākhyātam/sattvapradhānāni nāmāni/tad yatrobhe bhāvapradhāne bhavataḥ pūrvāparībhūtam bhāvam ākhyātenācaṣṭe vrajati pacatīti/upakramaprabhṛtyapavargaparyantaṁ mūrtaṁ sattvabhūtaṁ sattvanāmabhiḥ vrajyā paktir iti*, 'These (items included in the list traditionally handed down) are nominal forms, verb forms, pre-verbs and particles, these four classes of words which are (recognized). Among these, this is the characteristic set forth for a nominal and a verbal form: a verb form has bhāva as its principal meaning, nominals have substantial beings as their principal meanings. Where both have bhāva as their main meanings, one expresses a sequential bhāva by means of a verb form: *vrajati, pacati*; (one expresses a bhāva) from its inception to its completion as embodied, become a substantial being, by means of names of substances: *vrajyā, paktiḥ*.' The term *bhāva* ('being, state') is here obviously used with reference to activities like going and cooking. The use of this term reflects, I think, an analysis such that all verbs are viewed as signifying particular states. Additional details of interpretation cannot be considered here.
18. Nirukta 1.12 (Sarup 36): *tatra nāmāny ākhyātajānīti śākaṭāyano nairuktasamayaś ca/na sarvāṇīti gārgyo vaiyākaraṇāmāṁ caike*, 'With respect to these (four classes of words), Śākaṭāyana says that nominals arise from verbs, and this is also the convention of etymologists; Gārgya and some grammarians say that not all (nominals arise

from verbs).' A similar statement is made in a ślokavārttika cited in Patañjali's Mahābhāṣya on Aṣṭādhyāyī 3.3.1 (Abhyankar II.138, lines 14, 16): *nāma ca dhātujam āha nirukte vyākaraṇe śakaṭasya ca tokam*, 'One says in nirukta that a nominal arises from a verb, and in grammar (so says) the son of Śakaṭa.'

19. Nirukta 1.12 (Sarup 36): *atha cet sarvāṇy ākhyātajāni nāmāni syur yaḥ kaśca tat karma kuryāt sarvaṁ tat sattvaṁ tathācakṣīran/ yaḥ kaścādhvānam aśnuvītāśvaḥ sa vacanīyaḥ syāt* . . ., 'Now, if all nominals arose from verbs, one would refer to any entity that performed a given action in a manner appropriate to this; any one that covered a path should be called *aśva*.'
20. A compound with the locative *puri-* and the agent noun *śaya-* derived from *śī*, 'lie'; see above note 14. In Nirukta 2.3, Yāska gives this as one of three alternative explanations of *puruṣa*.
21. Nirukta 1.13 (Sarup 36): *athāpi ya eṣāṁ nyāyavān kārmanāmikaḥ saṁskāro yathā cāpi pratītārthāni syus tathaināny ā cakṣīran*, 'Moreover, (there should obtain) for them, the regular grammatical derivational procedure found in nominals that derive from verbs, and one would refer to the (entities in question) in a manner such that the activities which constitute the bases of the meanings would be directly understood.'
22. Nirukta 1.14 (Sarup 37): *paśyāmaḥ samānakarmaṇāṁ nāmadheyapratilambham ekeṣāṁ naikeṣām yathā takṣā* . . ., 'We see that some of several entities involved in the same activity take a particular name, others do not; for examle, *takṣā*.'
23. Nirukta 1.14 (Sarup 37): *santy alpaprayogāḥ kṛtaḥ* . . ., 'There are derivates with kṛt affixes that are rarely used.'
24. Nirukta 2.1 (Sarup 44): *atha nirvacanam// tad yeṣu padeṣu svarasaṁskārau samarthau prādeśikena vikāreṇānvitau syātāṁ tathā tāni nirbrūyāt athānanvite'rthe'prādeśike vikāre'rthanityaḥ parīkṣeta . . . na tveva na nirbrūyāt*, 'Now, etymological explanation. Words in which accent and grammatical derivation are capable (of accounting for the meanings in question) and accompanied by a verbal modification one should explain in that manner. In case, however, the meaning in question is not accompanied by (such obvious grammatical derivation) and there is no (obvious) verbal modification, one should examine it always with the meaning in mind . . . One should *not*, however, *not* give an etymological explanation.' I omit considering some terminological and textual difficulties, especially concerning *prādeśikena vikāreṇa* and the reading with *guṇena* instead of *vikāreṇa*. The gist of the argument is patent.
25. Pāṇini refers to a set of post-verbal affixes, starting with *uṇ* (*uṇādayaḥ*). There is also a work of uṇādi-sūtras, traditionally attributed to Śākaṭāyana, which includes rules for deriving nominal bases like *go*. However, as Pāṇinīyas like Patañjali point out, such nominals are treated as underived (*avyutpannāni*) in the Pāṇinian system.
26. Aṣṭādhyāyī 1.1.16: *sambuddhau śākalyasyetāv anārṣe* (*ot* 15, *pragṛhyam* 11), 'According to Śākalya, *-o* conditioned by a vocative singular

ending and followed by *iti* that does not emanate from a ṛṣi is called *pragṛhya*.'

27. Affixes are introduced not only as signifiers (*vācaka*) but also introduced as cosignifying (*dyotaka*) elements, which serve to bring out, together with bases, meanings which are directly attributed to these bases. In addition, Pāṇini operates with affixes that neither signify nor cosignify meanings but nevertheless have to be recognized as elements distinct from bases. In more modern terms, he recognizes empty morphs.
28. In Pāṇinian terms, an aṅga is a unit beginning with an item after which an affix is introduced and followed by that affix: Aṣṭādhyāyī 1.4.13: *yasmāt pratyayavidhis tadādi pratyaye'ṅgam*, 'The element beginning with a unit after which an affix is introduced and followed by that affix is called *aṅga*.'
29. Aṣṭādhyāyī 3.1.1: *pratyayaḥ* is a major heading, whereby items introduced by rules included in the following sections, through the fifth adhyāya, have the class name *pratyaya*. The class of affixes includes suffixes, prefixes, and infixes. The vast majority of affixes are suffixes, so that, in 3.1.2: *paraś ca*, Pāṇini provides that an element called *pratyaya* regularly follows (*paraḥ*) the item to which it is introduced.
30. Aṣṭādhyāyī 1.4.14: *suptiṅantaṁ padam*. The abbreviations ***sup*** and ***tiṅ*** respectively denote nominal endings and verb endings. A pada need not necessarily contain an overt ending in a final utterance; it does, however, always have such an ending at an early stage of derivation.
31. Aṣṭādhyāyī 1.4.17: *svādiṣv asarvanāmasthāne* provides that an element followed by suffixes of the set beginning with ***su*** (nom. sg. ending) other than endings called *sarvanāmasthāna* is called *pada*. That is, stems followed by nominal endings other than nom. sg., du., pl., acc. sg., du. as well as by certain other affixes have word boundaries after them. The nominal endings in question, moreover, are only consonant-initial. Additional details need not concern us here.
32. Aṣṭādhyāyī 3.4.69: *laḥ* (*kartari* 67) *karmaṇi ca bhāve cākarmakebhyaḥ*. For references to other sūtras of the Aṣṭādhyāyī providing for the operations mentioned here and in what follows, see Cardona (1988, 169–85).
33. Aṣṭādhyāyī 1.1.9: *tulyāsyaprayatnaṁ savarṇam* provides that a sound is *savarṇa* with respect to another if it is produced with the same effort at the same place of production in the oral cavity (*tulyāsyaprayatnam*). This is over-general, so that the next sūtra (1.1.10: *nājjhalau*) provides that a vowel and a consonant (*ajjhalau*) which would be classed as homogeneous with respect to each other by the preceding sūtra are not (*na*) so classed.
34. Aṣṭādhyāyī 6.1.77: *iko yaṇ aci*: a sound denoted by the abbreviation ***yaṇ*** replaces a sound denoted by ***ik*** if a sound denoted by ***ac*** follows.
35. Aṣṭādhyāyī 6.4.77: *aci śnudhātubhruvāṁ yvor iyaṅuvaṅau*.
36. Aṣṭādhyāyī 6.4.81: *iṇo yaṇ*. This provides that ***iṇ***, 'go', undergoes semivowel replacement before a vowel.
37. Aṣṭādhyāyī 61.101: *akaḥ savarṇe dīrghaḥ*: a sound denoted by ***ak*** and

a following homogeneous sound (*savarṇe*) are both replaced by a single long vowel (*dīrghaḥ*). This rule comes under the heading 6.1.84: *ekaḥ pūrvaparayoḥ*, whereby a single (*ekaḥ*) element substitutes for both preceding and following (*pūrvaparayoḥ*) elements given in following rules.

38. Aṣṭādhyāyī 1.4.2: *vipratiṣedhe paraṁ kāryam*, 'If there is conflict (*vipratiṣedhe*) that is to be done (*kāryam*) which is (provided for) later (*param*).'
39. Aṣṭādhyāyī 2.3.18: *kartṛkaraṇayos tṛtīyā* provides for endings of the third triplet (*tṛtīyā*) to follow a nominal if an agent or instrument (*kartṛkaraṇayoḥ*) is to be signified.
40. Aṣṭādhyāyī 1.4.42: *sādhakatamaṁ karaṇam* assigns the class name *karaṇa* to a participant in an act which, more than other participants in that act, functions as means of accomplishing it (*sādhakatamam*).
41. According to Aṣṭādhyāyī 1.4.54: *svatantraḥ kartā*, a participant which functions independently (*svatantrah*) with respect to other possible participants in an action is called *kartṛ*.
42. In his thirty-second vārttika on Aṣṭādhyāyī 1.4.1, Kātyāyana states explicitly (*karaṇaṁ parāṇi sādhv asiś chinatti*) that kāraka class names assigned by rules following 1.4.42 (*parāṇi*: see note 40) take precedence over the class name *karaṇa*, and he gives (4) as an example.
43. Aṣṭādhyāyī 1.4.105: *yuṣmady upapade samānādhikaraṇe sthāniny api madhyamaḥ*, 1.4.107: *asmady uttamaḥ*.
44. *Pramāṇa* designates authoritative means of acquiring knowledge, including direct perception (*pratyakṣa*), inference (*anumāna*), and verbal transmission (*āgama, śabda*).
45. The sūtra (*samarthaḥ padavidhiḥ*) states that an operation provided relative to padas (*padavidhiḥ*) applies to padas which are syntactically and semantically linked (*samarthaḥ*). Vārttika 5 (*tatra nānākārakān nighātayuṣmadasmadādeśapratiṣedhaḥ*) argues that, under a particular interpretation of what constitutes being samartha, namely, if this is considered to be the mutual dependence that constituents have towards each other, one must disallow certain operations.
46. Aṣṭādhyāyī 8.1.28: *tiṅṅatiṅah* (*anudāttaṁ sarvam apādādau* 18). The heading given in parentheses specifies that the element in question is one that does not occur at the beginning of a verse section (*apādādau*).
47. In the context of ritual performance, if particular elements called for are not available, one may substitute for them, but the sacrificer is not replaceable.
48. Vākyapadīya 3.7.101–102: *prāganyataḥ śaktilābhān nyagbhāvāpādanād api / tadadhīnapravṛttitvāt pravṛttānāṁ nivarttanāt // adṛṣṭatvāt pratinidheḥ praviveke ca darśanāt / . . . svātantryaṁ kartur ucyate*. The last is illustrated by examples like *asti*, '. . . is', where the verb ending designates an unspecified agent.
49. Vākyapadīya 3.7.103: *dharmair abhyuditaiḥ śabde niyamo na tu vastuni /kartur dharmavivakṣāyāṁ śabdāt kartā pratīyate*.
50. Aṣṭādhyāyī 1.3.88: *aṇāv akarmakāt cittavatkartṛkāt*.

51. See Cardona (1976, 230–31, 294) for references to studies concerning the interpretations of Naiyāyikas as well as of Mīmāṁsakas (below, section 5.4).
52. Nirukta 2.2 (Sarup 45): . . . *athāpi prakṛtaya evaikeṣu bhāṣyante vikṛtaya ekeṣu / śavatir gatikarmā kambojeṣv eva bhāṣyate . . . vikāram asyāryeṣu bhāṣante śava iti / dātir lavanārthe prācyeṣu dātram udīcyeṣu*, 'And bases are used in some, derivates in some; *śav* meaning "go" is used only in Kamboja; people use a derivate of this in the Ārya country: *śava*. *dā* in the meaning "cut" (is used) among easterners; among northerners, *dātra* (is used).'
53. Abhyankar I.9, line 25–10, line 1: . . . *śavatir gatikarmā kambojeṣv eva bhāṣito bhavati vikāra enam āryā bhāṣante śava iti / hammatiḥ surāṣṭreṣu raṁhatiḥ prācyamadhyeṣu gamim eva tvāryāḥ prayuñjate / dātir lavanārthe prācyeṣu dātram udīcyeṣu*. Pāṇinian commentators generally interpret the locative *vikāre* of this passage to refer to a modification of some thing, in particular to a corpse, which is a modification of the living body. This interpretation goes back at least to Bhartṛhari, who also mentions that *śava* could refer to a modification of going, namely its cessation. Moreover, Bhartṛhari here refers to the comparable discussion in the Nirukta, and remarks that there the term *vikāra* is used with reference to a part of the derivate *śava*, which ends in the suffix *ac*. Additional details concerning these passages and the discussion in Mīmāṁsā texts need not be considered here.
54. The Iranian term is *arya-* (Avestan *airya-*, Old Persian *ariya-*). Achemenid rulers not only spoke of themselves as being of Arya seed (*ariya cissa*) but also as speakers of an Arya language.
55. See recently Cardona (1988, 655–6).
56. See recently Cardona (1988, 632).
57. Vākyapadīya 3.3.30ab: *asādhur anumānena vācakaḥ kaiścid iṣyate.*
58. Vākyapadīya 3.3.30cd: *vācakatvāviśeṣe vā niyamaḥ puṇyapāpayoḥ*, 'Alternatively, given that there is no distinction with respect to signifying, there is a restriction with respect to merit and sin (*puṇyapāpayoḥ*).'
59. See Cardona (1988, 635)
60. Abhyankar I.3, line 22: *mahatā devena naḥ sāmyaṁ yathā syād ity adhyeyaṁ vyākaraṇam*. See Cardona (1988, 635).
61. Vākyapadīya 1.131.
62. Vākyapadīya 1.74: *pade na varṇā vidyante varṇeṣv avayavā na ca / vākyāt padānām atyantaṁ pravibhāgo na kaścana.*
63. The abstraction (*apoddhāra*) of component units involves substitution in frames and a mode of reasoning which allows concluding that given elements are causes of one's understanding particular meanings; see Cardona (1988, 499–503).
64. Vākyapadīya 2.12cd: *anvayavyatirekau tu vyavahāranibandhanam*, 'Anvayat and vyatireka (see n. 63) are the means (*-nibandhanam* 'cause') of speaking about (bases and affixes).'
65. Vākyapadīya 2.13ab: *śabdasya na vibhāgo'sti kuto'rthasya bhaviṣyati*, 'There is no division of a speech unit. Why should there be one of its

meaning?' Some maintain that the syntactic word is the unanalysable unit, others that whole utterances of normal discourse are units.

66. Vākyapadīya 2.238cd: *asatye vartmani sthitvā tataḥ satyaṁ samīhate.*
67. Vākyapadīya 1.1: *anādinidhanaṁ brahma śabdatattvaṁ yad akṣaram / vivartate'rthabhābena prakriyā jagato yataḥ.*
68. Vākyapadīya 1.143: *api proyoktur ātmānaṁ śabdam antar avasthitam / prāhur mahāntam ṛṣabhaṁ yena sāyujyam iṣyate.*
69. Bhartṛhari describes the three speech types in several places of his autocommentary on the first kāṇḍa of the Vakyapadīya; see Cardona (1976: 302) for a brief outline and references to more detailed studies.
70. Vākyapadīya 1.144ab: *tasmād yaḥ śabdasaṁskāraḥ sā siddhiḥ paramātmanaḥ.*
71. Vṛtti on Vākyapadīya 1.14: . . . *sādhuprayogāc cābhivyaktadharmaviśeṣo mahāntaṁ śadbātamānam abhisambhavan vaikaraṇyaṁ prāpnoti.*
72. Vākyapadīya 1.14ab: *tad dvāram apavargasya vāṅmalānāṁ cikitsitam.*
73. Aṣṭādhyāyī 1.1.68: *svaṁ rūpaṁ śabdasyāśabdasaṁjñā.*
74. In Sanskrit terms, the distinction is between *prasajyapratiṣedha*, negation (*pratiṣedha*) of something once this could tentatively apply (*prasajya*) and *paryudāsa* (*pratiṣedha*), excepting (*paryudāsa*) an entity from something.
75. Just what semantic contrasts are pertinent to a particular grammar depends, of course, on the particular language being described, and Pāṇini's categories can hardly be considered universal or intended to be of universal value.
76. For references, see Cardona (1976, 1989).

Bibliography

ABHYANKAR, KASHINATH VASUDEV (1962–72) *The Vyākaraṇa = Mahābhāṣya of Patañjali*, third edition, ed. by F. Kielhorn. Revised and furnished with additional readings, references and select critical notes, 3 vols, Bhandarkar Oriental Research Institute, Pune.

BELVALKAR, SHRIPAD KRISHNA (1915) *An Account of the Different Existing Systems of Sanskrit Grammar, Being the Vishwanath Narayan Mandlik Gold Medal Prize Essay for 1909*, The author, Pune.

BIARDEAU, MADELEINE (1964) *Théorie de la connaissance et philosophie de la parole dans le brahmanisme classique* (Le monde d'outre-mer passé et présent, première série, études, 23), Mouton, Paris–La Haye.

CARDONA, GEORGE (1976) *Pāṇini, a Survey of Research* (Trends in Linguistics. State-of-the-art Reports), Mouton, The Hague/Paris. Reprinted, Motilal Banarsidass, Delhi, 1980.

CARDONA, GEORGE (1986) Phonology and Phonetics in Ancient Indian Works: the Case of Voiced and Voiceless Elements, *Studies in South Asian Languages*, ed. by Bh. Krishnamurti, C. Masica, Motilal Banarsidass, Delhi, 60–80.

CARDONA, GEORGE (1988) *Pāṇini, his Work and its Traditions. Vol. I: Background and Introduction*, Motilal Banarsidass, Delhi.

CARDONA, GEORGE (1989) Pāṇinian Studies, in *New Horizons ofResearch in Indology*, edited by V. N. Jha (Silver Jubilee volume of the Centre of Advanced Study in Sanskrit, Pune), Centre for Advanced Study in Sanskrit, University of Poona, 49–84.

COWARD, HAROLD G. and K. KUNJUNNI RAJA (1990) *Encyclopedia of Indian Philosophies, Vol. 5: The Philosophy of the Grammarians*, Princeton University Press, Princeton.

FILLIOZAT, PIERRE-SYLVAIN (1988) *Grammaire sanskrite pāninéenne* (Collection Connaissance des Langues), Bocard, Paris.

JHA, V. N. (1987) *Studies in the Padapāṭhas and Vedic Philology*, Pratibha Prakashan, Delhi.

JUNNARKAR, P. J. (1977–88) *An Introduction to Pāṇini*, 4 vols, Shanti Dighe, Baroda.

KATRE, SUMITRA MANGESH (1987) *Aṣṭādhyāyī of Pāṇini*, University of Texas Press, Austin.

KUNJUNNI RAJA, K. (1969) *Indian Theories of Meaning*, second edition, The Adyar Library, Madras.

RAU, WILHELM (1977) *Bhartṛharis Vākyapadīya. Die Mūlakārikās nach den Handschriften herausgegeben und mit einem Pāda-Index versehen* (Abhandlungen für die Kunde des Morgenlandes XLII, 4), Franz Steiner, Wiesbaden.

SARUP, LAKSHMAN (1927) *The Nighaṇṭu and the Nirukta, the Oldest Indian Treatise on Etymology, Philology and Semantics; Critically Edited from Original Manuscripts and Translated for the First Time into English* ... University of the Panjab, Lahore. Reprinted by Motilal Banarsidass, Delhi, 1967.

SCHARFE, HARTMUT (1977) *Grammatical Literature* (A History of Indian Literature, Part II, Fascicle 2), Harrassowitz, Wiesbaden.

SHARMA, R. N. (1987) *The Aṣṭādhyāyī of Pāṇini, Volume I: Introduction to the Aṣṭādhyāyī as a Grammatical Device*, Munshiram Manoharlal, Delhi.

SHARMA, R. N. (1990) *The Aṣṭādhyāyī of Pāṇini, Volume II: English Translation of Adhyāya One with Sanskrit Text, Translation, Word-boundary, Anuvṛtti, Vṛtti, Explanatory Notes, Derivational History of Examples and Indices*, Munshiram Manoharlal, Delhi.

SUBRAMANIA IYER, K. A. (1969) *Bhartṛhari, a Study of the Vākyapadīya in Light of the Ancient Commentaries* (Deccan College Building Centenary and Silver Jubilee Series, 68), Deccan College, Poona.

SUBRAMANIA IYER, K. A. (1983) *Vākyapadīya of Bhartṛhari (An ancient Treatise on the Philosophy of Sanskrit Grammar), Containing the Ṭīkā of Puṇyarāja and the Ancient Vṛtti, Kāṇḍa II; with a Foreword by Ashok Aklujkar*, Motilal Banarsidass, Delhi.

VARMA, SIDDHESHWAR (1953) *The Etymologies of Yāska* (Vishveshwaranand Indological Series, 5), Vishveshvaranand Vedic Research Institute, Hoshiarpur.

YUDHIṢṬHIRA, MĪMĀṀSAKA (1973) *Saṁskṛta vyākaraṇa-śāstra kā itihāsa (tīn bhāgoṁ meṁ pūrṇa)* [A history of Sanskrit Grammar, complete in three volumes], Bhāratīya Prācyavidyā Pratiṣṭhān, Ajmer.

Note: Yudhiṣṭhira, Mīmāṁsaka (1973) is the most complete survey of Sanskrit grammatical literature available, although much of the chronology adopted is open to doubt. It is also written in Hindi, so that it remains inaccessible to many Western scholars. Scharfe (1977) covers a broader field, including sections on work concerning early modern Indo-Aryan languages; however, its style is not felicitous and what is said reflects the author's less than desirable knowledge of the field. Belvalkar (1915) is out-of-date in many respects, but still gives a clear and sober picture of the various systems of Indian grammarians. Cardona (1976) covers the major part of secondary literature and editions in the Pāṇinian school, with critical assessments of scholarly work done in this field up to 1975. Cardona (1989) covers major work done in this area since 1975. Junnarkar (1977–88) is an excellent introduction to the Pāṇinian system, with rules reorganized according to the author's scheme of presentation. A general introduction to Pāṇini's grammatical system appears also in Cardona (1988), the first of eight projected volumes, in which Pāṇini's work is to be treated in detail, with full consideration of arguments presented in commentatorial literature. Another general introduction appears in Filliozat (1988). Sharma (1987), is the introductory volume preceding a complete translation of the Aṣṭādhyāyī, of which the first part has appeared (Sharma 1990). Katre (1987) is the most recent and best English translation of the entire Aṣṭādhyāyī available at present, although the text adopted is a conflated version; the text and examples appear in transliteration. The most complete introduction available to Bhartṛhari's views is Subramania Iyer (1969); considerable space is devoted to Bhartṛhari also in Biardeau (1964), but in a broader context of Indian thought. The best general treatment of Indian thoughts on semantics is Kunjunni Raja (1969). Coward and Kunjunni Raja (1990) contains a general survey of Indian grammarians' views on language from a philosophical viewpoint together with summaries of major works by various contributors and a substantial bibliography compiled by Karl H. Potter.

3

Linguistics in the Ancient Near East

E. Reiner

3.1 Introduction*

Of the great written cultures of the ancient Near East the largest body of material concerned with linguistic matters, reflections on linguistic diversity, and attempts at contrastive linguistics comes from Mesopotamia. Of the other languages of the area with written records dating to the second and first millennia BC – Elamite, Hurrian and its cognate Urartian – much less written material is extant; their interpretation is too uncertain to attempt to identify such linguistic data. Only Hittite (of the Anatolian branch of the Indo-European family) has a substantial written corpus, but their preoccupations with language are best considered along with those of other Indo-European peoples, and similarly data from Ugaritic are best considered along with Hebrew linguistics. Here we consider Hittite and Ugaritic only insofar as they impinge on the great cultures writing in cuneiform script, Sumerian and Akkadian.

In ancient Egypt, it is mostly from the Ptolemaic period, after the conquest of Egypt by Alexander the Great, that a preoccupation with the structure and the diverse grammatical constructions of the language is attested. The need for communicating and interacting with the Greeks no doubt furthered an interest that is attested, albeit sporadically, before contacts with the Greeks.

It stands to reason that in Mesopotamia more attention was focused on linguistic matters than in Egypt, since from the earliest times of recorded history there co-existed native speakers of two languages as dissimilar as Akkadian (also called Assyro-Babylonian), a member of the Semitic language family and hence an

* See Note, p. 62.

inflected language, and Sumerian, a language with no known relatives, of an agglutinating structure, typologically closest to such languages of the area as those of the Caucasus, and perhaps genetically related to a now extinct language of that family.

The need for communication, for teaching the scribes how to write in a language that was not their own, and for preserving literary and religious material for cultic use and possibly for prestige purposes as well long after Sumerian had ceased to be spoken, all must have contributed to the awareness of the structural differences between the two languages and to the attempts to present them in some classified way.

It is, however, characteristic of Sumero-Akkadian civilization that ideas and procedures were not formulated in an abstract form but were to be extrapolated from concrete examples. This holds true for mathematics as much as for, for example, legal situations where problems and not theorems, a casuistic and not a codifying approach, were set down. As for the observation and classification of the world around him, Mesopotamian man compiled lists of objects and phenomena but whether the purpose of these lists was the classification of such objects and phenomena as some early version of the natural sciences or whether they constituted word lists for learning the language or writing is not clear (Oppenheim 1978, 635f.).

Linguistic phenomena are dealt with in a similar fashion. Both lists and casuistic formulations exist, but not what could be called a theoretical approach to linguistics. Thus, the presentation of the achievements of these cultures in the field of linguistics is necessarily different from that of the more abstractly-thinking cultures of the ancient world.

Note

The Egyptian writing system indicates consonants only. By convention Egyptologists normally insert a short *e* or sheva where a cluster of consonants would otherwise be difficult to pronounce. In the case of the laryngeals and semi-vowels which influence the quality of the vowel, ꜣ (alef) and ʿ (ayin) are usually pronounced as an *a*-vowel, ʾ/ and *y* as an *i*-vowel, and *w* as an *u*-vowel. Also by convention, the letters used in transliterating ancient Egyptian are pronounced as in modern English, with the following exceptions: *ḥ* is pronounced as a slightly stronger *h*; *ḫ* as a *kh*, *ẖ* somewhere between *kh* and *sh*, *š* as *sh*, *ṯ* as *tj* or *tsh*, and *ḏ* as *dj*.

By convention, transliterations and transcriptions for Sumerian and Akkadian are pronounced as if they were Latin. Macrons and circumflexes mark length. The consonants *ṭ*, *q* and *ṣ* are called, conventionally, emphatics and seem to have been glottalized or pharyngealized. A haček (ˇ) over *s* (*š*) is used for a pronunciation [ʃ].

Subscripts and accents are used to distinguish apparently homophonous signs: the first homophone is marked with an acute accent, the second with a grave accent, successive ones with subscripts starting with 3: e.g. *ab*, *áb*, *àb*, ab_3, ab_4, ab_5 . . . These diacritics have no phonological value.

3.2 Ancient Egyptian Linguistics

Janet H. Johnson

3.2.1 Introduction

Literacy was a basic requirement for admission to the middle or higher level of the ancient Egyptian bureaucracy and there is evidence from earliest times of the importance of the scribe in Egyptian society. However, outside this rather large and highly complex bureaucracy there is little evidence for general literacy. Professional scribes were available for hire to write personal letters or other documents and it is only at an unusual village such as Deir el-Medina, inhabited by the workmen who carved and decorated the royal tombs in Thebes, that we find jottings and notes made by a major segment of the population. Kings and members of the royal family were, at least sometimes, literate; references to women who could read and write are rare.

Although an individual might personally instruct his own son, or other potential successor, scribal training usually began with 'classroom' instruction by a teacher of a number of students, during which time the student learned the basics of reading, writing, mathematics, and so on. Study usually involved solving mathematical and geometrical problems and copying model letters, famous pieces of literature, and didactic treatises intended to instruct the student on proper behaviour (Old Kingdom), to instill loyalty to the ruling monarch (Middle Kingdom), and to provide students with a sense of pride in their profession (Middle and New Kingdom). Following this training, the student was apprenticed to an office or official in the secular or religious bureaucracy where he received further, more specialized, training.[1]

Most of the evidence for formal Egyptian concern with the structure and functioning of their own language comes from the period following Egypt's conquest by Alexander the Great in 332 BC. From this period when Egypt was ruled first by the Ptolemaic successors of Alexander and then by the Roman Emperors there exist several school texts with grammatical exercises or word-lists and a couple of formal papyri which may have been intended as reference materials for teachers or for scribes attached to a temple, the last repositories of ancient Egyptian science and literature as well as religion. From this period there are also numerous bilingual texts, both official government decrees and private documents, and some evidence of actual bilingual training in Egyptian and Greek.

There were three different Egyptian scripts in use during this period and at least two different stages of the Egyptian language. The original hieroglyphs were limited fairly exclusively to religious and royal inscriptions carved on the walls of temples, on public stelae, and the like. The more cursive script derived directly from the hieroglyphs, called hieratic, was likewise fairly limited in usage, being found especially in religious texts written on papyrus. Both scripts were used to write an archaic stage of the Egyptian language retaining many of the characteristics of Middle Egyptian, which remained the classical literary language from the Middle Kingdom (c. 2000–1800 BC) through the Roman period. The bulk of the Egyptian material from the late period, including literary and scientific texts, business documents, letters, legal texts, and the like, were written in a much later stage of the language called demotic and in a very cursive script called by the same name.[2]

3.2.2 School Texts

Students began their study of Egyptian with demotic and all the school texts which we have from this period are written in demotic, including all the grammatical exercises and most of the word-lists. The grammatical exercises occasionally involved practice with noun formations. An ostracon originally published by Brugsch (Hess 1897) contains a series of compound nouns formed using the nominal prefix *rmṯ ỉwf*, 'a man who' (and see Devauchelle 1984, 47–9, and Bresciani 1984, 3). Similarly, two unpublished Strassburg ostraca (Spiegelberg hand-copies 174 [=1188] and 1617) contain lists of professions built using the nominal prefix *s n*, 'a man of'. More frequently, however, the student practised various verbal constructions. Several examples consist of a series of sentences using the same basic construction but changing the verb, the subject, or similar (e.g. P. Berlin 13639 [Erichsen 1948]).

More instructive about Egyptian concepts of the organization and functioning of their language are those examples where paradigms are written out, rather than full sentences. For analytic compound verb-forms, which consisted of an auxiliary followed by the subject which was in turn followed by the infinitive of the lexical verb being conjugated, these paradigms often practice only the auxiliary and the subject (usually pronominal). This indicates that the scribe recognized the distinction between the two parts of the conjugation pattern and was practicing the abstract combination of auxiliary plus subject, not writing complete grammatical units.

When dealing with synthetic verb forms based on the *sḏm/f* (*sḏm* being the verb 'to hear' and *f* being the third person masculine singular suffix pronoun 'he') where the practice paradigms could not omit the conjugated verb, the scribe often showed his awareness of the abstract quality of his paradigm by labelling the whole with the infinitive form of the verb involved. Very good examples of both kinds of verbal paradigms are found in P. Vienna D6464 (Kaplony-Heckel 1974, 244–5).

Column (× +) 5	Column (× +) 4	Column (× +) 3	Column (× +) 2
wḏꜣ/t	ḥn/k	bn ỉw/t	. . .
wḏꜣ/w	ḥn/f	bn ỉw/w	. . .
wḏꜣ/n	ḥn/s	bn ỉw/n	. . .
wḏꜣ/tn	ḥn/t	bn ỉw/tn	. . .
wḏꜣ pꜣ. . .	ḥn/w	ỉỉr/y	. . .
wḏꜣ pꜣy/f. . .	ḥn/n	ỉỉr/k	. . .
wḏꜣ . . .	ḥn/tn	ỉỉr/f	bn-pw/s
w[ḏꜣ . . .]	rẖ	ỉỉr/s	bn-pw/t
wḏꜣ . . .	rẖ/y	ỉỉr/t	bn-pw/w
. . .	rẖ/k	ỉỉr/w	bn-pw/n
. . .	. . .	ỉỉr[/n]	bn-pw/t[n]
you (f.s.) are well	you (m.s.) ordered	you (f.s.) will not	. . .
they are well	he ordered	they will not	. . .
we are well	she ordered	we will not	. . .
you (pl.) are well	you (f.s.) ordered	you (pl.) will not	. . .
the . . . is well	they ordered	it is . . . that I	. . .
his . . . is well	we ordered	it is . . . that you (m.s.)	. . .
. . . is well	you (pl.) ordered	it is . . . that he	she did not
[. . . is we]ll	to know	it is . . . that she	you (f.s.) did not
. . . is well	I knew	it is . . . that you (f.s.)	they did not
. . .	you (m.s.) knew	it is . . . that they	we did not
. . .	. . .	it is . . . that [we]	you (pl.) did not

Something half-way between the two is found in O. Bodleian Egyptian 683 (Kaplony-Heckel 1974, 246) where, in the middle of a sentence, the scribe gives a series of alternative possibilities with different subject pronouns. In constructing their paradigms, Egyptian scribes consistently presented the pronoun subjects in the order: 1 singular, 2 masculine, 3 masculine, 3 feminine, 2 feminine, 3 plural, 1 plural, 2 plural[3] (although not all possible pronouns are found in all examples). Only infrequently was a noun subject given in parallel to the pronominal ones (e.g. in the fully preserved final column of P. Vienna D6464, above). There are also a few texts which combine practice of various verbal paradigms with practice of noun formations and the formation of prepositional phrases (e.g. a badly damaged Michaelides papyrus published by Bresciani [1963, 18–24] and P. Strassburg 182 + 300 [referred to by Kaplony-Heckel 1974, 231–2]). Note also O. Griffith (Reich 1924) where, rather than practising a simple *sḏm/f*, the student, using the verb *ḏ*(*d*) 'to say', first ran through the forms of the nominalized relative form based on the *sḏm/f* (*pꜣy-ḏ* . . . 'that which . . . said') and then wrote a series using the nominalized relative form with 3 plural subject (*pꜣy-ḏ/w*) followed by the dative preposition *n* 'to, for' plus a range of possible pronominal objects of the preposition.

Column B		Column A	
pꜣy-ḏ/w n/y	what they said to me	pꜣy-ḏ/y	what I said
pꜣy-ḏ/w n/k	what they said to you (m.s.)	pꜣy-ḏ/k	what you (m.s.) said
pꜣy-ḏ/w n/f	what they said to him	pꜣy-ḏ/f	what he said
pꜣy-ḏ/w n/s	what they said to her	pꜣy-ḏ/s	what she said
pꜣy-ḏ/w n/w	what they said to them	pꜣy-ḏ/w	what they said
pꜣy-ḏ/w n/n	what they said to us	pꜣy-ḏ/n	what we said
pꜣy-ḏ/w n/tn	what they said to you (pl.)	[pꜣ]y-ḏ/tn	[what] you (pl.) said

In one of these texts, P. Carlsberg 12 vo., Volten claimed to find the germs of a systematizing grammar and even the embryo of a theoretical grammar (1952, 507–8).

3.2.3 Word-Lists

These texts which include practice on a wide range of grammatical constructions also include reference word-lists, of which there are two kinds: those arranged by subject matter and those arranged by assonance, that is 'alphabetically'. Demotic word-lists arranged by subject matter occur on both ostraca and papyri and include lists of such things as parts of the human body, metal vessels and tools, and occupations (Tait 1984). Long geographical lists and lists of gods and their epithets are also examples of such word-lists. There are also late period hieratic papyri which are word-lists. The long papyri, and especially the hieratic ones, probably were written not by students but by professional scribes, many of whom were attached to Egyptian temples.

More interesting as indicators of Egyptian concepts of language are the 'alphabetical' lists, which group together words which begin with the same letter. In one list of personal names found in a Michaelides papyrus (Bresciani 1963, 15–16), the names all begin with the letter *h*. Since all the names are written using the uniliteral sign *h*, it is possible that the names were grouped together because of the way they were written. However, the verso of P. CCG 31169 (Spiegelberg 1908, 270–80) contains a list of personal names beginning with the letter *ỉ* where the written form of the names includes the *ỉ* in several different ligatures as well as being written occasionally with the uniliteral sign. For this reason, the organizing principle must be phonetic, that is assonance, not graphic, and one may conclude with Iversen (1958, 7) that 'Egyptians somehow or other must have considered an initial *ỉ* in a way which seems to correspond to our conception of an ordinary letter'. Other 'alphabetical' word-lists contain not personal names but ordinary nouns (e.g. P. Carlsberg 12 vo. [Volten 1952]).

In text 27 from Saqqara are two lists of birds. In the first each bird is said to be on a specific tree or bush where at least the initial sounds of the name of the bird and the name of the tree are identical (e.g. 1.2, *pꜣ hb ḥr pꜣ hbyn* 'the ibis is upon the ebony-tree'). In the second list each bird is said to have gone away to a place and again at least the initial sounds of the name of the bird and the geographical location are identical (see the discussion of this text, and related 'alphabetical' texts, by Smith and Tait (1983, 210–12), where they conclude that 'the lists are plainly evidence of an interest in the individual sounds of language, beyond the mere use of assonance as a literary device'). Two texts list words beginning with *ḥ*; many of the words in one are from the root *ḥ-t-r* (see Erichsen 1948, 10), leading Kaplony-Heckel (1974, 234) to suggest that, if the scribe realized that all these words were related, this might even be an 'etymological dictionary'.

A more likely candidate for an etymological dictionary is P. Carlsberg 7 (Iversen 1958), of which only the first two pages are preserved. In the first, right-hand, column of each is written a series of signs in cursive hieroglyphs or very clear hieratic. For each of these signs, the left-hand column gives the phonetic rendering of the word written by the sign and a commentary explaining the meaning and usage of the sign and providing a mythically based explanation why that sign had that meaning or usage. The left-hand column is written entirely in hieratic. Each of the words presented on page one begins with either *h* or *ḥ*. These two sounds, originally distinct, had by this period coalesced and it thus seems likely that this text was, like some of the word-lists, organized 'alphabetically'. Given this observation, it becomes significant that the first word on the first page is *hb*, 'ibis', the sacred animal of the god Thoth, the Egyptian patron deity of writing. Classical authors record the tradition that Thoth was the inventor of writing and that the ibis was the first letter of the Egyptian 'alphabet'.[4] Despite the 'not very clear, but nevertheless irrefutable evidence' that the Egyptians did develop 'certain alphabetic conceptions' (Iversen 1958, 8), the main purpose of P. Carlsberg 7 was to establish mythical etymologies for the words by means of alliterations. It was presumably from texts such as this, but deprived of their phonetic underpinnings,[5] that Horapollo and other classical authors derived their ideas of the nature of Egyptian hieroglyphs (Iversen 1958, 12–13; 1972). This text is perhaps the closest to a philosophical treatise on language and writing which has survived from ancient Egypt.

The only preserved text which bears any resemblance to P. Carlsberg 7 is the so-called 'sign papyrus' (Griffith 1889), a massive text (33 pages are preserved) giving a series of hieroglyphs in the right-hand column and their hieratic equivalent, plus the name of the sign or a short comment, also written in hieratic, in the left-hand column. For the first several pages the hieroglyphic signs are arranged by subject matter (e.g. men, women, animals, parts of the body, astronomical bodies, etc.), but for the last several pages no organizing principle (type of object, shape of sign, phonetic value, etc.) has been identified. Unlike P. Carlsberg 7, this sign list was not intended to provide mythical etymologies by which to explain the usages of the signs but simply to provide a list of current hieroglyphs and hieratic equivalents (Iversen 1958, 9) and would equally well have served a scribe attached to a temple and responsible for writing inscriptions in hieratic and hieroglyphs or a teacher called upon to teach these relatively rare scripts.

3.2.4 'Bilingualism'

In addition to such texts in which hieroglyphs are explained in hieratic there are also texts where demotic is combined with one of the earlier forms. This is sometimes in the form of short demotic glosses or interlinear additions to a hieratic manuscript. In other cases, a complete text is given in demotic as well as the earlier script. Examples of the latter include both the numerous private funerary stelae which have the dedicatory text and name of the owner carved in both hieroglyphs or hieratic and demotic and official royal decrees such as the Rosetta Stone. In the latter case it is clear that the hieroglyphic text is a translation of the demotic. The reverse is true in an astronomical treatise which quotes, in hieratic, from texts found in Ramesside tombs (there written in hieroglyphs) and then translates the quote into demotic and adds a demotic commentary. The astronomical texts themselves were written in Middle Egyptian and can be shown by their contents to have originated in the Middle Kingdom (Lange and Neugebauer 1940; see also Parker 1955).

Such texts indicate the mastery by at least some Egyptian scribes of several different Egyptian scripts. The same, combined with a knowledge of Greek, is provided by the Roman period magical texts. These texts were written largely in demotic but have words or phrases in the running text written in hieratic and have some Greek words and magical words written in an 'alphabetic' demotic script developed to indicate clearly the pronunciation of words so written.[6] Many of the words written in the demotic 'alphabetic' script, and some others as well, are glossed interlinearly in what has been termed 'Old Coptic', an alphabetic script composed of Greek capital letters plus additions from demotic for sounds not present in Greek (see Griffith and Thompson 1921; Johnson 1977a,b).[7]

Earlier evidence for Egyptian-Greek bilingualism occurs in both official and private documents. The royal decrees such as the Rosetta Stone also include a Greek version of the decree and although the earliest examples of such decrees include evidence that the Greek was the original text and the Egyptian are translations, the later examples of the corpus have been argued to have been composed in Egyptian and then translated into Greek. But aside from official texts there are also several private archives of legal documents and personal papers, some in Greek, some in Egyptian, written by and for the same individual. Such people would have been bilingual, as would many of those Egyptians who became members of the government bureaucracy and those others for whom there is evidence that they bore both Egyptian and Greek personal names. Although there is evidence for a fair amount of Egyptian-Greek bilingualism in post-Alexander Egypt, the exact nature and extent of the bilingualism is still in need of careful study.[8] A few bilingual 'aids' have been preserved: a papyrus in Munich (Spiegelberg 1928) has a list of demotic words, most or all of which may be personal names, where a Greek transcription has been written above the line; P. Heidelberg 414 (Bilabel 1938, 79–80) contained a Greek-Egyptian glossary written in Greek letters.[9]

3.2.5 Pre-Ptolemaic Evidence

It has often been suggested that the consciousness of their own language which is evidenced by some Ptolemaic and later scribes is due to contact with the Greeks (e.g. Iversen 1958, 6; 1972, 67) and with Greek methods of education. Indeed, such contact may well have spurred the Egyptians to greater awareness. However, there are examples of each of the kinds of texts which have been discussed for the post-Alexandrian period already in the New Kingdom (c. 1600–1100 BC). Two Ramesside ostraca have practice writings of verbal auxiliaries with subject pronouns. O. Petrie 28 (Černý and Gardiner 1957, pl. 8, no. 7) presents the pronominal subjects in the order: 1 singular, 3 masculine, 2 masculine, 1 plural, 3 plural (archaic form), 3 plural, 2 feminine. Both ostraca omit the infinitive necessary to make a complete grammatical form and thus seem to indicate an awareness of the distinction between the two parts of the conjugation pattern. It is interesting to note that, as with several of the later examples, O. Petrie 28 combines this grammatical exercise with a word-list (of words written with the 'stick' determinative used to indicate that the object was made of wood).

Column 1	
n/k	(dative) to, for you (m.s.)
ỉw/ỉ	I
ỉw/f	he
ỉw/k	you (m.s.)
ỉw/n	we
ỉw/w	they (younger form)
ỉw/sn	they (older form)
ỉw/t	you (f.s.)
. . .	. . .

All other examples of word-lists known from before the time of Alexander the Great, both school texts and several long formal hieratic papyri, are also organized by subject matter. The formal texts, which are attested as early as the Middle Kingdom,[10] are said to be 'for learning all things that exist' and although lexicography was not the major aim of such texts, philological considerations played an important secondary role in these and the related 'miscellanies' (Gardiner 1947, 2*, 4). There is also from the Ramesside period a very badly damaged, fragmentary papyrus now in Turin (Pleyte and Rossi 1869–76, pl. 144) which originally contained a series of individual signs written in cursive hieroglyphs or hieratic to each of which is added a description of the sign. This text may be seen as ancestral in kind, if not directly, to the late 'sign papyrus' and reflects some Egyptian concern for their writing systems. Although there are no preserved early examples of word-lists organized phonetically, by the assonance of the first letter,[11] the pre-Ptolemaic Egyptians were aware of and interested in phonetics, as is clearly shown by their propensity for punning and various other types of word-play dependent on phonetics; such punning occurs already in the earliest preserved texts, the Pyramid Texts (see, most recently, Gilula 1982).

Translations from one stage of Egyptian to another are also found in the new Kingdom. For example, one copy of the Ritual for Repelling the Aggressor contains not only the Middle Egyptian original but a Late Egyptian translation of the text. Similarly a school tablet dated to Dynasty 22 (c. 945–730 BC) has the title to the wisdom text known as the Maxims of Anii first in Middle Egyptian and then translated into Late Egyptian (Erman 1894). Contemporary with this tablet is a papyrus, part of which consists of alternating Middle Egyptian and Late Egyptian 'variations on a theme', as if a teacher had set a language exercise similar to the *chria* of Latin rhetoricians (Caminos 1968).

One aspect of Egyptian consciousness about their own language which was not explicitly mentioned in late texts but to which reference is made in a New Kingdom text is the existence of different dialects spoken by people from different geographical regions of the country. Thus, in the 'satirical letter' in which one scribe is berating another for the latter's ignorance, the writer says 'Your tales . . ., there is no interpreter to translate them; they are like the words of a man of the (Delta) marshes with a man of Elephantine' (Gardiner 1911, 80).

In this same letter the writer shows off his erudition by twice including a short passage in a Semitic language. The Semitic was written in these passages in 'group writing', which had, perhaps, been developed for writing foreign words which had come into Egyptian (see Gardiner 1957, 60 and nn.). How much real knowledge there was of Semitic languages by Egyptian scribes is hard to determine. The Amarna tablet which lists cuneiform numbers in one column and Egyptian numbers, written phonetically, in another and then includes a list of miscellaneous vocabulary, mostly objects made of wood, was perhaps intended for a cuneiformist learning Egyptian (Smith and Gadd 1925); the Maxims of Anii do make reference to teaching Nubians and Syrians to speak Egyptian (Volten 1937, 49–50). However, there are, from the Old Kingdom on, people who bear the title 'interpreter'. At least some of these 'interpreters' were Egyptians since in a Fifth Dynasty scene a group of Asiatics is shown in the company of Egyptian 'interpreters'.

3.2.6 Coptic Evidence

Thus, although there are no theoretical treatises on language from early Egypt, there is enough evidence to indicate that even before contact with Greeks, some Egyptians were concerned with different aspects of their language, if only mainly for pedagogical purposes. During the Coptic period, after Egypt converted to Christianity and began writing in Coptic, outside influence on language study becomes much more evident. In the schools students learned to read and write by drawing up syllabaries identical in form to ones used by Greek students (e.g. Husselman 1947). Coptic-Greek bilingualism is suggested by, among other things, a British Museum ostracon giving parallel conjugations of the verb 'to teach' in various tenses in the two languages (Leclercq 1913, 212), various Greek-Coptic glossaries, a Greek-Coptic phrase list, and a Greek-Coptic dictionary arranged in alphabetical order according to the Greek (see Kammerer 1950, 102–5).

But after Egypt was conquered by the Arabs, and the Arabic language began to replace Egyptian (something which even Greek had never succeeded in doing), varius Coptic bishops and monks began compiling vocabulary lists, often bilingual Arabic-Coptic lists of the vocabulary which occurred in specific books of the Bible, and writing grammatical treatises on Coptic (see Sidarus 1978). These, which date from the eleventh to the fourteenth centuries, are clearly based on the works of Arab grammarians (Mallon 1906; 1907).[12]

Notes

1. For a full discussion of Egyptian schools and scribal training, see Williams (1972) and the references therein for the Pharaonic period and Kaplony-Heckel (1974) and Devauchelle (1984) for the period post-Alexander the Great.
2. These three names (hieroglyphs, hieratic, and demotic) are derived from classical authors who, in explaining the Egyptian writing system, noted that, in their day, the former two were used primarily for sacred materials while the third was used by the general populace for everyday needs (see Iversen 1972, and the translations of some of the relevant passages from non-Christian classical authors in Marestaing 1913).

3. P. Berlin 23597 (Zauzich 1969, 43), a conjugation of the *sḏm.f* of the verb *ꜥnḫ*, 'to live', misplaces the 2 masculine after the 3 feminine.
4. Note also that the first bird mentioned in Saqqara text 27 is *hb*, 'ibis' (see Smith and Tait 1983, 212–13 and n. 2, p. 212).
5. Mythical explanations for the use of hieroglyphs are also given occasionally in literary texts, e.g. the Myth of the Sun's Eye (Spiegelberg 1917).
6. In addition, some words are written in a cipher script developed to hide the identity of secret ingredients of magical potions.
7. This whole series of texts is part of a much larger corpus of magical texts found in Egypt, most of which are written in Greek but incorporate extensive Egyptian mythology, etc.
8. See most recently Peremans (1983). Clearly, the Greek script is much easier to learn than the Egyptian writing systems and so it would have been much easier for a literate bilingual speaker with an Egyptian background to become capable of writing in both languages than for such a person with a Greek background. But that at least a few Greek speakers did learn Egyptian is indicated by a letter (Wilcken 1927, 635, no. 148), written in Greek, in which the writer of the letter indicates how pleased she is that the recipient is learning Egyptian, so that he will be able to get a teaching job.
9. In this text, as in 'Old Coptic' and Coptic, sounds for which there was no equivalent in Greek were written with signs from demotic. Perhaps one of the most interesting texts preserved from the early Roman period is a quadrilingual text in the Bodleian Library with short accounts (?) written in Greek, Latin, demotic, and an unidentified fourth script (Coles 1981).
10. And note the related scribal tablet from the Fifth Dynasty (c. 2550–2400 BC) found in a private tomb at Giza (Reisner 1910).
11. But note that, in the Ramesseum Onomasticon from the Middle Kingdom, for every town name there is an identifying symbol, often a phonetic or graphic abbreviation for the town name. The use of a 'letter of the alphabet' to designate a town whose name began with a triliteral sign implied to the editor of the text 'a consciousness of the alphabet as such' (Gardiner 1947, 12).
12. Occasional trilingual texts also occur, e.g. a Latin-Greek-Coptic text from the fifth or sixth century (Schubart 1913) and an interesting Arabic-Coptic-French vocabulary and phrase list from the thirteenth century (Maspero 1888).

Bibliography

BILABEL, F. (1938) Neue literarische Funde in der Heidelberger Papyrussammlung, *Actes du Vᵉ Congrès International de Papyrologie*, Fondation Égyptologique Reine Élisabeth, Bruxelles, 72–84.

BRESCIANI, E. (1963) *Testi demotici nella collezione Michaelidis*, Centro per le Antichità e la Storia dell'Arte del Vicino Oriente, Roma.

BRESCIANI, E. (1984) Testi lessicali demotici inediti da Tebtuni presso l'Istituto Papirologico G. Vitelli di Firenze, *Grammata Demotika. Festschrift für Erich Lüddeckens*, ed. by H.-J. Thissen and K.-Th. Zauzich, Gisela Zauzich Verlag, Würzburg, 1–9.

CAMINOS, R. A. (1968) A Fragmentary Hieratic School-Book in the British Museum (Pap. BM. 10298), *The Journal of Egyptian Archaeology*, 54, 114–20.

COLES, R. (1981) A Quadrilingual Curiosity in the Bodleian Library in Oxford, *Proceedings of the Sixteenth International Congress of Papyrology* (American Studies in Papyrology, 23), Scholars Press, Ann Arbor, Michigan.

ČERNÝ, J., and GARDINER, A. H. (1957) *Hieratic Ostraca,* Oxford University Press, Oxford.

DEVAUCHELLE, D. (1984) Remarques sur les méthodes d'enseignement du démotique, *Grammata Demotika. Festschrift für Erich Lüddeckens*, ed. by H.-J. Thissen and K.-Th. Zauzich, Gisela Zauzich Verlag, Würzburg, 47–59.

ERICHSEN, W. (1948) *Eine ägyptische Schulübung in demotischer Schrift* (Det Kongelige Danske Videnskabernes Selskab, Historisk-Filologiske Meddelelser, 31/4), Munksgaard, København.

ERMAN, A. (1894) Eine ägyptische Schulübersetzung, *Zeitschrift für ägyptische Sprache und Altertumskunde*, 32, 127–28.

GARDINER, A. H. (1911) *Egyptian Hieratic Texts*, J. C. Hinrichs Verlag, Leipzig.

GARDINER, A. H. (1947) *Ancient Egyptian Onomastica*, Oxford University Press, Oxford.

GARDINER, A. H. (1957) *Egyptian Grammar*, third edition, revised, Oxford University Press, London.

GILULA, M. (1982) An Egyptian Etymology of the Name of Horus?, *The Journal of Egyptian Archaeology*, 68, 259–65.

GRIFFITH, F. L. (1889) The Sign Papyrus, *Two Hieroglyphic Papyri from Tanis*, Part 1, Egyptian Exploration Society, London.

GRIFFITH, F. L., and THOMPSON, H. (1921) *The Demotic Magical Papyrus of London and Leiden*, Clarendon Press, Oxford.

HESS, J. J. (1897) Demotica, *Zeitschrift für ägyptische Sprache und Altertumskunde*, 35, 144–49.

HUSSELMAN, E. M. (1947) A Bohairic School Text on Papyrus, *Journal of Near Eastern Studies*, 6, 129–51.

IVERSEN, E. (1958) *Papyrus Carlsberg Nr. VII, Fragments of a Hieroglyphic Dictionary* (Det Kongelige Danske Videnskabernes Selskab, Historisk-Filologiske Skrifter, 3/2), Munksgaard, København.

IVERSEN, E. (1972) The Hieroglyphs in Europe before Champollion, *Textes et langages de l'Égypte pharaonique* (Bibliothèque d'études, 64/1), Institut Français d'Archéologie Orientale, Cairo.

JOHNSON, J. H. (1977a) The Dialect of the Demotic Magical Papyrus of London and Leiden, *Studies in Honor of George R. Hughes, January 12, 1977*, ed. by J. H. Johnson and E. F. Wente (Studies in Ancient Oriental Civilization, 32), University of Chicago, Oriental Institute, Chicago.

JOHNSON, J. H. (1977b) Louvre E 3229: A Demotic Magical Text, *Enchoria*, 7, 55–102.

KAMMERER, W. (1950) *A Coptic Bibliography* (University of Michigan General Library Publications, 7), University of Michigan, Ann Arbor.

KAPLONY-HECKEL, U. (1974) Schüler und Schulwesen in der ägyptischen Spätzeit, *Studien zur altägyptischen Kultur*, 1, 227–46.

LANGE, H. O., and NEUGEBAUER, O. (1940) *Papyrus Carlsberg No. 1* (Det Kongelige Danske Videnskabernes Selskab, Historisk-Filologiske Skrifter, 1/2), Munksgaard, København.

LECLERCQ, H. (1913) Devoirs d'écoliers d'après une table et des ostraca, *Bulletin d'ancienne littérature et d'archéologie chrétienne*, 3, 209–13.

MALLON, A., S.J. (1906) Une école de savants égyptiens, *Mélanges de la faculté orientale, Université Saint-Joseph, Beyrouth (Syrie)*, 1, 109–31.

MALLON, A., S.J. (1907) Une école de savants égyptiens, *Mélanges de la faculté orientale, Université Saint-Joseph, Beyrouth (Syrie)*, 2, 213–64.

MARESTAING, P. (1913) *Les écritures égyptiennes et l'antiquité classique*, Geuthner, Paris.

MASPERO, G. (1888) Le Vocabulaire français d'un Copte du XIIIe siècle, *Romania*, 17, 481–512.

PARKER, R. A. (1955) The Function of the Imperfective *sḏm.f* in Middle Egyptian, *Revue d'Égyptologie*, 10, 49–59.

PEREMANS, W. (1983) Le bilinguisme dans les relations gréco-égyptiennes sous les Lagides, *Egypt and the Hellenistic World*, ed. by E. Van't Dack et al. (Studia Hellenistica, 27), Orientaliste, Lovanii, 253–80.

PLEYTE, W., and ROSSI, F. (1869–76) *Papyrus de Turin*, Brill, Leiden.

REICH, N. (1924) A Grammatical Exercise of an Egyptian Schoolboy, *The Journal of Egyptian Archaeology*, 10, 285–8.

REISNER, G. A. (1910) A Scribe's Tablet Found by the Hearst Expedition at Giza, *Zeitschrift für ägyptische Sprache und Altertumskunde*, 48, 113–4.

SCHUBART, W. (1913) Ein lateinisch-griechisch-koptisches Gesprächbuch, *Klio*, 13, 27–38.

SIDARUS, A. Y. (1978) Coptic Lexicography in the Middle Ages, *The Future of Coptic Studies*, ed. by R. W. Wilson, Brill, Leiden, 125–42.

SMITH, H. S., and TAIT, W. J. (1983) *Saqqâra Demotic Papyri*, vol. 1 (Texts from Excavations, 7), Egypt Exploration Society, London.

SMITH, S., and GADD, C. J. (1925) A Cuneiform Vocabulary of Egyptian Words, *The Journal of Egyptian Archaeology*, 11, 230–9.

SPIEGELBERG, W. (1908) *Catalogue général des antiquités égyptiennes du Musée du Caire. Die demotischen Denkmäler 30601–31270, 50001–50022. Vol. 2, Die demotischen Papyrus*, Dumont Schauberg, Strassburg.

SPIEGELBERG, W. (1917) *Der ägyptische Mythus vom Sonnenauge (Der Papyrus der Tierfabeln – 'Kufi') nach dem Leidener demotischen Papyrus I 384*, Schultz, Strassburg.

SPIEGELBERG, W. (1928) *Demotica II* (Sitzungsberichte der Bayerischen Akademie der Wissenschaften, philosophisch-historische Klasse, 6/2), München.

TAIT, W. J. (1984) A Demotic List of Temple and Court Occupations, *Grammata Demotika. Festschrift für Erich Lüddeckens*, ed. by H.-J.

Thissen and K.-Th. Zauzich, Gisela Zauzich Verlag, Würzburg, 211–33.
VOLTEN, A. (1937) *Studien zum Weisheitsbuch des Anii* (Det Kongelige Danske Videnskabernes Selskab, Historisk-Filologiske Meddelelser, 23/3), Levin and Munksgaard, København.
VOLTEN, A. (1952) An 'Alphabetical' Dictionary and Grammar in Demotic, *Archiv Orientální*, 20, 496–508.
WILCKEN, U. (1927) *Urkunden der Ptolemäerzeit*, de Gruyter, Berlin.
WILLIAMS, R. J. (1972) Scribal Training in Ancient Egypt, *Journal of the American Oriental Society*, 92, 214–21.
ZAUZICH, K.-TH. (1969) Neue demotische Papyri in Berlin, *XVII Deutsches Orientalistentag* (*Zeitschrift der Deutschen Morgenländischen Gesellschaft*, Supplementa 1/2), Steiner, Wiesbaden, 41–7.

3.3 Sumerian

Miguel Civil

3.3.1 The Language

Sumerian is an isolated language, written on clay tablets in cuneiform script using a mixture of logograms (a symbol for a word) and syllabograms (a symbol for a syllable). Sumerian was used in ancient Mesopotamia (Iraq) in the area that extends from Baghdad to the Arabian Gulf; as a written culture language it reached at various times as far as south-west Iran (Susa), Central Anatolia (Boghazköy), north-west Syria (Ebla, Ugarit), and Egypt (El-Amarna). Sumerian texts appear for the first time during the Uruk III/IV periods (c. 2900 BC) and continue to be written until almost the beginning of the Christian era. During the Old Babylonian period (1894–1595 BC), and possibly much earlier, Sumerian is no longer a living language and survives only as a literary language used in administrative, legal, scholarly, and religious texts. From very early in its history the language coexisted with languages of the Semitic family. Other significant languages in the area are Subarian or Hurrian, Elamite, and Amorite. Their influence cannot be gauged since little is known about them. Late languages such as Kassite or Aramaic can be safely assumed to have had no influence on the Sumerian lexicon or grammar. The term for 'Sumerian' is *eme-gir*$_7$ ('tongue' + an adjective of uncertain meaning possibly related to the name of the country, *ke-en-gi*) and the women's dialect is known as *eme-sal* ('fine or thin tongue').[1]

3.3.2 Paradigms

What can be called scientific texts in Mesopotamia are classificatory lists with enumerations of lexical or grammatical sets. They are written on clay tablets often forming large collections known as 'series'.

The earliest examples of paradigms probably appear in the Fara period, c. 2500 BC, Deimel (1923, 41 vi 7ff., 42 ix 2ff., 63 iv 19ff.) and certainly in the Ebla archives, c. 2300 BC. They consist of short lists of contrasting verbal forms inserted in word repertories used in scribal training:

Transitive verb:

in-na-sum 'he will give to'
ì-na-sum 'has been given to him'
nu-ì-na-sum 'has not been given to him'
ḫe-na-sum 'let it be given to'

Intransitive verb:

ba-til 'has been finished'
nu-til 'is not finished'
in-til 'he finishes'
ḫe-til 'let him/her/it finish'

(Pettinato et al. 1981, 208 v 12ff.)

It can be safely assumed that the purpose of such lists is to teach apprentice scribes the proper use of the forms (note that in the case of Ebla we are in a peripheral area where Sumerian is a foreign, 'technical' language). More ambitious and comprehensive paradigms appear in the eighteenth to seventeenth centuries BC (Old Babylonian Grammatical Texts, henceforth OBGT).[2] We now have large tablets written in a minute script with extensive and detailed verbal paradigms. The paradigm of the verb *gen* = *alāku*, 'to go' (i.e. Sumerian *gen* is translated by Akkadian *alāku*) has 318 entries and the one of *gar* = *šakānu*, 'to place' has 227. In addition to the verbal paradigms there are long paradigms of pronominal forms with various prepositional and conjunctive elements, adverbial phrases, etc. OBGT I, one of these paradigms, must have had in its original form about 1200 entries. These tablets are bilingual with the text arranged in two subcolumns, the Sumerian on the left, the Akkadian on the right. Such an arrangement, however, cannot be taken as an indication that Sumerian is necessarily to be considered the primary language. It is true that this arrangement is found in Sumero-Akkadian glossaries but it is also the one found in Akkado-Sumerian glossaries such as Nabnitu (see section 3.2.3). The OBGTs have been extensively studied by Jacobsen (1965, 1974), Foxvog (1975), Black (1984), Kang (1968), Edzard (1971), and Yoshikawa (1964, 1966–73), but many doubts remain about their value and interpretation. The fundamental question –

are these paradigms descriptive or prescriptive? – has never been explicitly formulated, much less answered, although there is widespread scepticism about their descriptive adequacy. Note that these texts date from a time when Sumerian was no longer a spoken language and was used by Akkadian speakers as a learned language.

As an example of pronominal paradigm one may quote OBGT I:

(324) lú-ne-a 'this one' (loc.) = anniam 'this one' (accus.)
'man' + deictic + locative demonstrative accusative
(325) lú-ne-er 'this one' (dat.) = anniam
'man' + deictic + dative
(326) lú-e-ra 'this one' (dat.) = anniam
'man' + deictic + dative
(327) lú-e-meš-a 'these ones' (loc.) = annūtim 'these ones' (accus.)
'man' + deictic + plural + locative
(328) lú-ne-meš-ra 'these ones' (dat.) = annūtim
'man' + deictic + plural + dative

On the positive side, the compiler shows sufficient flexibility to recognize that a dative or locative in one language may correspond to an accusative in the other, depending on the surface cases required by particular verbs; on the negative side, note that, judging from the attested ordinary language of the preserved texts, (1) a noun of the animate class such as *lú* 'man' does not take the locative, (2) the plural *-meš-* is a copula, not a nominal suffix – the correct form would be *-ene* – (3) the locative or dative suffixes cannot follow *-meš* unless the form is nominalized, and (4) there is a normal Sumerian accusative – represented by a zero case – which is not listed. Except for lines 325 and 326, these forms are artificial constructs which do not respect the constraints of morpheme distribution and, not suprisingly, are not attested in real contexts.

The verbal paradigms often start with non-indicative, volitive forms (OBGT VI):

(1) gar-ra = šu-ku-un 'place!' (2 sg.)
(2) ga-gar = lu-uš-ku-un 'I want to place' (1 sg.)
(3) ḫé-gar = li-iš-ku-un 'may he place' (3 sg.)

The correspondences are normal and correct. In the rest of the paradigms the usual sequence is third, first, second person:

(130) mu-un-da-gar = iš-ku-un-šu 'he placed him'
(131) mu-da-gar = aš-ku-un-šu 'I placed him'
(132) mu-da-gar = ta-aš-ku-un-šu 'you placed him'

The infix *-da-* is a comitative 'with' and is not used in Sumerian to represent the direct object. However, the verb *gál*, 'to be (somewhere)' has a construction with *-da-* which is the equivalent of a transitive: *mu-e-da-gál* 'it is with you' = 'you have'. This construction has been incorrectly extrapolated to other intrinsically transitive verbs. Similarly, the locative infix *-ni-* and the locative-terminative infix *-*e/i-* are used to translate the Akkadian causative which has no direct counterpart in Sumerian. Nevertheless, there is much in these paradigms that reveals obscure details of the verbal structure as long as the data are critically interpreted. For instance, a contrast between *a*-prefixes for the stative and *i*-prefixes for the perfect, a contrast which seems to be unsubstantiated by texts contemporary with the OBGTs, turns out to have existed at the end of the third millennium.

The general impression, however, is that the compiler tried, whenever possible, to create one-to-one correspondences between his native Akkadian and the Sumerian, forcing the Sumerian morphology in the process. Except for rare cases, notably the school dialogue 'The Father and His Misguided Son', composed in Ur sometime before the end of the eighteenth century BC,[3] and some royal inscriptions, the forms prescribed by the paradigms are seldom used in literary texts. It would seem that these grammatical texts represent a last-ditch effort to salvage a moribund language.

3.3.3 Lists of morphemes

Although one can find in lexical lists isolated instances of bound morphemes already in Old Babylonian times, the first lists of morphemes (still mostly unpublished) seem to have been composed in Middle Babylonian times before the twelfth century BC. Large systematic lists ('Neobabylonian Grammatical Texts', henceforth NBGT),[4] however, are preserved only from much later periods (fifth to fourth centuries BC).

Two tablets, one with 462 lines and another with 279, and several fragmentary texts are known. As an example one may quote NBGT I:

(272) e-a = ana kuata 'to you'
(273) ri/ra
(274) ra-da
(275) a-ra
(276) e-ra
(277) e-ši
(278) e-da
(279) e-ta

(280) zu-a
(281) za
(282) za-ra

The Akkadian translation applies to all successive entries. The list gives all forms – nominal suffixes, verbal infixes, and independent pronouns – that can be considered as representations of the second person indirect object. Morphophonemic variants are included: *ri*/*ra*, *a-ra*/*e-ra*. The syllabic writing prevented the isolation of the morpheme in its 'basic' form. Another example from the same text:

(308) mu = aššum 'because'
(309) mu-šè
(310) ke_4-eš = aššum KI.TA 'because, suffix'
(311) nam
(312) ke_4-nam
(313) mu-aš = aššum AN.TA $MURUB_4$.TA 'because, prefix (and) infix'[5]

The passage illustrates the use of grammatical terms. In line 308 the term AN.TA 'prefix' is understood.

The NBGTs deal with pronouns, conjunctions, prepositions, and verbal particles; a brief section lists suppletive forms of some very common verbs. Apparently the preserved tablets are part of a larger series or collection; one of the lost tablets may have had verbal paradigms as shown by its preserved title [gá-n]u = al-ka 'come!'

3.3.4 Lexical Compilations

The largest number of Sumerian texts of linguistic interest consists of word lists.[6] They have been found among the oldest tablets discovered in Mesopotamian sites (Uruk, levels IV-III, 2800(?) BC). These lists survived, unchanged, in all Mesopotamian sites and peripheral areas (Elam, Ebla) until the end of the third millennium. At this time they were replaced by lists similar in content but differently arranged. The word lists were originally unilingual; bilingual lists appear sporadically in Ebla (c. 2300 BC) but become common only around the eighteenth to seventeenth centuries BC. Later lexical compilations are normally Sumero-Akkadian bilinguals. Although the central core remains unchanged, the texts from the nineteenth to the twelfth centuries show a great deal of textual variation, which may be explained by a strong oral element in their transmission. They were standardized ('canonical' recensions) before the twelfth century BC and they continued to be copied virtualy unchanged, until almost the beginning of the Christian era.

The main types of lexical lists are as follows.

(a) Repertories of signs arranged according to their shape
In their most complete form these repertories include: (1) pronunciation given in syllabograms, (2) the sign itself, (3) the sign's name or description, and (4) its Akkadian translation. For instance (series Ea, tablet IV):

	(1)	(2)	(3)	(4)	
(95)	ki-i	KI	kikû	= erṣetu	'earth'
(101)	ḫab-ru-da	KI × U	ša kigāku gešpa igub	= ḫurru	'earth hole, cave'
(106)	na-a	NA	nanû	= abnu	'stone'
(228)	la-al	LÀL	ša tatāku duga igub	= dišpu	'honey'

(b) Lists of words according to their meaning
For instance, from a list of boats and their parts (series ḪAR-ra, tablet IV):

	Sumerian	Akkadian	
(262)	giš.má	= eleppu	'boat'
(263)	giš.má-gur$_8$	= makurru	'"magur"-boat'
(264)	giš.má-tur	= maturru	'small boat'
(265)	giš.má-u$_5$	= rukūbu	'ceremonial boat'
(266)	giš.má-lal	= malallû	'raft'
(267)	giš.má-sal-la	= mašallû	'narrow boat'
(268)	giš.má-ti-la	= muballittu	'lifeboat'
(269)	giš.má-gíd-da	= makkītu	'long boat'
(270)	giš.má-gud$_4$-da	= makkūtu	'short boat'

And so on. The boat section has no less than 136 entries. The linguistic and cultural interest of such word lists hardly needs to be stressed.

One can also find collections of pairs or triplets of semantically related terms (series Erimḫuš, tablet VI):

192 kuš-è	= kâṣu	'to flay'
193 zil	= qalāpu	'to peel'
194 gar-ra	= šahātu	'to rinse off (hides)'

(*c*) *Lists of words according to their graphic shape (c1) or etymology (c2)*

(c1) The following example lists compounds with the sign á (series Izi, tablet Q):

57 á-lá	= kamû	'to tie'
58 á-lá	= kasû	'to tie'
59 á-sukud	= aškuttu	'door bar'
60 á-sùḫ	= ammatu	'forearm'
61 á-sùḫ	= kiṣir ammati	'elbow'
62 á-ág-gá	= têrtu	'command'

(c2) Akkado-Sumerian word-lists group the Sumerian words according to the consonant pattern of their Akkadian translations. The following example gives Sumerian words whose Akkadian translations include the triliteral *š-ḫ-r* (series Nabnitu, tablet IX):

222 si-si-ga	= šuḫarratu	'silence'
225 ḫúb-šú	= šuḫar šēpi	'a part of the foot'
226 dug.saḫár	= šuḫarratu	'a type of clay pot'
227 sa-ḫir	= šaḫirru	'sack'
228 é-suḫur-ra	= šaḫūru	'tent'

Some of these lexical compilations are extensive: the series quoted above sub (a) has close to 14,000 entries, the one quoted sub (b) 9700. The latter forms a sort of encyclopaedic lexicon divided into twenty-four tablets listing legal and administrative terms (tablets 1 and 2), trees (3), wooden objects (4–7), reeds and implements made of reeds (8–9), pottery (10), hides and copper (11), other metals (12), domestic (13) and wild (14) animals, parts of the animal body (15), stones (16), plants (17), birds and fish (18), textiles (19), geographic terms (20–2), and foods and drinks (23–4). This ḪAR-ra compilation is completed by other thematic monographic lists; for instance, an extensive lexicon of professions, kinship terms, and various human activities and conditions (1300 entries), or a list of parts of the human body (270+ entries).

The bilingual vocabularies offer no definitions, only single-term correspondences. In the case of Akkadian homonyms or to indicate semantic restrictions, the formula *X* = *Y ša Z*, 'X [Sumerian] = Y [Akkadian] (said) of Z' is used. For instance, du_8 = *peḫû ša eleppi*, 'to caulk (lit. to close), (said) of a boat', *úš* = *peḫû ša karpati*, 'to seal, (said) of a clay pot'; or, *gú* = *aḫu ša amēli*, 'side, (said) of a human', *aḫu ša nāri*, 'bank, (said) of a river'. As shown by the latter example, Sumerian homonyms are disambiguated only by their translations. When an entry represents only a syllabic value it is labelled *ka-ka-si-ga* (Sumerian) or *ša tēlti* (Akkadian) both meaning 'of pronunciation'. If a syllabogram has a restricted distribution, it is indicated by the formula *X* = *Y* = *ša Z* + *Y* = *W*, '*X* is (the pronunciation of) the sign *Y* in [the Sumerian word] *Z* + *Y* = (Akkadian) *W*'. For example, *sa-al* = *NI* = *ša GIŠ.NI* = *qâlu*, '*sa-al* is the pronunciation of the sign *NI* in the word *GIŠ.NI* (i.e., *giš-sàl*), Akkadian *qâlu* ('to pay attention')'.

In the Neo-Babylonian period there start to appear commentaries, titled 'traditions, sayings, and questions of the masters', which explain obscure terms in both lexical compilations and literary or scientific works. Although one can find in these commentaries useful remarks about derivations, semantic equations, and quotations illustrating the use of a word, most of these texts consist of mythological or astrological hermeneutics of scant linguistic interest.[7]

3.3.5 Other Sources

Dialogues used in scribal schools for training purposes include occasional information about grammar. The most remarkable is a Middle Babylonian (or perhaps later) bilingual composition in which a teacher questions his pupil. One of the questions deals with grammatical terms, another with pronominal forms and suffixes. Tablets with drill exercises can indirectly throw some light on grammatical contrasts as perceived by the natives. Some of these are intended for scribal training:

Are you a scribe?
I am a scribe!
Is the one over here a scribe?
The one over there is a scribe, etc.

Others aim at instructing administrators and foremen on how to give orders and conduct their business in Sumerian. Thus one text lists the expressions needed in preparing malt in a brewery, another in weaving reed mats. The 'Instructions to a Farmer' are not so much advice on how to farm as on how to administer a farm using the Sumerian language.

Statements about linguistic matters are infrequent in literary texts. King Šulgi (2094–47 BC) boasts on two occasions of being capable of conversing and administering justice in five languages. Interpreters (*eme-bal*) of several languages are mentioned in administrative documents. A passage of difficult interpretation, inserted in an epic tale, tells how all countries used to speak a single language but Enki, the god of wisdom, 'changed mankind's tongues that used to be one', apparently because of quarrels among rulers.

3.3.6 Grammatical Terms

The NBGTs contain a number of terms qualifying grammatical forms. Some of these terms already appear in lexical lists which must be dated in the Middle Babylonian period, but so far there is no evidence to suggest an earlier, Old Babylonian origin. These terms do not seem to be used systematically in NBGT and some of them are exceedingly rare. The following list gives the grammatical terms known so far and their meaning, when ascertainable; the words in quotation marks give the literal meaning of the term, the forms in capital letters represent logograms (i.e. expressions written with Sumerian logograms, instead of syllabically, in Akkadian contexts):

1. *elītu (AN.TA) 'superior', prefix or anterior element in a clause
2. qablītu ($MURUB_4$.TA) 'middle', infix
3. *šaplītu (KI.TA) 'inferior', suffix
4. ša ištēn (DIŠ) 'of one', singular
5. ša ma'dūti (MEŠ) 'of many', plural
6. ḫamṭu (*UL_4) 'quick', and
7. marû (ŠE) 'fat, slow', are a contrasting pair that designate the two themes or aspects of the verb (roughly perfect and imperfect, respectively); it is not clear whether the terms qualify the verbal action itself or the general phonological shape of the themes
8. rīqu/rīqtu 'empty', vocalic affix with no following consonant
9. malû 'full', vowel + consonant affix
10. gamartu (TIL) 'complete', perfect?
11. riātu 'leading(?)', a verbal form with movement toward speaker? antecedent?[8]
12. šusḫurtu (NIGÍN) 'which causes to go back, to turn around', pronominal affix?
13. atartu (*SI.A) 'additional', grammatical meaning unknown
14. uḫḫurtu 'late', grammatical meaning unknown

In a single case the suffix *-ta* (sometimes used instead of *-a*) is described as *ša kīma A ītenerrubu* 'which "comes in" instead of *-a*', showing that *erēbu* 'to enter' was used in the sense of 'to affix'.

3.3.7 Conclusions

The grammatical legacy of the Mesopotamian scribes consists essentially of lists of forms, implicitly classified and with no labels (OBGT). The rudimentary labelling of some categories of morphemes is first detectable around the twelfth to eleventh centuries BC and is well attested in tablets of the Persian period and after (NBGT). The criteria for classification of Sumerian forms is derived in most cases from the categories of the very different Semitic Akkadian. The compilers indulge in what seem to be combinatory exercises of morphemes with insufficient empirical control. There are no definitions or general statements about the distribution or use of grammatical elements. The remark about the affixes *-ta-* and *-a-*, quoted in the preceding paragraph, is the closest the Mesopotamians came to a grammatical statement. What is known about school activities, however, suggests that a more developed, now lost oral tradition lies behind the terse data of the tablets, even in the earlier periods. The grammatical lists are at present the oldest instance of man looking at his speech and, despite their shortcomings, an invaluable source for the reconstruction of Sumerian.

The motivation behind the creation of the grammatical texts has to be sought in the bilingual situation and in the status of Sumerian as a disappearing or extinct language. Judging from literary texts, the linguistic fact that most impressed the Mesopotamians was linguistic diversity.

Notes

1. The women's dialect is used by women speakers, regardless of the sex of the hearer, and in one of the genres of religious poetry. The differences between female and male speech consist in changes in the articulation of certain sounds and in lexical alternations. See Diakonoff (1975, 113–16) and Yoshikawa (1963–4, passim).
2. All grammatical texts known before 1956 were published by Landsberger et al. (1937–, vol 4). Important texts from Ur have been published in Gurney (1974, nos 98–102) and discussed by Black (1984). There are some unpublished fragments from Nippur in the University Museum in Philadelphia.
3. Edited by Sjöberg (1973).
4. Published in Landsberger et al. (1937–, vol. 4. 129–78).
5. In an Akkadian context the use of capitals indicates that a word is written with a Sumerian logogram the Akkadian translation of which

may not be known. In a Sumerian context it indicates that the pronunciation of the sign is unknown or doubtful.

6. For an overview of the native lexical material, see Civil (1975), and for some rules of interpretation, Cavigneaux (1976). A complete edition of all lexical texts is to be found in Landsberger et al. (1937–) with seventeen volumes already published.
7. On commentaries in general, see Civil (1974) with previous literature. Important examples of commentaries to lexical texts can be found in Landsberger et al. (1937–, vol. 14, 267–70, 273–5, 323–8).
8. I assume that *riātu* is a derivation from *(w)arû*, 'to lead', analogous to *ṣiātu*, 'exit', from *(w)aṣû*, 'to go out'.

Bibliograhy

BLACK, J. A. (1984) *Sumerian Grammar in Babylonian Theory* (Studia Pohl. Series Maior, 12), Biblical Institute Press, Rome.

CAVIGNEAUX, A. (1976) *Die sumerisch-akkadischen Zeichenlisten: Überlieferungsprobleme,* PhD Dissertation, Ludwig-Maximilians-Universität, München.

CIVIL, M. (1974) Medical Commentaries from Nippur, *Journal of Near Eastern Studies*, 33, 329–38.

CIVIL, M. (1975) *Lexicography*, in Lieberman (1975), 123–57.

CIVIL, M. and KENNEDY, D. A. (1986) *Middle Babylonian Grammatical Texts* (Materials for the Sumerian Lexicon. Supplementary Series, 1), Pontificium Institutum Biblicum, Roma, 72–91.

DEIMEL, A. (1923) *Schultexte aus Fara* (Wissenschaftliche Veröffentlichungen der Deutschen Orient Gesellschaft, 43), J. S. Hinrichs, Leipzig.

DIAKONOFF, I. M. (1975) Ancient Writing and Ancient Written Texts, in Lieberman (1975), 99–122.

EDZARD, D. O. (1971) Grammatik, in *Reallexikon der Assyriologie*, 3, Walter de Gruyter, Berlin, 610–16.

FOXVOG, D. A. (1975) The Sumerian Ergative Construction, *Orientalia,* 44, 395–425.

GURNEY, O. R. (1974) Middle Babylonian Legal Documents and Other Texts, in *Ur Excavations Texts* vol. 7 (Publications of the Joint Expedition of the British Museum, and of the University Museum), British Museum, London.

HYMES, D. (ed.) (1974) *Studies in the History of Linguistics: Traditions and Paradigms*, Indiana University Press, Bloomington/London.

JACOBSEN, TH. (1965) Introduction to the Chicago Grammatical Texts, in Landsberger, et al. (1937–), 4, 1*–50*.

JACOBSEN, TH. (1974) Very Ancient Texts: Babylonian Grammatical Texts, in Hymes (1974), 41–62.

KANG, S. T. (1968) *A Study of the Sumerian Verb in Bilingual Grammatical Texts*, PhD Dissertation, m.s., Hebrew Union College, Cincinnati.

LANDSBERGER, B. et al. (1937–) *Materialien zum sumerischen Lexikon*, Pontificio Istituto Biblico, Roma.

LIEBERMAN, S. (ed.) (1975) *Sumerological Studies in Honor of Thorkild*

Jacobsen (Assyriological Studies, 20), University of Chicago, Chicago/London.

PETTINATO, G. in collaboration with R. Biggs, M. Civil, P. Mander, D. Owen, F. Pomponio, T. Vino and T. Viola (1981) *Testi lessicali monolingui della Biblioteca L.2769*, in *Materiali Epigrafici di Ebla* (Istituto Universitario Orientale di Napoli, Series maior, 3), Napoli.

SJÖBERG, Å. W. (1973) Der Vater und sein Missratener Sohn, *Journal of Cuneiform Studies*, 25, 105–69.

YOSHIKAWA, M. (1963—4) A Study of Emesal, *The Minato*, 10, 55–92; 12, 1–16.

YOSHIKAWA, M. (1964) On the Reliability of Babylonian Grammatical Texts, *Gengo Kenkyū*, 46, 1–11.

YOSHIKAWA, M. (1966–73) On the Grammatical Terms in Neo-Babylonian Grammatical Texts, in *Hiroshima University Studies, Literature Department*, vols 26–32.

3.4 Akkadian

Erica Reiner

3.4.1 Introduction

Akkadian represents an eastern branch of the Semitic family of languages. The first written records date from c. the middle of the third millennium BC. Since it coexisted with Sumerian, the awareness of linguistic diversity was lively among Akkadian speakers.

Among the first problems to be solved was how to write Akkadian with a writing system that had evolved for Sumerian and was not adequate to express Akkadian phonological differences, such as emphatic (i.e. probably, glottalized) consonants (the emphatic stops *ṭ* and *q* in addition to the voiced and voiceless dental and velar stops, and the emphatic sibilant *ṣ*) and the glottal stop. The orthographic solutions to this problem were different in various periods and areas, and only in the second half of the second millennium did certain spelling conventions become standardized. For example, on the one hand one among several quasi-homophonous syllabic signs was chosen to represent the emphatic sibilant in syllable initial, and on the other, one sign was secondarily differentiated according to whether the laryngeal fricative /x/or the glottal stop /ʔ/ was intended. Other conventions, such as expressing in writing a morphologically distinctive consonant doubling – not expressed in other Semitic writing systems, but made possible by Sumerian writing conventions – were never fully observed.

On the levels of morphology and lexicon – to a lesser extent syntax – the schooling of the scribes included contrastive lists and paradigms for writing Sumerian; these are described in the preceding section. However, the large scholarly literature of a linguistic character may have been due not only to the necessities of coexistence, but presumably also to the intellectual curiosity of the Akkadians. This scholarly literature included, besides the earlier mentioned Sumero-Akkadian bilingual vocabularies (that can be likened to present-day bilingual dictionaries) and grammatical paradigms, (a) bilingual dictionaries for other languages; (b) Akkadian-Akkadian lists (the so-called synonym lists); (c) lists of technical terms (plant and stone names); and (d) commentaries to scientific texts (including vocabularies) and difficult Akkadian literary texts; (e) partial or full translations accompanying Sumerian religious and literary texts; and finally (f) scattered comments about the foreign provenance of certain words and the difficulty of pronouncing or writing foreign words.

3.4.2 Bilingual lists

Apart from the Sumero-Akkadian bilingual vocabularies discussed above there exists a Kassite-Akkadian word list.[1]

The list contains 48 items, mostly such divine names and words as enter into compound names of Kassite kings and other personal names; for example the elements of the royal name *Kadašman-Harbe* are listed as *kadašman* = *tukultu* 'trust' (line 39) and *Harbe* = *Enlil* (line 2). These names also appear, occasionally in a somewhat different form, in another Kassite-Akkadian list which contains personal names with their translation (Balkan 1954, 2f.). The 48-item list also includes words for heaven, earth, parts of the body (head, foot), and a few other terms, e.g.:

ha-mi-ru = še-e-pu 'foot'
sa-ri-bu = še-e-pu 'foot'
ya-šu = ma-a-tum 'land'
áš-rak = mu-du-ú 'knowledgeable'
šir = qa-áš-tu 'bow'

(Balkan 1954, 3f. lines 32–6)

A number of Kassite words, predominantly in the field of horse-training, such as descriptive names of horses (e.g. 'roan') and words for trappings and chariot parts, have entered Akkadian as loanwords.

Outside Mesopotamia, native speakers of the area also compiled bilingual lists of their own language with Akkadian translation, for example Hittite and Akkadian, or provided Sumero-Akkadian bilingual lists used in the scribal training with a third, and sometimes a fourth, column adding equivalents in the language of the area, such as Hittite in Anatolia, or Ugaritic – and as a fourth column also Hurrian – in Ugarit in Syria.

3.4.3 Synonym lists

Synonym lists are arranged, like bilingual lists, in two sub-columns. The left sub-column lists the rare term, the right the more common one; usually several entries of the left sub-column are equated with the same word on the right. For example, the synonym list called, from its incipit, *malku* = *šarru* 'king', begins:

malku (West Semitic 'king') = šarru 'king'
maliku (phonetic variant of same) = ditto
lulīmu 'stag' = ditto
parakku 'throne' = ditto

(Kilmer 1963, 24)

The left sub-column may contain not only less common, poetic, or metaphoric terms, but also words of foreign origin. Those which are – or are borrowed from – Elamite or Hurrian are usually marked as to their origin by adding *NIM* '(in) Elam' or *SU.BIR*$_4$ '(in) Subartu' to the equivalent in the right sub-column, but words from another Semitic language are not marked. Before Assyriologists recognized this pattern, they took West Semitic words occurring in the left sub-column to be Akkadian; thus, they took the word *aqrabu* to be the Akkadian word for 'scorpion' whereas, as the entry *aqrabu* = *zuqaqīpu* in Malku V 54 shows, *aqrabu* is a West Semitic word (Heb. *ᶜaqrāb*, Ar. *ᶜaqrab*^{un}), and the Akkadian word is *zuqaqīpu*.

3.4.4 Lists of technical terms

Identification as Subarian (i.e. Hurrian), Elamite, and even Kassite, also accompanies some entries in technical (pharmaceutical) lists, although the relationship between the two sub-columns in such lists is not always clear.

3.4.5 Bilingual texts

Sumerian literary texts – mythological poems, magical texts – were sometimes provided with an Akkadian translation. The usual format is interlinear, though side-by-side translations, similar to the list format, also exist. Interlinear texts give the Sumerian line first; the Akkadian translation follows beneath it and is usually indented. If the line is short, the translation is sandwiched in the centre, between the two halves of the Sumerian line, and is set off at the beginning and the end by a mark consisting of two superposed wedge-heads, thus resembling our colon, with which it is often transcribed.

lú-u_{18}-lu-bi : amēla ['man', acc.] šu-a-tum ['that'] i-duk ['kill' 3rd sing pret.] -ma ['and'] : ba-an-gaz-eš 'it killed that man'
(Weiher 1983, 22 col. i, 15)

Royal inscriptions from the eighteenth century BC, which exist in both a Sumerian and an Akkadian version, written either in two adjacent columns on the same tablet or object or on two different tablets or objects, are probably not to be considered bilingual texts in the above sense, but may have been composed independently in the two languages.

A group of bilingual texts, composed in the late second or in the first millennium, betray through their mistakes in Sumerian and especially through their syntax which is a calque on the Akkadian, that their primary version was Akkadian and that the Sumerian version was secondarily added, either because of the need for a Sumerian version for cultic recitation or simply to lend authenticity to the text. Eventually even text genres which had no antecedent in Sumerian literature, for example, omen texts deriving predictions from strange terrestrial and celestial phenomena, were composed in a bilingual version (Hunger 1976, 90ff., no. 85).

3.4.6 Commentaries

Commentaries attempt to deal with rare or obsolete words in poetry and with ambiguities of interpretation in scientific texts. Some commentaries have a subscript *ṣâtu šūt pî u maš'altu ummâni*, 'traditions, sayings, and questions of the master'; others are labelled *ṣâtu*, 'traditions', or *mukallimtu*, 'exposition', alone; the distribution of these two terms has not yet been sufficiently investigated.

There are two types of commentaries. The first is essentially a word-list, and the second a discursive type.

In the first type, a Sumerogram (a Sumerian word, usually transcribed in capital letters, in the Akkadian text) or a rare Akkadian word from the text commented upon is displayed in the left sub-column, and its explanation in the right; thus, even in its layout, it resembles bilingual vocabularies and synonym lists, although the equations are occasionally preceded by a quotation of the line or phrase in which the commented word occurs.

LUGAL IM.GI	= LUGAL ha-am-ma-'u	'despotic king'
LUGAL	= šar-rum	'king'

IM	= e-mu-qu	'strength'
GI	= ta-ka-lu	'to trust'

(Leichty 1969, 214 lines 72–5)

DINGIR.MEŠ ina SU KUR BAD.MEŠ (gloss:) in-né-su-u 'the gods will retreat from the land'

i-dim$_{\text{BAD}}$	= né-su-u	'to retreat'
né-su-u	= ru-u-qu	'far'

(*ibid.*, 215 lines 108–9a)

Occasionally, if the commentator does not know the explanation, he writes *ul idi,* 'I don't know':

ina kar-ka-ti DU.MEŠ : ul i-di
(CT 41 33 rev. 3, and passim) (see Labat 1933, 70f.)

In the second type of commentary, the quotes, words commented upon, and their explanations are written in a continuous fashion, divided only by the colon-like mark.

Commentaries use as source Sumero-Akkadian vocabularies and synonym lists. If in a bilingual vocabulary the Sumerian word has two or more Akkadian glosses, the commentator may cite the Akkadian words in the form of an equation, omitting the Sumerian tertium comparationis, so that the entry looks as if it were taken from a synonym list.[2]

When the commentator wants to clear up an ambiguity in a divinatory text or change an unfavourable interpretation into a favourable one, he has to resort to a more complex scheme. For example, he may adduce a Sumerian word that has two diametrically opposite Akkadian equivalents:

GI = šalāmu, GI = lapātu 'GI (means) favourable, GI (also means) unfavourable'

(Thureau-Dangin 1922, no. 5, rev. 39)

and thus arrive at an opposite portent.

Some commentaries employ the device – also known from medieval commentaries – of analysing the word into its component syllables (which are not necessarily the word's constituents) and explaining each syllable until the chain of equivalences has led to the desired explanation. In this process, not only the morpheme structure of the word is ignored, but so is its linguistic affiliation. Thus, an Akkadian word is divided into syllables or rather strings of vowels and consonants, and each of these is treated as if it were a Sumerian word and given an Akkadian translation:

> šá-am-nu : ni-ig GAR sin-niš-tim : am : ze-ri : nu : ba-nu-u šá-niš i NI šá-am-nu : i : aṣû ša zēri. This is a morph by morph interpretation: 'šamnu ('oil') : (with the reading) *nig* (the sign) GAR (i.e. šá) = sinništim ('woman'), am = zēru ('seed'), nu = banû ('to create'), secondly (with the reading) *i* (the sign) NI = šamnu, i = aṣû ša zēri ('to sprout, said of seed')'
>
> (Civil 1974, 332 lines 11f.)

Such explanations should not be taken to mean that the commentator was not aware of mixing two languages; rather, he exhibited his learning.

Some explanations are etymological, in the sense that they give the word's derivation, usually introduced by the word *aššum* 'because of', for example *alit aššum la'āti 'alit* ('swallowed') because of *la'ātu* ('to swallow')' (Leichty 1969, 229 line 250).

Such etymologies are often fanciful; in the cited example *alit* derives in reality from *alātu* 'to swallow' and not from *la'ātu*, with the same meaning. Popular etymologies can also be found: the name of the goddess *Zarpānītu* is etymologized as if being a compound of *zēru*, 'seed, progeny' and *bānītu*, 'creatress', according to the comment *Zarpanītu ša kīma šumišama bānât zēri*, 'Zarpanītu who, according to her name, is the creatress of progeny' (see the dictionaries sub *Zērbānītu* and *Ṣarpānītu*).

Late commentaries, as mentioned in the previous section, seem less interested in the linguistic aspect than in a mythological or theological explanation. To achieve this, the word commented upon is divided into its constituent syllables and each syllable is explained, either from a Sumerian or an Akkadian base. The foreign name *Šulak* is thus commented upon as follows:

> Šulak imahhassu : Šulak : ša iqbû ŠU : qa-tu : LA : la-a : KÙ : el-lu . . . qātāšu la ella ana muhhi qabi. This is a morph by morph interpretation: '(the demon) Šulak will strike him: Šulak : as they say (i.e. in the oral explanation) : (Sum.) ŠU = (Akk.) qātu ('hand'), (Akk.) LA = (Akk.) la ('not'), (Sum.) KÙ = (Akk.) ellu ('pure'), 'his hands are not pure' it is said about it.'
>
> (Hunger 1976, 57, no. 47, lines 5–7)

3.4.7 Linguistic competence

Due to the many contacts – through conquests, trade relations, and so forth – Babylonians and Assyrians had with peoples of the ancient Near East, as far as India in the east and Syria, Anatolia, Egypt in the west, the need for interpreters arose. Interpreters (Sum. *eme.bal* 'who changes the tongue') are attested as early as c. 2300 BC and they are designated as 'of' Meluhha (probably India), Marhaši (probably also in the east), Guti (in the north-east), and Amurru (the west). The Akkadian term *targumannu* – the same as our *dragoman* – first appears in the nineteenth century BC; they are 'of' Hanigalbat (i.e. Hurrian), Egypt, and, in the seventh century BC, from the land of the Manneans (in the north).

It is occasion, therefore, for great wonderment when a messenger from king Gyges of Lydia arrives in Assyria and, as king Assurbanipal puts it, 'among all the languages from east to west that (my god) Aššur had given into my hands there was no one who mastered his language – his language was strange and his words were not understood' (Piepkorn 1933 16, col. v, lines 1–13).

Assurbanipal himself, like the Sumerian king Šulgi, boasts of his learning, having 'read the artfully written texts whose Sumerian (version) is obscure and whose Akkadian is difficult to unravel' (Streck 1916, 256, lines 17f.). While his boasts may be exaggerated, he certainly knew how to read cuneiform, as shown by letters and reports addressed to him in which sometimes even simple words are glossed, no doubt to enable the king to read these communications himself.

The foreign words included in lists are sometimes identified as to their origin. In addition to such entries in lists, identifications of foreign words or names also appear in other texts. For example, first a plant's Akkadian name is given and then its name 'in the language of Hatti' or 'in the language of Nairi' is added (Köcher 1955, no. 33, lines 17 and 23); in historical texts we have such notations as 'a portico that they call *bīt-hilāni* in the language of Amurru [i.e. the west]' (Luckenbill 1924, 97, line 82, etc.); '(so-and-so) whom they call *ir-ru-pi*' (*ir-ru-pi* is the transcription of the Hurrian word *erwi* 'king') (Budge 1902, 41, column ii, line 26); 'the country Til-Aššūr that is called *Pitānu* in the mouth of the people of Mihrānu' (Borger 1967, 51 Episode 10).

The difficulty of writing foreign words is expressed in the inscription of king Sargon, at the end of the list of booty from the land Urartu (the language of which is related to Hurrian): '120 copper objects the names of which are not easy to write' (Thureau-Dangin 1912, line 364).

The word for *lišānu* 'tongue' is used, however, not only to designate a language in our sense, but is also the term used when referring to a dialect, technical language, or argot; a Sumero-Akkadian bilingual text describing the schooling of the scribe (Sjöberg 1975, 142ff., lines 25–6) enumerates among the subjects the 'tongue' of the shepherd, the 'tongue' of the silversmith, and so on. The same term *lišānu* also designated a synonym list or commentary. For the two main languages Sumerian and Akkadian the simple adjectives *šumeru* 'Sumerian' and *akkadû* 'Akkadian' suffice; for example a list of songs summarizes the various sub-groups as 'so-and-so-many Sumerian (*šumeru*)' or 'Akkadian (*akkadû*) songs', and rubrics of texts in which bilingual and Akkadian sections alternate occasionally state that the foregoing section is to be recited *akkadû* 'in Akkadian'.

No written records survive to document the transition in the second half of the first millennium to Aramaic as the spoken language in Babylonia, presumably because texts that would document the awareness of the linguistic problem were written, if at all, in Aramaic alphabetical script on such perishable materials as parchment and papyrus.[3] The scribe who wrote Aramaic was designated by a new term, *sēpiru* (the active participle of the verb *sepēru*) or *sepīru* (a form of the same verb, suggested by the Aramaic borrowing *s^efīr*) as opposed to the scribe who wrote in cuneiform, *ṭupšarru*, from Sumerian *dub.sar* 'tablet writer', and 'to write in alphabetic script' was expressed by the verb *sepēru*, which is documented in a letter to king Sargon, in which the writer says 'if it please my lord, I will write on an [Aramaic] document' and the king answers: 'why do you not write on an Akkadian document [akkadattu]?' (Dietrich 1967, 90, citing CT 54 10).

Neither has any evidence survived of the teaching or learning of Greek under Seleucid rule, with the exception of a few fragments of Sumero-Akkadian vocabularies and school texts with the cuneiform text on the obverse and a transcription into Greek letters on the reverse (Sollberger 1962, 63ff., Geller 1983, 114ff., Maul 1991, 87ff.). Of a total of 16 such fragments with Greek letters, seven are lexical, six literary (including two bilingual texts) and three are unidentifiable.

Notes

1. Kassite was the language of foreign conquerors who ruled Babylonia from c. 1730 to 1155 BC; their linguistic affiliation is not known, but their language contains a number of Indo-European loan words, including names of gods such as *Buriaš*, presumably = *Boreas*.

existence to such excerpts of two or more entries from the Akkadian sub-column of a bilingual vocabulary.

3. On the other hand, Aramaic religious texts could be written on clay in cuneiform script, e.g. Thureau-Dangin (1922) no. 58.

Bibliography

BALKAN, K. (1954) *Kassitenstudien. 1. Die Sprache der Kassiten* (American Oriental Series, 37), American Oriental Society, New Haven, Conn.

BORGER, R. (1967) *Die Inschriften Asarhaddons Königs von Assyrien* (Archiv für Orientforschung, Beiheft 9), Biblio-Verlag, Osnabrück.

BUDGE, E. A. WALLIS (1902) *The Annals of the Kings of Assyria*, British Museum, London.

CIVIL, M. (1974) Medical Commentaries from Nippur, *Journal of Near Eastern Studies*, 33, 329–38.

DIETRICH, M. (1967) Neue Quellen zur Geschichte Babyloniens (I), *Die Welt des Orients*, 4, 61–103.

DUPONT-SOMMER, A. (1942–4) La tablette cunéiforme araméenne de Warka, *Revue d'Assyriologie et d'archéologie orientale*, 39, 35–62.

GELB, I. J. (1968) The Word for Dragoman in the Ancient Near East, *Glossa*, 2, 93–104.

GELLER, M. J. (1983) More Graeco-Babyloniaca, *Zeitschrift für Assyriologie und vorderasiatische Archäologie*, 73, 114–20.

HUNGER, H. (1976) *Spätbabylonische Texte aus Uruk, Teil I* (Ausgrabungen der Deutschen Forschungsgemeinschaft in Uruk-Warka, 9), Gebr. Mann, Berlin.

KILMER, A. D. (1963) The First Tablet of *Malku* = *Šarru* together with its Explicit Version, *Journal of the American Oriental Society*, 83, 421–46.

KÖCHER, F. (1955) *Keilschrifttexte zur assyrisch-babylonischen Drogen- und Pflanzenkunde* (Deutsche Akademie der Wissenschaften zu Berlin, Institut für Orientforschung, 28), Akademie-Verlag, Berlin.

LABAT, R. (1933) *Commentaires Assyro-Babyloniens sur les Présages*, Imprimerie-Librairie de l'Université, Bordeaux.

LEICHTY, E. (1969) *The Series Šumma Izbu* (Texts from Cuneiform Sources, 4), J. J. Augustin, Locust Valley, NY.

LUCKENBILL, D. D. (1924) *The Annals of Sennacherib* (The University of Chicago Oriental Institute Publications, 2), The University of Chicago Press, Chicago.

MAUL, S. (1991) Neues zu den 'Graeco-Babyloniaca', *Zeitschrift für Assyriologie und vorderasiatische Archäologie*, 81, 87–107.

OPPENHEIM, A. L. (1978) Man and Nature in Mesopotamian Civilization, *Dictionary of Scientific Biography*, ed. by Ch. C. Gillispie, vol. 15, Scribner, New York, 634–66.

PIEPKORN, A. C. (1933) *Historical Prism Inscriptions of Ashurbanipal, I* (Assyriological Studies, 5), The University of Chicago Press, Chicago.

SJÖBERG, Å. (1975) Der Examenstext A, *Zeitschrift für Assyriologie und vorderasiatische Archäologie*, 64, 137–76.

SOLLBERGER, E. (1962) Graeco-Babyloniaca, *Iraq*, 24, 63–72.

STRECK, M. (1916) *Assurbanipal und die letzten assyrischen Könige bis zum Untergange Niniveh's* (Vorderasiatische Bibliothek, 7/2), J. C. Hinrichs, Leipzig.

THUREAU-DANGIN, F. (1912) *Une relation de la huitième campagne de Sargon* (Musée du Louvre, Textes cunéiformes, 3), Geuthner, Paris.

THUREAU-DANGIN, F. (1922) *Tablettes d'Uruk* (Musée du Louvre, Textes cunéiformes, 6), Geuthner, Paris.

WEIHER, E. VON (1983) *Spätbabylonische Texte aus Uruk, Teil II* (Ausgrabungen der Deutschen Forschungsgemeinschaft in Uruk-Warka, 10), Gebr. Mann, Berlin.

4

Hebrew linguistics

Raphael Loewe

4.1 Introduction*

A prudent scholar will be reluctant to generalize in regard to the attitude of 'Jews', or that allegedly integral to 'Judaism', towards most subjects: but it is perhaps less hazardous to use broad strokes when describing Jewish ideas as to the nature, function, and role of the Hebrew language. On the one hand, a markedly conservative approach transcended chronological periods from late antiquity until approximately 1879 (the date of the publication of E. Ben-Yehuda's seminal article *She'elah Nikhbadah* ('A Matter of Moment')),[1] and had itself been retrojected by tradition into the culture and the purported religious notions of biblical Israel. And on the other, the revised evaluation of Hebrew that has emerged over the last hundred years has – despite some initial opposition, still sustained in exiguous pockets – come to enjoy well-nigh universal Jewish endorsement. At the time when the conventional picture was taking shape, that is during the formative period of rabbinic Judaism or approximately the four centuries 200 BCE to 200 CE, Hebrew was certainly intelligible to Palestinian Jewry, for many of whom it was still their vernacular: but at the latest by the turn of the eras the Jewish diaspora, which in Mesopotamia spoke Aramaic and from Egypt westwards spoke Greek, was overtaking Palestine demographically,[2] and in the West Jewish familiarity with Hebrew was rapidly shrinking to token liturgical proportions. In such a situation even literary bilingualism, to say nothing of complete bilingualism, was the characteristic of a learned elite; but this did not modify the popular estimation of the religious and indeed the metaphysical quality deemed to be inherent in the

* See beginning of Notes.

Hebrew language by those who remained faithful to the synagogue. With the descendants of Jews who became assimilated into gentile Christianity it was of course different, and by the fourth century St Augustine would castigate St Jerome for the priority which he accorded to the *hebraica veritas* of the Old Testament over the Greek version that had become part of the Bible of the Western Church.[3]

One contributory reason for this consistency may link up with a feature of Hebrew itself which, although it is paralleled to some extent in the character of the sister-languages in the semitic group, corresponds to Jewish psychological traits thrown into relief by their contrast to the host environments in the West. If there is any substance to this suggestion, it might go some way towards explaining the continuing influence of a characteristic of the language long after Jewish vernacular use of Hebrew had gone into extended hibernation. What is here referred to is the way in which speech itself is regarded in Hebrew. First to consider are the two verbal stems which mean *to say* (*'amar*) and *to speak* (*dibber*) and their corresponding nouns. We may observe that in Arabic the corresponding verb *'amara* means not *say* but *command*; and even though too much ought not to be made of etymology or comparative lexicography, it remains true that the Hebrew notion of speech communication is a self-assertive one, and that in Hebrew, as in all Semitic languages, the effectiveness of the written word is proportionate to the extent that it permits the reader to recreate the spoken original.[4] Thus, not only are the Ten Commandments prefaced by the statement[5] that 'God spoke all these *words*' (*debharim*: post-biblical Hebrew still calls them *dibhroth*, not *miṣwoth* = *commandments*); but the following sentence, 'I am the Lord thy God . . .' is regarded in the Jewish enumeration not as preamble, but as the first of the ten 'words' – the assertion of a divine identity through acknowledgement of which its corollaries are to be accepted.[6] Nor do biblical and rabbinic Hebrew (in the latter of which there are incipient Western influences) distinguish between *word* and *thing* –*dabhar* is used indiscriminately. It is in virtue of there being a word for it that the identity of any thing is established; and, *per contra*, the *word*, as being the extension of the speaker who utters it, has a force which, particularly in the case of those possessed of particular power (men when blessing,[7] cursing, etc.; God when 'speaking') has an irreversible effect. Another feature is but a different facet of the foregoing. The Hebrew word *shem* ought never be translated *name, tout court*, as if it were a mere label; *shem* covers *nature*, *character*, *personality*, *reputation*, and so on, and, as such it constitutes the summation of the individual or item to which it refers. Hence the significance attached to name-giving and, even more so, to name-changing (*Jacob-Israel*),[8] which is understood to effect a complete change of personality. No less meaningful is the description in the creation-myth[9] of God's forming the animals and parading them before Adam, 'and whatever the man called it, that was its name'. Individual names for domestic animals and pets, unheard of in Jewish literature or in the folk-custom of the east-European ghettoes, begin under westernizing cultural influence only. Since the Hebrew word *kelebh* (= dog) is conceived to be the fullest possible expression of 'caninity', to give a dog an individual name would be pointless. One contrasts Odysseus's hound Argos[10] with 'the dog' in the fuller recension of the apocryphal book of *Tobit* (translated into Greek from a mainly lost Hebrew original) that accompanies Tobias and the archangel Raphael on their journey.[11]

All this contrasts strikingly with Western notions of speech communication, especially insofar as they bear the imprint of Greek. The Greek *λέγειν* occasionally means, alongside its commonest value *say*, also *pick* or *select*; and where the Hebrew *'amar*, *dibber*, *dabhar* assert, and, often enough, implicitly purport to initiate action or occurrence, *λόγος* describes, and frequently analyses. So it still does, in fields of European intellectual and scientific interest, through its many descendants. In religion, however, God's creative word (*dabhar*) in the Hebrew Bible, having in hellenistic times been rendered into Greek by *λόγος*, imposed its own strong personality upon its 'mate'; and in their descendants, it is the genes of the Hebrew *dabhar* that are dominant, as any translation of the first words of St John's gospel will show. But the Hebrew impress on emergent Christianity lies outside our scope, except inasmuch as there is now in Israel a small Christian group whose vernacular is modern Hebrew. Its impact may be ignored, however, and it is indeed negligible as compared with the powerful forces of secularization, the effect of which on modern Hebrew will be noted below (see pp. 137f.).

4.2 Time concepts

There is another element in the language itself that seems to have contributed powerfully to the Jewish attitude towards Hebrew – an attitude which, as we shall see, is closely integrated with the Jewish sense of religious and ethnic identity. Although the categories that are reflected in the tense-system and syntax of biblical Hebrew are perfectly adequate to express most time-distinctions, they are not themselves primarily time-orientated. The Western tense system evolved at an early date to correspond to an intellectual universe in which the difference between past, present and future is accorded an importance that has rendered possible the development of scientific thought and historiography; and the crucial significance in these of time-categories has led to the Western toleration of their dominance over virtually all other spheres, albeit often operating as a strait-jacket. Music, and some forms of drama and painting, are examples of rare instances in which the West is prepared to suspend its subordination to the dictates of chronology. The original Hebrew attitude treated time-categories as but a convenience that ought to be kept in its place. By approximately the turn of the eras post-biblical Hebrew begins to reflect a sharpened time-awareness, derived ultimately, no doubt, from Greek, but principally mediated through contemporary Aramaic, which was itself surrendering to the advances of Greek time-categories (pp. 121ff.). The Jewish scholar Rab (the Master: i.e. ʾAbba ʾArekha, died 247 CE) recognized that 'there is no [overriding] chronological system in the Torah',[12] but it was not before the middle ages that Jewish grammarians would produce terminology to distinguish the present from past and future.[13] Even after that, Hebrew was to continue to resist more or less complete subjection to Western time-patterns in its tenses until the development of modern Hebrew during the last hundred years. This is to a large extent because, although Jews have used other languages as their vernacular for two millennia, their liturgical familiarity with the Hebrew Bible and the intensity of their education in the classical sources of rabbinic Judaism kept them (including the least educated in their midst) familiar with the (apparent) nonchalance of Hebrew itself in regard to distinctions between past, present and future. This, combined with the circumstance that biblical myth was presumed not to be myth at all, but factual account, and biblical historiography was deemed to be no less 'accurate' than the chronologically dominated Western historiography, made it all the more natural for popular Judaism to retroject into the remote biblical past its own axiomatic thinking in regard to Hebrew and the contents of the Bible. It also allowed popular Judaism to assume that the symbolic value which, ever since rabbinic times at least, the language had embodied for Jews, had similarly been appreciated and endorsed by their primeval forbears.[14]

4.3 Language and metaphysics: Torah, Hebrew and Babel

The biblical legend of the dispersal of the nations after abandonment of the building of the Tower of Babel is an attempt to account for linguistic diversity which presupposes the interdependence, if not indeed the identity, of language and ethnicity.[15] The list of peoples descended from Noah's sons is classified (at least in part, and despite some anomalies) according to language [-groups],[16] and the totality of peoples, traditionally taken as numbering 70, is referred to indifferently in post-biblical Hebrew as 'seventy nations'[17] or 'seventy tongues'.[18] Such expressions nearly always occur where Jewish distinctiveness from the gentile world is being stressed, and (probably like the Babel story itself) they reflect the assumption that the primeval language was Hebrew, used by God Himself when, by the mere utterance of his word, He effected creation:[19] and that it had been subsequently preserved in Shem's line by Eber,[20] the eponymous ancestor of the '[H]ebrews', to become the language of Abraham and so of Israel. And since it had been the speech current in paradise during the idyllic period that preceded Adam's sin, intelligible until then perhaps to all the animals[21] and certainly to the serpent,[22] eschatological symmetry dictated that Hebrew would once again be the vernacular in the messianic age, when God 'will turn to the peoples in "pure speech" (*saphah berurah*, literally *purified lip*) for all to call upon God's name'.[23] It was a notion which would, in the fullness of time, find powerful echoes among the puritans of seventeenth-century England.[24]

Jewish confidence in the reliability of both scripture (as exegetically embellished) and traditional ideas about the golden age to come view the role of Hebrew both in the beginnings and at the messianic climax of humanity as clearly lying upon the historical plane – providential history, perhaps, but none the less 'history'. But this taking of Hebrew for granted is complemented, and indeed outweighed by axiomatic assumptions as to its metaphysical function. For Hebrew is the language of the Torah, or pentateuch (although the Torah in its plenary sense is possessed of a dynamism that mystically transcends any circumscription apparently inherent in its reduction to a biblically encoded text). When God created the world, He did not merely call it into existence by uttering words in the same language as that in which the Torah would, in due course, be written down by Moses,[25] but He actually consulted the Torah as the blueprint of the creative process.[26] For the Torah, although not co-eternal with God, is one of the items that 'pre-existed creation'[27] – in its case, by a period of 974 generations.[28] And since, as a pre-existent 'document' it must have already possessed a notionally written form, the metaphysical quality of its language communicated itself to the Hebrew alphabet in which it is to be deemed to have been so 'written'. Probably no other ethnic or religious group (including Islam) that invests great emotional capital in its own language has insisted so intensely upon the integral link between its language and its script as has Jewry, with its pride in the idiosyncratic uniqueness of both. The book of Esther records how the king of Persia 'wrote to every province according to its script, and every people according to its tongue, and to the Jews according to their script and language':[29] a formulation that attracted the rabbinic comment 'just as [the Jews'] language has never changed, neither has their mode of writing'.[30] Out of this associative veneration for the written word there developed the custom of respectful interment not only of tattered sacred texts, understood in a wide sense that includes talmudic elaboration of biblical laws and so forth, but also of 'secular' documents in Hebrew script (irrespective of the language that they embodied), such as discarded letters and accounts.[31] And parallel to this, the feeling that the use of Hebrew was a hall-mark of Jewish identity ensured its continued use by Jews as a medium, within the Jewish community, for writing (and printing) various non-Hebrew vernaculars of their adoption (Arabic, German, Spanish, Italian, etc.) – a folk-custom that maintained itself for a surprisingly long time despite advanced Jewish acculturation into the host environment. The greater openness of medieval Karaite Judaism towards use of the Arabic script, even for the writing of Hebrew texts,[32] is symptomatic of its rejection of rabbinic tradition as being supposedly supererogatory in favour of a severely biblical-based interpretation of Jewish institutionalism.

It is the foregoing *midrashim*, i.e. exegetical elaborations of the bare bible story, which constitute the symbols that encapsulate the values – emotional, mystical, and indeed political values – which would, in due course, determine the lines of speculative address to the significance of Hebrew on the part of medieval philosophers of Judaism, and also, reinterpreted in secularist terms, of nineteenth- and twentieth-century Zionist thinkers and protagonists of the revival of Hebrew (see below, pp. 135f.). But it ought not to be supposed that, for a culture so much alive to both the positive and the negative aspects of social reality as is the culture of Israel, metaphysical models or political paradigms in regard to the function of Hebrew constitute the complete picture.

4.4 Late Antiquity. Languages in Palestine and in the Jewish Diaspora

The linguistic pluralism in which Jewish historical experience was involved from antiquity onwards made it impossible for Jews to ignore the importance, the power, and the prestige of at least the successive *linguae francae* of the near east and mediterranean area

– Aramaic, Greek, and Arabic – as well as, later on, Spanish and German: particularly since all these were becoming the vernacular of numbers of Jews whose own knowledge of Hebrew was fast becoming attenuated, sometimes to the point of complete disappearance. For the moment, we may restrict our horizon to late antiquity, and leave till later (see pp. 109f.) the impact of Arabic and of European languages other than Greek, which was already making its mark by the second century BCE at the latest. Greek-speaking Jews in Alexandria and elsewhere felt the need for a translation of (at least part of) the Hebrew scriptures – a need that was met by the accumulation of versions of the individual books that goes under the name of the Septuagint.

But we must start from the more intimate socio-linguistic situation of Hebrew in Palestine. From a modern point of view, it seems surprising that late-antique Judaism evinces no academic interest in the close relationship of Hebrew to the other semitic languages – a relationship which springs to the eye and ear, being, in the case of Hebrew's own sub-group, at least as close as that obtaining within the romance or the teutonic groups of Indo-European. Increasing economic and cultural contacts, and a historical experience in which some measure of bilingualism played a part,[33] will have ensured that some speakers, at least, were aware of the relationship. But aside from occasional talmudic observations regarding cognate words (or, as we nowadays would rather say, 'roots') which are for the most part exegetically motivated,[34] no attention was given to the phenomenon as a whole. Philological interest did not loom large in Western antiquity either, but there is more awareness in Latin writers[35] of the close relationship obtaining between Greek and Latin than there is in the Talmud of that obtaining between Hebrew and Aramaic; and it was not until late in the first Christian millennium that Jewish scholars in Spain whose vernacular was Arabic became aware of the possibilities of a comparative philological approach to Arabic, Hebrew, and Aramaic.[36]

But irrespective of any academic awareness, the fact that great numbers of Jews were themselves using a language other than Hebrew as their vernacular forced those to whom Jews turned for leadership in spiritual, political, and metaphysical thinking to come to terms with the facts of life. A Babylonian Jewish authority purported to show from scripture that Aramaic was a language, perhaps even *the* language, spoken by Adam.[37] Hebrew was undoubtedly the appropriate language for prayer, both for the sake of Jewish historical integrity and because the angels, whose sponsorship in presenting prayer was sometimes considered desirable, allegedly do not understand Aramaic.[38] But even for the *Shema'*, that is the cardinal affirmation of Judaism taken from Deut. 6,6, 'Hear, O Israel, the Lord is thy God, the Lord is one', around the proclamation of which the daily liturgy is constructed, authority had to be found to legitimize the fact that Jews were reciting it in their various vernaculars; and it was discovered in the very word with which the formula begins. '*Shema'* – *Hear*: in whatever language you can hear [i.e. understand]'.[39] Despite the authenticity of this ruling, the opposite view expressed by Rabbi Judah the Patriarch (c. 200 CE) reflects what was soon to become the dominant Jewish attitude, that prayers are to be offered in Hebrew only, with minor concessions for women: an insistence that went virtually unchallenged until the rise of reform Judaism in Germany in the nineteenth century. While no doubt xenophobiac considerations were a contributory factor, this traditional conservatism corresponds to a conviction in Judaism that it is prayer – with which public rehearsal of scriptural texts is integrally involved – that constitutes the essential form of communication of which language is the instrument (cf. below, pp. 132f.). However, a sober understanding of social realities sufficed to keep these two contrasting approaches in tension. Thus we find two views in rabbinic sources as to the value of the Greek translation of the Bible, the origins of which attracted legendary elaboration designed to authenticate the inspirational quality of the version for those who used it in default of ability to read the divinely inspired original.[40] The circumstance that by the second century CE the vast majority of such readers were gentile Christians no doubt accounts for the negative Jewish view, according to which the day when the Torah was translated into Greek was as fraught with trouble for Israel as the day on which they made the golden calf,[41] and the world was dark for three days.[42] As against this there stands the opinion that 'investigation showed that the only language into which the *Torah* could be adequately translated was Greek',[43] and the interpretation of Noah's blessing of Japheth (the ancestor of the Greeks, Gen. 9.27, 10.2), 'may God extend Japheth's bounds and let him dwell in the tents of Shem', as meaning 'may the words of the *Torah* be uttered in the language of Japheth within the tents of Shem', the ancestor of Israel.[44] This positive appraisal is of a piece with the appreciation, outward-looking in a way relatively rare in rabbinic sources, that at least some languages other than Hebrew have qualities that render them particularly fitted for sundry differentiated functions:

> Rabbi Jonathan of Beth Gubrin said: 'four languages are appropriate for general use, *viz.* the common vernacular (*la'az*, i.e. Greek) for song;

> Roman (i.e. Latin) for war; Syriac (i.e. Aramaic) for lament; and Hebrew (*'ibhri*) for speech'. Some also say 'Assyrian (which here probably means square Hebrew characters) for writing'.[45]

Although the last item is a red herring, its inclusion underscores the intimate link referred to above[46] which Judaism sees between the Hebrew language and its script as being twin aspects of God's revelation in the Torah. As regards the remainder, it may be noted that Jonathan of Beth Gubrin (Eleutheropolis) was a third-century Palestinian. The passage is an important one, quite apart from the aesthetic sensitivity that it reflects. First, the assertion that the province of Hebrew is speech (*dibbur*, cf. above, pp. 98f.). Although *dibbur* sometimes means the divine *Word* – clearly not applicable here – it can also mean *talking*: and its occurrence would not invite comment were it not for a variant recension of Rabbi Jonathan's *dictum*[47] in which *'ibhri*, Hebrew, is replaced by *'asshurith*, 'Assyrian' (see above), and instead of its being credited with particular aptitude for *dibbur*, *speech*, it is allocated *tefillah* = *prayer*. Even though this recension is doubtless corrupt[48] the error is significant, as pointing towards a consciousness that although Hebrew might be subjected to casual use, its real function was as the vehicle of Israel's prayerful response to the divine address. This links up with the fact that the use of *'ibhri(th)* as here meaning the Hebrew language is, in traditional texts, very unusual indeed. *'Ibhri* is used as a gentilic adjective in biblical (and post-biblical) Hebrew to describe persons, for example Jonah:[49] talmudic Hebrew also uses it to distinguish the palaeo-Hebrew script from the later, 'Assyrian' script, the ancestor of the square Hebrew in use to-day.[50] The passage with which we are dealing is one of perhaps two only in the whole of pre-medieval Hebrew literature in which *'ibhri(th)* is applied to *language*.[51]

It is illuminating to take note of what terms are in fact used where reference is made to the Hebrew language. *Yehudith*, i.e. 'Judaean', is contrasted both with Aramaic[52] as a language, and with *'ashdodith*, the language (or dialect?) spoken in Ashdod.[53] Quite unequivocal is the reference, in the course of a prophecy concerning Jewish settlement in Egypt, to the time when five cities there, including Heliopolis, would speak 'the language of Canaan'.[54] In post-biblical (and indeed in later, pre-modern) Hebrew the term regularly used is 'the holy tongue' (*leshon haqodesh*). For example, the preamble to the priestly benediction in Numbers 6.23, 'thus shall ye bless . . .', elicited the following piece of exegesis: 'in the holy language; for wherever the adverbs *thus*, *so*, occur in connection with [prescriptive] address or response, they indicate [the indispensability of] the holy language'.[55] Medieval Hebrew is generally consistent with this. Thus the pupils of Menahem ibn Saruq taunted Dunash ibn Labrat in tenth-century Spain with having 'corrupted the holy language, which would survive in perpetuity provided that it maintained "Hebrew" metres (*be-shoqelo ha-'ibhrith*), by introducing foreign metres'.[56] In the following century the classical commentator Rashi (i.e. Solomon b. Isaac of Troyes) normally refers to 'the holy language', as for example in Gen. 2.23, citing an older source,[57] although he does occasionally use the term *'ibhrith*,[58] no doubt relying on its use with reference to speech by R. Jonathan in the 'four languages' passage discussed above.[59] The prevalent modern use of *'ibhrith* for [the] Hebrew [language] began with the (mildly iconoclastic) *haskalah* (*'intelligentsia'*) movement in eighteenth-century Germany (and later in Russia: see below, pp. 133f.) that followed in the wake of the German *Aufklärung*: and in view of the extreme paucity of earlier examples, it must be considered essentially a calque on the German *hebräisch*, itself derived from the Latin [*lingua*] *hebraica*. It was thus adopted with enthusiasm by the Zionist movement that emerged in the nineteenth century, conscious as it was of the enormous political potentiality with which a revived Hebrew would be pregnant (see below, pp. 135f.), and determined that the revival should be free of subservience to religion. It is consequently no surprise to find that the traditionalism inherent in the three most important vernaculars adopted by Jews ensured the retention of *leshon ha-qodesh*, the holy tongue, as a loan-word: in Yiddish (i.e. Judaeo-German) *loshn qodesh*, in Ladino (i.e. Judaeo-Spanish) as *lăshon aqodes(h)*, and in Arabic as *lisān a(l)-quds*. It was not until the latter part of the nineteenth century that *hebräisch* penetrated Yiddish, and the Spanish *hebreo* probably never penetrated Ladino at all in this sense.[60]

4.5 Jewish language-satellites

Before we proceed to review some medieval Jewish thinking about the Hebrew language, it is convenient to deal here with the Jewish use of other languages as a vernacular and with Jewish attitudes towards them. Although these 'Jewish languages' may sometimes have been slightly bent so as to 'echo' Hebrew, they are but idiosyncratically adapted variants of vocabulary, and occasional hebraisms in syntax or word-order, of the speech of the gentile environment (in the same way that Christian Latin was, in its origins, an adaptation);[61] and they may be properly classified as 'Jewish' if written by Jews in Hebrew characters, instead of in the alphabet commonly used by the literate members of the wider speech community. The ideological aspect of this extended use of the Hebrew alphabet for Arabic, Spanish, German, and so on, has been touched upon above (see p. 102), and it has a Christian analogue in the use of the Syriac script (called when thus applied *karshuni*) for Arabic and, in India, for Malayalam; but ideology must be complemented by taking account of the economics of medieval and later Jewish education. Because of the importance of sending the Jewish child (or strictly speaking, boy) forth from school adequately equipped to follow the readings from the Bible and the prayers in communal worship, elementary education concerned itself with inculcating the ability to read and write Hebrew; teaching of other scripts at the primary stage of education does not begin in Jewry until acculturation is far advanced, that is in modern Europe from the seventeenth century among the Sephardim (of Iberian antecedents) in Italy, Holland, etc., and among the Ashkenazim of northern, central, and eastern Europe scarcely before the nineteenth century on any large scale. In those areas where acculturation occurred rapidly because Jewish settlement was, at first, sparse – meaning, in effect, England and the United States of America before 1880 – Jewish educational resources were never strong enough to 'impose' use of the Hebrew script for the local vernacular. There is consequently no 'Judaeo-English' to set alongside Judaeo-German, Judaeo-Greek, Judaeo-Italian, Judaeo-Persian, and so on.

Only four of these 'Jewish languages' [62] need concern us here, as having been used (not always to the same degree throughout their history) by substantial numbers of Jews over extended periods of time: Jewish Aramaic, Judaeo-Arabic, Judaeo-Spanish, and Judaeo-German. Their common features, in varying intensity – apart from the circumstance that each was both spoken in the home in the Jewish community and was also generally intelligible (at least at first) to gentile speakers, though not readers, of the language concerned – are as follows:

1. use for correspondence, business records, casual memos, and so on;
2. use for literary purposes and quasi-literary purposes in an oral form, including translation of the Hebrew Bible and a few prayers for use in elementary or popular education;
3. the circumscribed admission of vernacular translations alongside the Hebrew original to public worship, either generally, or for the use of women only;
4. partly because of the seal of Jewish approbation implicit in 3,

> a literary or sentimental 'half life' (occasionally, indeed, a 'three-quarter life') when the language concerned has ceased, for historical reasons or because of mass migration, to be used for vernacular speech.

Similar features would be evinced by other Jewish languages besides these four main ones, each of which must now be considered independently since generalization cannot be pursued beyond the points already established.

In antiquity, the great Aramaic-speaking zone of the middle east included areas in which Jewish communities were both numerous and demographically strong, especially in 'Babylonia' (i.e. Mesopotamia); and the need for a vernacular version of parts of the Hebrew Bible must have made itself felt certainly no later than the turn of the eras, since the early history of the Syriac (i.e. Christian Aramaic) version of the Hebrew Bible (the *Peshiṭta*) can be shown to be intertwined with that of the Jewish Aramaic version(s) (*targum(im)*), even though the extant, written *targumim* are several centuries younger. Because of the great Jewish population in the Mesopotamian area and the importance of the Babylonian Jewish academies in the centuries following the destruction of Jerusalem by the Romans in 70 CE, liturgical use of the *targum* entrenched itself in areas far beyond Mesopotamia. It survives today, even in the West in a residual, token form, albeit as not much more than a curiosity. That it has done so is due to the two recensions of the Talmud – the Palestinian and the Babylonian – consisting of scholarly discussions, or contrived literary versions of such, recorded basically in Aramaic with liberal Hebrew insertions. The Talmud (and more especially the longer, Babylonian recension) has, down the ages, constituted the classical text of Jewish secondary education. The importance for Judaism of its content has outweighed the fact that, quite apart from the all but complete disappearance of Aramaic as a spoken vernacular among both Jews and gentiles, the later scholars who studied the Talmud had themselves lost full grammatical and syntactical control of the language in which it had been written down (rather as, for example, a medieval French or Italian apothecary might be able to read volumes of *materia medica* and write a prescription in Latin, even though he was unable either to speak or write Latin for other purposes himself). But despite this grammatical handicap, the capacity to handle (i.e. to follow an argument in) talmudic Aramaic came to be the hallmark of Jewish academic (i.e. quasi-professional) competence; and it is the medium in which, until this very day, rabbinical luminaries formulate their jurisprudential *responsa*. In view of the high proportion of Jewish youth who, in strong Jewish centres such as pre-war Jewish Poland, studied the Talmud intensively during their secondary education even though they did not enter the rabbinate professionally, the 'half-life' of Jewish Aramaic since its disuse for daily speech has been remarkably tenacious. It was, indeed, strong enough to stimulate a few 'revivalist' endeavours among medieval and renaissance Jewish hymnologists, and, more importantly, to be used by Moses de Leon in twelfth-century Spain as the language in which he wrote his great mystical commentary on the pentateuch known as the *Zohar*, representing it as having been composed in Palestine in the second century CE. The *Zohar* rapidly became the classical document of Jewish mysticism (the *Kabbalah*), and it was accorded by its wide circle of devotees a status analogous to that of the Talmud. The importance (religious and educational) of Aramaic was thus correspondingly enhanced.

In view of this long *symbiosis* of Aramaic and Hebrew, it is not surprising that rabbinic and later traditional Hebrew is replete with Aramaic loan-words and influences, or that Jewish tradition has regarded knowledge of Aramaic as being but a degree less necessary than a knowledge of Hebrew, even though 'the angels do not understand it' (see above, pp. 103f.). It is eloquent of the secularizing *tendenz* of modern Hebrew than in editing his great *Complete Dictionary of Ancient and Modern Hebrew* (1910–59) Eliezer Ben-Yehuda adopted a rigorous policy of excluding Aramaic from its entries almost entirely.[63]

Judaeo-Arabic, on the other hand, has been in continuous use as a vernacular in Iraq, Yemen, North Africa, and so on until modern times; and plentiful evidence of the written purposes to which it was applied in the middle ages has been recovered from documents disposed of in the Cairo *Genizah*.[64] The extensive literary productions of Jews who wrote in Arabic include bible translation, commentaries both on the Bible and on rabbinic writings, medical and other scientific works, translations (at second hand) of Greek texts, and religious philosophy – the most famous item within this category being Maimonides' *Guide for the Perplexed.* But despite the importance of some of this writing for such integrally Jewish concerns as talmudic jurisprudence and case-law (*halakhah*, 'procedure'), Arabic never came to be regarded by Jews as a virtually indispensable tool for Jewish expertise in the way that Aramaic was considered. On the contrary: the classics composed in Judaeo-Arabic such as Judah Hallevi's *Kuzari* and Maimonides' *Guide* were themselves translated into rather stylized Hebrew (in the case of the *Guide*, during Maimonides' own lifetime), because of the interest that they attracted among European Jews who could not read them in the original. For those Jews in the east, in North Africa, Spain, the Sicily of Frederick II of Hohenstaufen ('*stupor mundi*', reigned 1198–1250), and also those in southern France for whom Arabic was either their vernacular or else a very strong second language, its significance was as a channel up which the tide of Islamic intellectualism could flood. But despite the advantages that they derived from it, Arabic-speaking Jews seem never to have felt any strong emotional link with their vernacular, possibly taking it for granted because no expulsion or forced migration interrupted its currency among them. It is significant that although some liturgical items have been translated into Arabic and printed in some modern prayer-books, the little Arabic poetry known to have been written by Jews down the centuries does not include religious pieces. Solomon ibn Gabirol and Judah Hallevi, both of them masters of Arabic prose, wrote their hymns in a magisterial Hebrew.

If continuity of domicile and environmental culture accounts for the matter-of-fact attitude towards Judaeo-Arabic of those who spoke (or still speak) it, the place occupied by Judaeo-Spanish (generally called *ladino*, sometimes *judezmo*) in the hearts of the Sephardim, with ancestral links to the Iberian peninsula, is due essentially to discontinuity. There had been a Jewish presence in Spain before the coming of the Muslims: and although it is certainly true that after their arrival it was by the Arabic language and eastern element in *mudéjar* (i.e. Moorish) culture that Spanish Jews were principally influenced, the integration of Christian, Muslim and Jewish elements in Spanish society is typified by the quadrilingual inscription – Spanish, Latin, Arabic, and Hebrew – placed on the tomb of Ferdinand III in Seville by order of Alfonso X ('*el sabio*').[65] However, from 1391 onwards aggressive Christianity and forced conversions drove many Spanish Jews into crypto-Judaism, and the recovery of the last Moorish outpost, Granada, in 1492, coincided with the expulsion of all professing Jews from Spain: expulsion from Portugal followed in 1497. Sephardi Jewry was thus riven asunder. Those of the exiles who settled in North Africa and Turkish lands, from Salonica to Palestine, brought with them both a residual affection for the Spain that they had left behind, and also a European culture quite different from that of their new environment, which – to the exiles – seemed inferior. They consequently cherished their Spanish vernacular, which remained in wide use until 1939, for secular, educational, and para-liturgical purposes. For scholarly works the descendants of the exiles used Hebrew, sometimes also translating their books into Judaeo-Spanish; but apart from ballads and songs (*romanzas*, many of which had been brought from Spain), there was little creative writing. The very existence of these *romanzas*, acknowledged as specifically Sephardi, underscores the hold that Spanish continued to exercise on the descendants of the exiles for nearly five centuries.

The other branch of Iberian Jewry went underground in Spain and Portugal. It retained a fierce loyalty to Judaism which, as in the course of one or two generations these so-called *marranos* or *conversos* lost all knowledge of Hebrew, they had to foster in an attenuated form of Jewish ceremonial practised in secret, to the accompaniment of prayers in Spanish. In south-western France there existed a few communities of 'Portuguese', whose crypto-Jewish identity was common knowledge to the authorities despite the fact of Jews being forbidden to reside in the country; and as in due course such communities as these felt secure enough to put the text of their prayers onto paper, they naturally had to write or print them in Latin characters. With the establishment of openly tolerated ex-Iberian Jewish communities during the sixteenth century, in Italy and later in Holland, the former crypto-Jews and the descendants of such who constituted them had their meagre Jewish knowledge reinforced through renewed contact with the Sephardim, the descendants of the 1492 exiles from the Ottoman empire. They began (especially in Ferrara and Amsterdam) to publish Spanish translations of the Bible and post-biblical Jewish classics (almost all of them in Latin type), as well as Hebrew books. Thus the two branches of Iberian Jewry, in recovering their contact, mutually reinforced the attachment to Spanish which, in each of them, ascended to different causes. As they came to adapt for everyday use the vernaculars of their respective environments – French, Italian, Dutch, German, or English – their continued love of Spanish was essentially the expression of their pride in their Iberian past and the richness of its cultural integration. In the Balkans particularly, Spanish remained in vernacular use and was maintained for religious educational purposes. A recent example of its ghostly survival is furnished by an order of service for the eve of Passover published in Athens in 1970, in Hebrew with a modern Greek translation as well as the traditional Judaeo-Spanish version in Hebrew characters. However, since the destruction of Jewish Salonica during the Second World War, there have been few in Greece who can still read it in Hebrew type; and it is therefore repeated in romanized form. In its essence, the living Judaeo-Spanish prior to 1939 was the symbol of a Jewish legitimization of cultural pluralism.

Persecution and discontinuity largely account for the linguistic sentiment of the Judaeo-Spanish segment of Jewry; but continuity and self-isolationism go far towards explaining the attitude to their vernacular of speakers of Yiddish. Judaeo-German would in the course of time develop its own distinct regional dialects, but it began as middle high German although its origins are now carried back as far as the tenth century.[66] Accepted as the language of daily speech, including its function as the medium of both elementary and higher (i.e. talmudic) Ashkenazi Jewish education, it was carried eastwards into Slavonic lands by increasing Jewish migration from the twelfth century onwards; the turning of the tide in the later seventeenth century carried it back into Holland and beyond the Rhine, while the vast Jewish emigration from Russia that commenced in the 1880s brought large, culturally self-sufficient Yiddish-speaking communities to areas subject to the British crown, in Latin America especially to the Argentine, and above all to the United States of America. Yiddish was thus, for centuries, the *lingua franca* for a progressively larger majority of the entire Jewish population, although Hebrew continued to be regarded by the intellectual aristocracy as constituting Jewry's essential linguistic bond. And despite the development of a literature, to be glanced at below (p. 113), Yiddish was for long regarded as being no more than an inevitable convenience. Its romanticization probably began with its role as link between emigrants to the west who were rapidly acquiring other vernaculars, especially English, and the kinsfolk whom they had left behind in eastern Europe. Its recent, retrospective sentimentalization is due to Hitler's physical extermination of the masses of its speakers.

The studied restriction of Yiddish to an ancillary role until the nineteenth century is explicable by reference to the high standard of elementary Hebrew education for boys – but not girls – maintained in the Ashkenazi Jewries of Germany (and its Western overspill), the Austrian empire, and in Russia and Poland. Folk tales, some of them drawing on midrashic, i.e. exegetical sources in Hebrew that embellish the biblical story, and some of them of non-Jewish origin, were being written down in Yiddish from the fourteenth century, but the liturgical 'embargo' tells its own story. Whereas Spanish translations of some scriptural items occasionally gained formal recognition within the Sephardic rite, Yiddish bible translation and prayers were produced specifically for the use of women, despite the paradox that Yiddish was the language in which the sermon would be delivered in synagogue. Hebrew prayer-books admitted it but only marginally, for use in rubrics and sometimes also by providing translations of the rarer liturgical pieces and abstruse hymns – versions which were doubtless gratefully used by men as well as women. It was this severely circumscribed Yiddish-Hebrew *symbiosis* that provided both the background and the incentive for Moses Mendelssohn's production, in the eighteenth century, of a bible version in correct German, albeit printed to begin with in Hebrew characters, with the object of promoting Jewish cultural integration into the Germany of the *Aufklärung*. Not surprisingly, Mendelssohn's followers, as protagonists of a Hebrew-based *Aufklärung* (*haskalah*), stigmatized Yiddish as being but a jargon; and the fact that *Jargon* came to be an alternative name for Yiddish reflects the love-hate relationship towards it entertained by its own traditionalist speakers. Conservative reluctance to countenance any Yiddish legitimization explains why the homilies – lasting several hours each – which the rabbinical leader (*ṣaddiq*) of a hasidic group would deliver were subsequently written down by a disciple or secretary for circulation in Hebrew. But the nineteenth century witnessed the beginnings of a Yiddish-speaking anti-clericalism that stimulated the emergence of a secular Yiddish literature, including poetry. More importantly for our purposes, it witnessed also the development of Yiddish journalism from purely literary enterprises into a full-scale press: and against it the forces of religious traditionalism (which was probably not particularly worried) and the 'enlightened' outlook of those interested in a wider literary revival of Hebrew, were equally powerless. But it is the occasional gesture that epitomizes the opposition. Thus Chaim Weitzmann, later the first president of the State of Israel, who sprang from a moderate milieu that smiled on enlightenment without repudiating Jewish institutional religion, recorded in his autobiography that although he regularly corresponded with his mother in Yiddish, on the one occasion that he wrote to his father in that language instead of in Hebrew, his letter was returned to him unanswered.[67] But it was not until the movement to revive Hebrew, not merely as the medium of scholarly correspondence and literary creativity which it had always been, but as a vernacular in the full sense of the word – a movement whose beginning was signalled by E. Ben-Yehuda's *She'elah Nikhbadah* published in 1879[68] – that those who were avowedly looking towards Hebrew as a political weapon for use in the endeavour to achieve independent Jewish statehood in effect declared war on Yiddish self-perpetuation. The classical statement of the nationalist case for Hebrew was propounded in an article by Ahad Ha'am (i.e. Asher Ginsberg) entitled *Riv Leshonoth* ('Battle of the Tongues') in 1911.[69]

4.6 Philological, philosophical and theological interests

Reference has been made above[70] to the late development within Jewry of any systematic address to the relationship of Hebrew to its cognate languages. When serious philological interest, as opposed to whimsical 'etymologizing', evinces itself during the middle ages, it is among Arabic-speaking Jewry in the middle east, North Africa, and Spain that it begins; and it owes its stimulus to Islamic cultivation of linguistic science. But inasmuch as Jewish endeavour was directed almost exclusively towards biblical Hebrew, the essential groundwork of fact-finding had already been completed by a group of scholars known as the Massoretes, or 'tradents', from their completion of the Masorah.[71]

The Hebrew word *massoreth*, tradition, refers specifically to the received consonantal text of scripture that lacks vowel-points, and the addition thereto of notation to indicate its correct vocal rendition. The form *masor(a)* is Aramaic, and had originally been adopted into Hebrew to mean *informer* (i.e. one who *hands over* another to malevolent authority); later, it was wrongly assumed to be a Hebrew noun with the feminine ending *ah*, and was applied to the listing of occurrences of the rarer root-stems or of their morphological forms, as well as the phonetically correct reading of the text in prayer.[72] The consonantal text had been essentially fixed since at least the middle of the second century CE, although minor variations, largely concerning orthography but occasionally affecting the sense, are attested in biblical manuscripts down to the age of print.[73] The enterprise of imposing on the consonants a system of symbols designed to standardize pronunciation was stimulated in part by Arabic concern with linguistic purism, upon which the paradigmatic position of the Qur'an conferred the status of a sacred science; but the immediate example seems to have been provided by the analogous endeavours of the Syrian church to preserve the rendition of its own, Aramaic biblical text (the *Peshiṭta*) – or more precisely, in the first instance the gospels – at a period when Aramaic as a vernacular was fighting a losing battle with Greek and later with Arabic. This Christian activity, which consisted in inserting diacritical points, or Greek vowels, above or below the Syriac consonantal text, is already attested in a codex of 411.[74] The first introduction of a similar apparatus into Hebrew codices cannot have preceded the sixth century CE, and although it cannot have post-dated the seventh, the systematic work of the Massoretes did not begin before the second half of the eighth. It is particularly associated with the names of two scholarly families, that of Ben-Asher – especially Moses b. Asher (active in 896) and his son Aaron – and Ben-Naphtali: the aforementioned two, as well as Moses (? Jacob) b. Naphtali (probably a contemporary of Aaron b. Asher) were located in Tiberias. Later tradition records approximately 850 instances of minor divergence between readings associated with the schools bearing these names, but it is now known that the evolution of the vocalization system is in fact rather more complex. From close study of biblical manuscripts first deposited in the Cairo *Genizah* and now preserved mainly in Cambridge (England) (i.e. discarded documents in the Hebrew script put aside to await reverent interment, but which remained untouched over centuries in a Cairo synagogue), P. Kahle[75] and subsequent scholars have distinguished different systems of notation, simple and more complex, supralinear and sublinear, that preceded the so-called 'Tiberian' punctuation as still used in printed Hebrew. Although each system is, in the main, internally self-consistent, they do not evince identical realizations of grammatical morphology. This manuscript evidence was digested in an apparatus of critical notes appended to the text of the Hebrew Bible published under the editorship of Rudolf Kittel and Kahle,[76] and when studied in connection with the consonantal orthography of the Dead Sea Scrolls and with the pre-medieval transliteration of Hebrew words and phrases into Greek and Latin characters, it may be used in order to reconstruct the form of the Hebrew language in antiquity. In this way, the Massoretes unwittingly provided modern scholarship with significant source material.

But the medieval Jewish grammarians who built upon their concordantial work (see below) regarded the Tiberian vocalization as definitive, since they assumed its identity with the 'mother', that is authority for traditional rendition (*'em la-massoreth*) which rabbinic axiom regarded as being co-eval and enjoying parity with the authority of the scriptural text (*'em la-miqra*),[77] both deriving from the Sinaitic revelation through Moses himself – an assumption not questioned within Jewry or the Church before the renaissance.[78] The massoretic concordances consist of textual notes, in a compressed and technical Aramaic, that indicate occurrences elsewhere in the Hebrew bible (or within one of its three canonical divisions) of the root-stem marked, or of the particular form of it evinced. In this way they identify *hapax legomena*, vocabulary characteristic of poetry and prose, and assemble statistics of the forms occurring of a given root-stem – information that is essential for any systematic study of either lexicography or grammar. The relevant texts for comparison are indicated by catchwords only, since Jewish *pericope*-divisions were not numbered; the chapter divisions to be found in printed Hebrew Bibles were taken over, with minor modifications, from the system evolved in the thirteenth century in Paris for the Latin Bible, in order to obviate confusion in the schools caused by students from different parts of Europe using various capitulation systems current in their countries of origin.[79]

Absence of such numerical references was less of a handicap than might appear, since the Massoretes could presuppose a readership closely familiar with the Hebrew text, including portions of it that figure neither in the liturgy nor in the scriptural lectionary cycle. Apart from the circumstance that the very common words and particles are ignored, the work in effect constitutes a biblical concordance. It was inscribed, in miniscule script, in the upper and lower margins of major Hebrew biblical codices, and is referred to as the Greater Masorah; being thus distinguished from the Lesser Masorah, which cites the relevant statistics but omits the catchwords that indicate the parallels concerned. The Lesser Masorah was set out in the inner and outer margins and between the columns, an arrangement that has been reproduced in print.[80]

Jewish attention to Hebrew lexicography and grammar began at the same period as that in which the Masorah was reaching its final stage, being stimulated by analogous Islamic interests, grammar following closely in the wake of lexicography. Sa‘adyah Ga'on of Sura, in Babylonia (see below, p. 125), halakhic, that is canonical jurist and philosopher of Judaism, discussed word-analysis in his *'Agron*, and also compiled a list of 70 biblical *hapax legomena* the meanings of which he explained by recourse to mishnaic Hebrew.[81] The fullest Hebrew and Aramaic biblical dictionary produced (in Arabic) in the tenth century was the work of a Karaite Jewish scholar, David al-Fasi of Jerusalem.[82] But it was in Andalusia that Hebrew linguistic science particularly flourished. Menahem ibn Saruq of Cordoba (tenth century), writing in Hebrew, was the author of a Hebrew dictionary known as *Maḥbereth* (‘Assemblage'),[83] and in order to appreciate the limitations of this work it is necessary to understand the phonological structure of Hebrew. Since his vernacular was Arabic, Menahem can scarcely have been unaware that, like Arabic, Hebrew is based on a triliteral root system: yet he deliberately chose to ignore this parallel, perhaps through conviction of the uniquely sacred quality of Hebrew. Since the position of any weak consonants (*h*, *w*, *y*, etc.) within a given root often means that they are not heard in pronunciation and disappear in writing thanks to assimilation, aphaeresis, or apocopation, Menahem arranged his dictionary according to a biliteral (or even occasionally an uniliteral) scheme of stems; with the result that disparate material is brought together under one heading, semantic connections being either strained or disregarded altogether. What we are presented with is a supposed ‘archaeology' of the language, rather than a lexicon. In spite of this, since it was written in Hebrew, Menahem's dictionary enjoyed wide circulation even after it had been superseded, particularly in northern Europe where Jews were ignorant of Arabic, being quoted by the classical commentator Rashi (Solomon b. Isaac of Troyes, 1040–1105). Menahem ibn Saruq's work was attacked when it appeared, albeit not on grounds of his lexical principle, by Dunash ibn Labrat[84] and his pupils, and was defended by his own.

Among these controversialists was Judah b. David Ḥayyuj[85] (c. 945–c. 1000), born in Fez but resident in Cordoba from about 960, who curiously supported ibn Saruq, even though his own grammatical works, written in Arabic, presuppose the triliteral root for Hebrew. For the sake of clarity, it will be convenient to postpone further consideration of grammar, and first to follow through the development of lexicography from beyond the middle ages up to modernity. The most influential dictionary of biblical Hebrew written in Arabic was that of Abu'l-walid Marwan ('Marinus') ibn Janaḥ,[86] who flourished in the first half of the eleventh century; after his Jewish education at the great rabbinical academy of Lucena he studied medicine at Cordoba, where he practised until its siege by the Berbers in 1012, subsequently settling in Saragossa. His last work, *Kitab al-tanqiḥ* ('Book of minute research') embraces both a grammar and a complete dictionary of biblical Hebrew (*Kitab al-'usul,* 'Book of roots'); translated into Hebrew by Judah ibn Tibbon (c. 1120–c. 1190) of Lunel in southern France, this for the first time provided Jews who did not know Arabic with a satisfactory biblical lexicon.[87] A complete survey of medieval Jewish lexicography cannot be given here,[88] and we must limit ourselves to noticing the *Sepher hashorashim* ('Book of roots') by David Qimḥi (Kimḥi), which, like ibn Janaḥ's dictionary, formed the second part of a work entitled *Mikhlol* ('Comprehensive [tract]') that also included a grammar, but, unlike ibn Janaḥ's work, was written in Hebrew. Qimḥi[89] (?1160–?1235), who lived in Narbonne, was himself the son and brother of grammarians. He based his lexicon on that of ibn Janaḥ, but he cites other authorities, including references to the *Masorah* and grammatical features, makes comparisons with post-biblical Hebrew and with Aramaic, and he also includes numerous Provençal glosses. This lexicon effectively replaced its predecessors, and became (with the companion grammar) the fundamental instrument of Christian Hebrew studies in renaissance Europe, the founders of which may be recognized in Pico della Mirandola[90] (1463–1494) in Italy and Johann Reuchlin[91] (1455–1522) in Germany. Reuchlin's Hebrew grammar and dictionary[92] are substantially based on Qimḥi's.

It is to be emphasized that all these works address themselves specifically to the Hebrew of the Bible, even if some of them occasionally appeal to the evidence of post-biblical Hebrew. In spite of the emulation of the biblical form of the language for liturgical and some literary purposes, Jewish axiomatic distinction between the two – a distinction rooted less in logic than in theological mystique – is made explicit in the talmudic statement that the language of the Torah and that of the sages are two self-contained entities.[93] Correspondingly greater significance attaches, therefore, to the compilation in Hebrew of an encyclopaedic dictionary of talmudic and midrashic Hebrew by Nathan b. Yeḥiel of Rome[94] (1035–c. 1110) entitled *'Arukh* ('Arrange[ment]'),[95] which adduces etymologies from Greek, Latin, Arabic, and Persian, and occasionally introduces Italian glosses. Thus, in his entry for *'skwl'* (i.e. *scholē*) which rabbinic exegesis had linked with the biblical Hebrew word *'eshkol* = *cluster*,[96] Nathan adduces the vernacular *'shqwl'*, that is, *iscuola*. A similar dictionary, compiled by another (adoptive) Italian, Elijah Levita[97] (1468/9–1549), Hebrew teacher to a number of humanists including Cardinal Egidio da Viterbo,[98] Paulus Fagius,[99] and Sebastian Muenster,[100] bears the hallmark of renaissance scholarship. Levita was the first to claim that the massoretic vocalization of the Hebrew bible dates from the post-talmudic period, and not from the law-giving at Sinai. His lexicon, entitled *Tishbi* ('Tishbite') in allusion to the author's first name (cf. 1 Kings 17,1), with a Latin translation by Fagius, appeared at Isny in 1541, as did his dictionary entitled *Meturgeman* ('Interpreter') of the Aramaic of the *targumim* (see above, p. 115, n. 78).

We may briefly round off Jewish lexicography here, by carrying the story beyond the middle ages. Building on the foregoing works, Christian hebraists of the sixteenth to eighteenth centuries such as the Buxtorfs[101] edited important dictionaries; but renewed Jewish endeavour had to await nineteenth-century Jewish emancipation and the emergence of Jewish scholars equipped with a Western university training. Pre-eminent are the two targumic and talmudic lexica in German by Jacob Levy[102] (1819–92), who had studied at Breslau and Halle, and in English (substantially based on Levy) by Marcus Jastrow[103] (1829–1903), whose universities were Berlin and Halle and who left Poland for Philadelphia in 1866. The impetus behind these enterprises was academic, possibly tinged with apologetic concern to make rabbinic sources more accessible, and thus less liable to misrepresentation, in the climate of a liberal century. But the end of the nineteenth century also witnessed the beginning of the revival of spoken Hebrew that went hand-in-hand with zionist political aspirations. This inspired the movement's protagonist, Eliezer Ben-Yehuda[104] (originally Perelman, 1858–1922) to embark on a comprehensive dictionary, in Hebrew. It was provided with title-pages in Hebrew, English, French, German, and Latin, the last reading sonorously and ambitiously *Thesaurus totius hebraitatis et veteris et recentioris.*[105] It was completed by his widow and son, assisted by the eminent philologist and biblical scholar N. H. Ṭur-Sinai (Torczyner)[106] (1886–1973). Subsequent major dictionaries are those (Hebrew–English and English-Hebrew) of 'Even-Shoshan[107] and (English-Hebrew) 'Alcalay;[108] the one currently in production at Oxford University Press and involving a team of Israeli and British scholars may be expected to be hailed as a landmark out of political considerations, whatever its lexicographical merits may prove to be.

We may now revert to the middle ages, and sketch briefly the work of some of the Jewish grammarians.[109] Already in the ninth to tenth century Judah ibn Ḥayyuj[110] in Algeria had indicated, in an Arabic tract addressed to the Jews of Fez, the family relationship of Hebrew with Aramaic and Arabic.[111] Note has already been taken (see p. 117) of the criticism of the *Maḥbereth* of Menahem ibn Saruq by Dunash and his disciples. Judah Ḥayyuj in his Arabic essay on Hebrew verbal grammar confined himself to weak stems containing *'aleph*, *waw*, or *yod* and those that duplicate the second radical letter.[112] This was translated into Hebrew in the eleventh century by Moses b. Samuel Gikatilla of Saragossa.[113] It was with the object of completing (and criticizing) Ḥayyuj's work that Jonah ibn Janaḥ first compiled his own 'Book of criticism' (*Kitab al-mustalḥaq*, Hebrew translation *Sepher ha-hassagah*) in 1012.[114] But his *magnum opus*, written in the 1040s, of which the second part is the lexicon (see above, p. 117), began with his grammatical treatise (*Kitab al-lum'a*, 'Book of greenery'),[115] which constituted the first full description of Hebrew accidence: a Hebrew translation was made by Judah ibn Tibbon c. 1171.[116] Enough grammatical works are known from the tenth to eleventh centuries – complete, fragmentary, or lost but known from references in medieval authors – some of them emanating from Karaite scholars (see above, p. 102, n. 32), to attest a lively interest in linguistic science among the Andalusian Jewish intelligentsia. But the next landmark is Abraham ibn Ezra[117] (1089–1164), a wandering scholar distinguished as much for his biblical exegesis and his mathematical and astronomical works as for his philological prowess. Apart from his Hebrew translation of Ḥayyuj (see n. 113) he himself composed, in Hebrew, three grammatical works, of which the most important was his comprehensive *Sepher ṣaḥoth* ('Book of clarity'),[118] written in Mantua in 1145. These grammatical treatises of Ibn Ezra exercised substantial influence, possibly bolstered by the importance of their author's biblical commentaries. His chief academic heirs were the

Qimḥis – Joseph, and his two sons Moses and David – of whom the latter (see above, p. 117) was perhaps 4 years old when Ibn Ezra died. His grammar first appeared in his *Sepher mikhlol*,[119] and it was the most popular Hebrew primer in use in the middle ages; from the date of its first printing (1532–4, Constantinople) if not indeed earlier, it was used by the Christian hebraists of the Renaissance, its occasional attestation in the holdings of monastic libraries and the early universities being evidence for this. In those countries where the reformed churches established themselves, with a reversion to the authority of scripture as against that embodied in the living tradition of the church of Rome, David Qimḥi's mark was particularly strong, being traceable in some of the vernacular bible versions, for example the English King James' Bible of 1611.[120]

Although the demographic pattern of medieval Spain meant that there was significant interaction between Jews whose vernacular was Arabic (except to some extent in the north) and speakers of early Spanish – as is shown, *inter alia*, by *ḥarjas* (conclusions) in Romance to a large number of Hebrew and Arabic poems – the heart-land of Jewish Spain was Arabic-speaking Andalusia. As Jewish interest in grammar began to be cultivated in southern France, Provence and Italy, it is possible to detect some unconscious ingestion by Jewish scholars of grammatical categories identified by Western grammarians as features of Indo-European speech. From some anonymous notes (*Pethaḥ debharai*) printed in Naples in 1492 and tentatively ascribed to Qimḥi[121] there comes what may well be the earliest application (in a grammatical context, it is to be stressed) of the Hebrew terms for past (*'abhar*), future (*'athid*), and present (*howeh* – the latter a neologism).[122] The adoption of this terminology assigns to the Hebrew so-called tenses a primarily time-orientated function, and in so doing belies their true nature (see above, pp. 99f.); an obscuration of their essential function, which appears to be that of either isolating an item or setting it in a serial context, that was to prove of far-reaching importance. (Naturally, the language operates syntactical devices that distinguish adequately between narrative anteriority and posteriority.) While this ingestion of Western time-concepts did, indeed, make it easier for scholars educated in Latin to get to grips with biblical Hebrew, it created a number of phantom-problems regarding biblical historiography both for Christian students as well as for Jews in Europe generally, inasmuch as their own vernaculars were variations of the Romance languages and of German (see above, pp. 100, 106f., below, pp. 121f., 123).

A striking lacuna in the substantial body of Jewish philological literature (of which we have here cited but a small fraction) is the almost complete disregard of syntax, despite the sensitivity of some of these same grammarians to nuances and their syntactical indications when they were themselves commenting on the biblical text. (An obvious touchstone is afforded by conditional clauses: does, or does not a given grammarian offer any systematic presentation of the various types of condition?) Such an approach is not, to my knowledge, attempted by Abraham ibn Ezra; and yet, commenting on Gen. 48.14, he points out that the particle *ki*, the commonest meanings of which are causal (*since*, etc.) and temporal (*when*, etc.) here has a concessive force (*although*).[123] Recognition of syntax as a substantive branch of philology was of long standing in the West. In the third century BCE the stoic Chrysippus wrote a book (now lost) *on syntax*,[124] and it was treated at length in the second by Apollonius Dyscolus.[125] Among Latin writers it is sufficient to mention Priscian[126] (c. 500 CE). Arabic grammarians, from Sībawayhi (a native of Persia, died 793 or 796)[127] onwards, acknowledged that syntax (*nahw*) merited study in its own right.[128]

Too much ought not to be made of the fact that *taḥbir*, the specific term for *syntax* now current in Hebrew, is not listed in Ben-Yehuda's dictionary (see above, pp. 118f.) that was completed in 1959, although its alphabetic position would fall within the final volume. It appears in 'Even-Shoshan's dictionary (1947–58) and in 'Alcalay's (1959–61),[129] and I am informed that its introduction, or at any rate its authentication by the Hebrew Language Academy (see below, p. 139), occurred in 1936.[130] Ibn Ezra no doubt subsumed syntax within what he terms *mishpaṭ ha-lashon*, 'the rule[s] of the language'.[131] Ibn Janaḥ had discussed word order,[132] but concerns himself with periodic sentence structure rather than with priorities within the clause; and Judah ibn Bal'am[133] (late eleventh century) of Seville composed, in Arabic, a lexicon of Hebrew particles.[134] Judah Ben-Ze'ev (Bensew)[135] (1764–1811), who worked in Berlin, Breslau, and Vienna, published a grammar in Hebrew in 1796, which Steinschneider,[136] following Luzzatto, declares to be *'prima cum syntaxi bene disposita'*.[137] However, already in 1523 Abraham de Balmes[138] had included in his grammar entitled *Miqneh 'abhram* a section on syntax, which he calls *harkabhah* (i.e. 'grafting') and *shimmush* (usage); but de Balmes was an Aristotelian scholar, who had taken doctorates of philosophy and medicine at Naples in 1492.

There is one feature only of biblical syntax that interested medieval Jewish scholars, owing to their unconscious assumption that Western time-concepts had been current as categories presupposed both immemorially and universally – an assumption the falsity of which is strikingly demonstrated by the Jewish writer of the (Greek) *Wisdom of Solomon* (first century BCE), when he makes his hero give thanks to God for having revealed to him knowledge of cosmology, natural science, astronomy, and 'the beginning, ending, and midst of times' (7, 18). Reference here is to the rules of sequence applicable to biblical Hebrew narrative prose and prescriptive writing, that is the consecutive *waw* commonly referred to nowadays as the 'conversive' *waw* (*waw ha-hippukh*).[139] Already in the late tenth century the karaite scholar Japheth ben 'Ali[140] of Jerusalem had referred to the *waw 'athidhi*, the '*waw* indicative of the future' preceding the verb *hayah* = *occur*.[141] Menahem ibn Saruq[142] distinguished the '*waw* referring to past time' as in *wa-yomer* ('and he said') from the '*waw* referring to future time', as for example, *we-'amar* ('and he will say'); and he states that the force of adding the *waw* to the verb is to *change* (*ḥalephah ha-millah*) the time-reference of the unprefixed verb. Qimḥi, who designates this usage of the *waw* as 'auxiliary' (*waw ha-sheruth*, i.e. the *waw* of service) states:[143] 'when you add the auxiliary *waw* to verbs in the past tense it indicates the future . . . if you add it to the personal pronoun prefixes [of the verb in the future], vocalizing it *wa-* it indicates the past'. Ben-Ze'ev[144] states that the *waw*, as well as its copulative force = *and* (*la-ḥabhor*), possesses also a *conversive* function (*la-haphokh*). It is probably this formulation that has generated the current terminology – *waw ha-hippukh* – the earliest occurrence of which I have been unable to trace.[145] It may be observed that correct usage would here require *haphikhah* rather than *hippukh*, but the misuse is attested already in medieval texts in other connections.[146]

As already mentioned (see pp. 117f.), medieval Jewish interest was focused almost exclusively on biblical Hebrew, even though mishnaic Hebrew and the cognate languages were sometimes cited to explain unusual phenomena. Systematic investigation and presentation of the morphology of the post-biblical language had to await modern times, a pioneer endeavour being M. H. Segal's *Grammar of Mishnaic Hebrew*.[147] Study of subsequent strata of the language (except for that of modern Israeli Hebrew, which has attracted continuous attention, some of it from reputable scholars) has been largely neglected, but a few tentative investigations of syntactical features, some presented according to the canons of modern descriptive linguistics, have been appearing since 1948,[148] perhaps the most useful being U. Ornan's outline, prefaced by an articulated list of its contents, in the *Encyclopaedia Judaica*.[149] Ornan begins by noting the traditional Jewish neglect of syntax, and accounts for it by appealing to the fact that, as compared with Greek, Latin, and classical Arabic, Hebrew is a much less heavily inflected language: and he assumes that this circumstance (to which one might add the relative paucity of particles as syntactical indicators, as compared with Latin and Greek) created the illusion that Hebrew does not have any syntax at all. As a result, the Western non-Jewish Hebrew grammarians, such as the German H. Gesenius[150] (1786–1842), imposed on the material they were describing a system derived from their own inherited assumption that Latin syntax is the most complete expression of both logic and reality. It may be added that the same unconscious assumption (*mutatis mutandis*) animated the revivers of spoken Hebrew (themselves born into a German or Yiddish-speaking environment), who in turn injected into Hebrew a Western-type syntax and word-order that can sometimes obscure, for the contemporary vernacular speaker, the true meaning (or at any rate the real emphasis) of a pre-modern Hebrew text (see below, pp. 138f.).

It may not be altogether implausible to suggest that considerations partly overlapping with the foregoing deterred medieval Jewish scholars from attempting any taxonomy of syntactical devices. They may be credited with having rejected the assumption, implicit in the heritage of Rome, that all human speech communication and writing is governed by logic; and they are likely to have viewed with mistrust any assertion to that effect, as stemming from the essentially humanistic 'wisdom of the Greeks', for whom the Protagorean dictum that man is the measure of all things was axiomatic. Their own alternative, which they would surely have insisted was axiomatic to Judaism, would have been to claim that it is not logic that is of central significance but rather *response* – at the human level indeed, but more especially as between man and God: a response of which mankind as a whole is potentially capable, even if it were in practice limited to the Jewish situation and to Hebrew as the medium of communication. The vocation of the Jew is to respond to the spiritual challenge inherent in the revelational address that is propounded in a document emanating from the Deity, and formulated in the language of God Himself. Insofar as that challenge stimulates an intellectual concern with the vehicle in which revelation is expressed, i.e. the language of the Hebrew Bible, study of it will naturally concentrate on a relatively small canonical corpus; and even though its language may be considered the appropriate model for (at any rate liturgical) poetry, such study will be less open-ended than is the study of the *Qur'an* and the pre-islamic poets for the Muslim student of Arabic grammar, who will find his material appropriate for wide literary purposes.

The foregoing considerations may explain why an academic approach to Hebrew exercised so little influence on those medieval Jewish philosophers who felt called upon to give some account of the significance of Hebrew *qua* language; and they would probably have concurred with the folk saying later to be formulated in Yiddish, that anyone who studies *gemara* (i.e. the Talmud) with grammar, understands nothing about it. This holds good even for Sa'adyah, who was himself a grammarian (see pp. 116, 125), and for Judah Hallevi, who was a poet (see p. 126). In language as a medium of purely human communication they were scarcely interested. For them, the essential points were theological ones, and they had already been enunciated in the Talmud and other rabbinic writings. Broadly speaking, the contribution of the philosophers was to rehearse traditional Jewish ideas about Hebrew with a greater degree of articulation than that evinced in their own sources, which were dealing with language but incidentally. An extra metaphysical dimension was added by some of the kabbalists in their mystical superstructure erected on Jewish tradition (see below, pp. 132f.). Within the compass of this article, no more will be attempted than to give a thumbnail sketch of the views advanced by a few of the most important writers.

It seems right to start by taking a look at the brief and enigmatic but none the less influential *Sefer Yeṣirah*,[151] or 'Book of Creation'. Compiled by a Jewish neo-pythagorean between the third and sixth centuries CE, it shows affinities with gnostic writings, a specifically Jewish feature being the mystical power identified in the 22 letters of the Hebrew alphabet as constituting the instrument used by the Deity in order to effect creation. The complete alphabet – which, in its full sequence, is here deemed to be one of the divine names – is classified into three divisions; and the 231 possible combinations of two letters, considered to be 'elements' (cf. the double meaning of the Greek *στοιχεῖα*), are deemed to underlie all created entities. For present purposes, what is significant is the dominant position of the traditional notion of the Torah, itself pre-existently 'written' in an alphabetic script, as God's blueprint for creation. As we have seen (pp. 99-101), this is paralleled in tradition by the concept of the divine word (*dabhar*), utterance of which is imbued with creative efficacy. But while it seems reasonable to suppose that in the classical form of this tradition the written alphabet – even if conceived to be a mystical tool in the hands of the creator – will have been thought of as a system by means of which individual words may be analysed, in the *Sefer Yeṣirah* the picture is inverted: and the alphabet is viewed as constituting those elements without which there could be none of the combinations that render possible articulate speech. Thus, the overriding interest is not in linguistics but in cosmogony. And the substantial number of medieval commentaries on the *Sefer Yeṣirah* emphasizes the fact that even those philosophers of Judaism who might set out from basically linguistic premises to account for the significance of Hebrew, are liable to have the orbit of their thinking captured by the magnetic pull of the cosmological function of the Torah, as being a document that the Deity saw fit to encode in Hebrew.

Sa'adyah b. Joseph (882–942), better known as Sa'adya Ga'on, who was born in Egypt and rose to scholarly eminence amid the so-called 'Babylonian' Jewry of Iraq, wrote his Arabic *summa* of Judaism (*amanat wa-'iqtidat*,[152] generally translated 'Beliefs and opinions' but rather meaning 'beliefs and obligations arising out of conviction') under the impact of the mu'tazilite *kalam*. His work exercised great influence, particularly upon the Jewish neoplatonists, and, as translated into Hebrew, on the Jewish *intelligentsia* down the centuries. His concern for the religious obligation to make responsible use of reason subsumes an awareness of the need for the accurate use of language and the understanding of idiom, and in particular of the idiom of biblical Hebrew.[153] But although Sa'adyah was himself the author of works on Hebrew grammar and lexicography, in his *magnum opus* he is not especially interested either in language in general or in Hebrew in particular. It is, however, noteworthy that in the context of a purely philosophical discussion of cognition he states, on the lines of the *Sefer Yeṣirah* noted above, that the articulate sounds produced by man 'consist' of the 22 letters of the (Hebrew) alphabet[154] (he did use Arabic script, but probably also wrote Arabic in the Hebrew alphabet: see above, p. 102, n. 32). This becomes more significant in that in his own, earlier commentary on the *Sefer Yeṣirah*[155] he had endeavoured to play down its system of 'alphabetical cosmology' in favour of conventional scientific atomic theory.[156] In connection with Sa'adyah's reference to human articulacy, it is pertinent to note that of the terms applied in the Hebrew version to translate Aristotelian psychology, one of the equivalents for the 'rational' (διανοητική) soul is *dabberanith*, i.e. 'endowed with speech'. It is perhaps first attested in the twelfth-century Hebrew translation of the *Improvement of Moral Qualities* (*Tiqqun middoth ha-nefesh*) of Solomon ibn Gabirol, the original Arabic of which was probably written in 1068. The word is similarly used in translations of philosophical texts to indicate humanity as opposed to the animal kingdom.[157]

Before we consider Sa'adyah's followers, it is apposite to take note that in its post-classical period (c. 1010–c. 1258) Arabic literature developed, alongside strictly philological writings, an interest in rhetoric and poetics. In the same way that the language of the *Qur'an* had been regarded as the perfect prototype for all Arabic, so pre-islamic poetry came to be considered the pre-eminently classical model worthy of emulation. The parallel in Judaism of reverence for the diction of the Hebrew Bible needs no elaboration; but it would be strange if Muslim interest in these topics, which was notably intense in Spain, had not stimulated Jewish writers to apply to Hebrew some of the critical categories that were establishing themselves in Arabic.[158]

Judah Hallevi (before 1075–1141) is generally regarded as the greatest of the medieval Hebrew poets. The power of his religious hymns, and in particular the pathos of his odes to Zion, combined with the idealism that led him to forsake his native Spain for Palestine (which he probably, but not certainly reached) has brought about his romanticization by Jewish folk-memory; and no doubt it is this circumstance that is principally responsible for his dialogue, the *Kuzari* (written by him in Arabic and later translated into Hebrew) being acclaimed as a major contribution to the philosophy of Judaism. In point of fact, the *Kuzari* is a work of apologetics written by one who, although well read in the philosophical literature available in Arabic, was content to beg all the essential questions, regarding them as his premises. In his poetry, Judah Hallevi displays a masterly control of the Arabic metrical schemes which his predecessors had adapted to fit the morphology of massoretically vocalized biblical Hebrew (see p. 114). It may be doubted whether he would have been temperamentally capable of writing his *Kuzari* in Hebrew himself: the technical vocabulary for translation into Hebrew of scientific and philosophical works written by both Jews and non-Jews in Arabic was being evolved largely in the century following his death.[159] These facts have to be appreciated if the paradox inherent in what Judah Hallevi has to say about language in general and Hebrew in particular is to be understood.

He starts, as one would expect, from the traditional position.[160] Abraham, at the confusion of tongues that followed the *débâcle* of the Tower of Babel, retained the primeval language (for religious purposes: see below). Articulate speech is not an eternal phenomenon:[161] all languages originated in a conventional manner, as is indicated by the fact that all of them form the various parts of speech – verbs, nouns, and so on. But it is in the second part of the *Kuzari*, in the context of a discussion of the importance of science, that Judah Hallevi is led – by way of admission that the world of his own experience associated science pre-eminently with Greece and Rome – to deal at greater length with the historical significance and the nature of the Hebrew language.[162] All the sciences popularly associated with the Greeks, and so on, stem ultimately from Israel, but the Jews had lost their original knowledge of them. Hebrew holds primacy among the languages, both in virtue of having been itself created and instituted by God and because of its fullness of meaning. In its original (i.e. biblical) form it is, indeed, the noblest of all languages, but it has degenerated, therein sharing the fortune of those that speak it. Abraham employed Hebrew for sacred purposes only, and in everyday speech used Aramaic (this seems to be a detail of Judah Hallevi's own invention). This language was brought, by his son Ishmael, to the Arabs, and hence the close cognate relationship of Hebrew, Aramaic and Arabic. The spiritual and intellectual stature of Moses and the prophets, of David and Solomon, renders it inconceivable that they could have been at all frustrated in verbal self-expression. Biblical Hebrew, together with its method of cantillation according to the massoretic accents (which Judah Hallevi takes for granted as co-eval with the origin of the text itself), represents the acme of oral communication, which is superior to written communication; and in virtue of being thus provided with accentual scoring, Hebrew is superior to the external poetic forms which other languages have to impose upon the sense of the words. Israel is to be criticized for its own contrariness in yielding to assimilative temptation and imitating [Arabic] prosody – as Judah Hallevi claims, forcing Hebrew into its mould, despite the adaptation noticed above (p. 126). 'Instead of being satisfied with the superiority mentioned above, we corrupted the structure of our language, which is built on harmony, and created discord'.[163]

Sentiments similar to Judah Hallevi's likewise animated Judah b. Solomon al-Ḥarizi ('The Rhymester', 1170–1235), his junior by about a century and, like him, a Spaniard who travelled through Palestine and the near east. But the thrust of al-Ḥarizi's criticism of his own people diverges from Judah Hallevi's; and whereas the latter deprecates his own subservience to the influence of Arabic poetic form, al-Ḥarizi finds Arabic literary influence both positive and indeed challenging. He was himself one of the pioneers of Hebrew translation literature, and produced the earlier version of Maimonides' *Guide for the Perplexed.* He also rendered into Hebrew the *maqamas* of Abu Muḥammad al-Ḥariri of Basra (1054–1122), which by the beginning of the century were already a literary classic in Moorish Spain. The *maqama* form (literally *session*, i.e. of anecdotage) is a bellelettristic convention in which is set a short story, written in rhyming prose; and al-Ḥarizi's experience in translating al-Ḥariri stimulated him to parallel (rather than slavishly imitate) the *genre* in Hebrew. He consequently produced (after 1220) a collection of such pieces, entitled *Sefer Taḥkemoni* ('A Book for Savants'). In his introduction (reminiscent in some ways of the *Satires* of Horace) he criticized the Jewish people not, as Judah Hallevi had alleged, for debasing biblical Hebrew, but rather for abandoning Hebrew altogether. A German translation published in 1845[164] substituted for the medium of rhymed prose regular rhymed couplets. In view of the rarity today of that publication, a straightforward though abbreviated English version is given here. Although the biblical imagery and allusiveness[165] with which al-Ḥarizi's style is replete cannot be effectively reproduced, hopefully a faint echo of the charm of his writing shows through the following rendering of his account of his own 'call', which he models on the biblical story[166] of how Abraham's servant identified Rebecca as a suitable wife for Isaac:[167]

> I was sleeping, but my heart was wakeful. Intelligence aroused me, bidding me bestir myself to gird me in zeal for the Lord of Hosts and the Holy Tongue – the language which the prophets spoke, now fallen on such disastrous times. 'Renew Thou her youth', said Intelligence, 'heal the wounds made in her by the fangs of infidel lions'. I protested my own unworthiness; constant travel had confused both my thinking and my powers of verbal expression. 'Nay', replied Intelligence, 'I will be at thy side: and all thy folk shall perceive the tremendous, God-inspired feats that I shall perform through thee.' Whereupon Intelligence touched my lips, as Isaiah's were once touched, with its searing coal, saying, 'behold, I have set my word in thy mouth, to be prophet of poetry to the gentiles'. Thus it was that God stirred up my spirit, to kindle from the effulgence of his very Presence a candle for the Holy Tongue, that all might know that it is beyond compare for the clarity of its vocabulary and for the aesthetic pleasure of its literary conceits – a veritable bride, decked out in figures of speech, her train perfumed with myrrh . . .
>
> In times past, the saints of the Most High took pleasure in the Holy Tongue; but nowadays, the rabble amongst our own folk, their taste having gone all sour, rain their dagger-blows upon it. Her sons have all abandoned their own language, becoming mere stammerers; so that every day she weeps her heart out to deaf ears, saying, with Jeremiah, 'what ill have ye found in me that ye have distanced yourselves from me – from me, that self-same language in which God spoke to your fathers? I it was that was then the intermediary; for though it was God's breath that formed the words that wrote themselves on the tablets of stone, it was in my language that they were engraved there. So long as God's glory dwelt in his temple, I was his consort: but your children have spurned me, becoming enamoured of the language of strangers – sacrificing to false gods, exchanging the speech of Israel for

the speech of the bedouin and saying, like Joseph's brethren, 'come, let us sell him to the Ishmaelites' . . .

I therefore bestirred myself to restore her fortunes, and arriving one day at a well, I uttered a prayer. 'Lord God', said I, 'let it so turn out that to whichever of these water-nymphs – discernment's daughters and the maids of mystery – I shall say, "give me, prithee, to drink of those mellifluous fountains of speech that flow from thy lips", and she shall say, "drink!" – let her prove to be the one whom Thou hast marked out for thy servant.' No sooner had I finished speaking to myself when there came a maiden, one of the daughters of wisdom, fair as the sun, with her pitcher on her shoulder. 'Drink', said she, 'from the fountain of my thoughts, for 'tis milk and honey beneath my tongue.' I asked her whose daughter she might be. 'An orphan am I, albeit my sire still lives', quoth she; 'my brothers – my own mother's sons – have scorned me. Time was that I was a very diadem, who am now no more than a doormat. I am thy true queen, the Holy Tongue: and, if thou wilt, I will be thy companion to glorify God and to render holy that great name of mine that the House of Israel have desecrated.' Whereupon I bowed down to God, and set my praises as her ear-rings and my own fairest language for her necklet, betrothing her to me in reverence and righteousness. And so, in course of time, she bore a child in God's very likeness: and the government was upon his shoulder, as the spirit of the Lord began to impel him, like Samson . . .

Now the occasion of my writing this book was as follows. Amongst the intellectuals of the Ishmaelites one of the foremost minds was al-Ḥariri. He was gifted with an easy-running, graceful Arabic style that threw all his rivals into the shade. He wrote a book – in Arabic, to be sure, although all its subject-matter and its figures of speech really derive from our own literature; so that were one to ask of any turn of phrase that he uses, 'what brought thee to the shores of Araby's tongue?', it must needs reply, like Joseph, 'I was indeed stolen from the land of the Hebrews'. No sooner had I seen this book than my heavens of joy were rolled up into glowering clouds that distilled raindrops heavy with mourning, as I considered how all other peoples are so punctilious about not offending against the canons of their language, whereas our tongue, once the envy of all eyes, is now reckoned a mere spent breath: its beauty become a reproach, its one-time grace taken for a curse, scoffed at by our own folk as being inadequate in power of expression and deficient in literary devices. Little do they realise that its alleged shortcomings reflect their own incapacity to understand it . . . I have consequently written this book to demonstrate to the holy people the power of the Holy Tongue. I have included in it many metaphorical conceits and items of essentially aesthetic significance – figures of speech, enigmas, apophthegms, poems, etc. – as well as reading the riot act, producing pictures of everyday life, *memento mori*, the importance of forgiving, the delights of love, a touch or two of ribald verse, wine, women and song, heroes locked in combat, the vicissitudes of kings, moral philosophy, the wiles of tricksters and the gullibility of their

> victims, and so on. The intention is that the book should be a garden of delights suited to all tastes . . . Those who themselves would fain write poetry, but succeed merely in hacking out broken cisterns in which to store brackish water, will find here a tree which, when thrown in, renders the water sweet . . . It is a book that should prove its worth wherever there are to be found those who can but limp their way through the Holy Tongue, mouthing it barbarically; for it can straighten their path and correct their speech, opening their eyes to their own folly so that they may realise that they are naked, and so, by stitching for themselves some fig-leaves of poetic language, they may make them girdles to conceal their shame. Unless I have overlooked something, there is nothing in this book that has been taken from the Arabic prototype, which many before have essayed to translate into the Holy Tongue . . . until I attempted the task . . . at the request of the [Jewish] grandees of Spain, who were so struck by the Arabic original that they asked me to translate it.[168] I could not disappoint them; but after completing the work I travelled beyond the seas, and I came to realise my own folly – and indeed my fault – in neglecting to produce a book consisting of our own literary treasures, choosing instead to translate those of others: as if God's living words were not to be found in our own midst. So, after having been in such a hurry to tend the vineyard of strangers whilst neglecting my own, I have now written this book, composed in a new style of literary flourish that is nonetheless sanctified by the Holy Tongue, in order to restore the language's dry bones to life.

It is hard to exaggerate the significance of this introduction. Acceptance of the validity of the myth of the origin of language is here tempered by realism, and linguistic chauvinism is checked by acknowledgement – in the spirit of the 'four languages' passage discussed above (pp. 104f.) – that other cultures as well can vaunt literary achievements worthy of inspiring a creative adaptation in Hebrew.

Moses b. Maimon (Maimonides, or, in Hebrew, acronymically, '*RaMbaM*'), who was born in Cordoba in 1135, lived mainly in Egypt, where he died in 1204; and the impact which he made upon his own generation has proved a continuing force in Jewish traditional life and thought ever since. Although he had by the age of sixteen composed a *Treatise on Logic*, Maimonides does not appear to have been particularly interested in language as such. In his (Arabic) *Guide for the Perplexed* he links an assertion that languages are conventional, and not natural 'as some have thought', with the biblical statement (Gen. 2,20) that it was Adam who assigned names to the animals.[169] In another passage, where sinfulness in thought as opposed to action is under review,[170] he makes the point that ribaldry in speech is to be shunned: God's gift of a 'tongue of learning' (*Isaiah* 50,4) should not be degraded by application to lascivious talk. It is not for nothing that Hebrew is called 'the holy language', since it is deficient in explicit terms for the generative organs, and so on, in referring to which it uses allusive or surrogate terms. (Maimonides is here carrying to its logical conclusion the earlier rabbinic observation of an alleged biblical tendency towards euphemism in such connections).[171] For him, as essentially for rabbinic Judaism throughout, the primary function of Hebrew is as a medium of communication between man and God. In his great compendium of Jewish law, the *Mishneh Torah*,[172] he says that the basic features of the statutory Jewish liturgy were formulated by Ezra (i.e. in the fifth century BCE) as a measure of reform; because of the Babylonian captivity and the developing diaspora, Jewish competence in Hebrew had become eroded by use of various vernaculars, so that those invited to take the lead in prayer were no longer capable of accurate Hebrew improvization. A fixed form of prayer was consequently needed in order to obviate their difficulties.

Maimonides' explanation of the conventional title of 'the holy language' for Hebrew was criticized by Moses b. Naḥman (Naḥmanides, *'RaMbaN'*) of Gerona (1194–1270), himself an anti-Christian apologist, mediator in the controversy to which Maimonides' *Guide* gave rise, and a bible-commentator who, while adopting a rationalist approach to the text, appreciated that if rationalism is to have any theological significance, it must be subsumed in and indeed transcended by a spiritually aware exegetical dimension. Commenting on the poll-tax of 'half a shekel of the "holy sheqel" [i.e. temple] standard' instituted by Moses for census-taking purposes,[173] he comments as follows:

> Moses established a silver coinage in Israel and called its unit a *sheqel* (i.e. *weight*), since the entire issue of specie was of full weight and unadulterated. Since that standard was applicable for holy purposes such as the redemption of first-born sons . . . scripture styles it the *holy* shekel. In my view, the same consideration accounts for the language of the Torah being styled by our sages 'the holy language', since it was the medium in which the Torah itself, prophecy, and all other sacred matters were communicated, as well as being the language in which the Holy One, blessed be He, spoke to his prophets and addressed the Ten Commandments to his own congregation. It is also the language in which were formed the divine names (*'elohim*, etc.) including that unique, ineffable Name through voicing which He effected creation and assigned names to heaven, earth, and all that is in them,[174] likewise to his angels and the heavenly host – Michael, Gabriel, etc. – as well as to the biblical heroes – the patriarchs, Solomon, etc. [for all of which names

Hebrew etymologies can be found]. The argument of the Master (i.e. Maimonides) that Hebrew is styled 'holy' because of its lack of explicit words for the sexual organs, etc. . . . is superfluous; for it is manifest that the language is the holiest of the holy for the reasons that I have set forth. Indeed, his own reasoning is faulty, since the very fact of there being massoretic directives for the substitution of innocuous synonyms for terms considered to be indelicate, as at, e.g. Deut. 28,30, indicates that the suppressed term is indeed itself explicit.

4.7 The cabbalistic transformer

Naḥmanides forms an appropriate bridge over which to pass on to a brief consideration of the significance of the Hebrew language for cabbalism. The *kabbalah* may be defined as a theosophical superstructure which presupposes institutional Judaism with all its self-expression through forms of worship and exuberant jurisprudence, but finds these, in themselves, to be spiritually incomplete. While the sense of privilege with which the *kabbalah*, together with non-mystical Judaism, accepts the discipline of halakhic observance excludes anti-nomianism, some of the more advanced notions of the cabbalists would, in due course, come to be exploited by an anti-nomian movement itself articulated on basically non-mystical premises. The terms of reference of the *kabbalah* being as they are, it is not surprising that it takes over the evaluation of Hebrew current in conventional rabbinic Judaism, but enhances it by jettisoning the recognition of the philosophers that all language has a conventional origin. The following formulation, by Scholem, is unsurpassable:[175]

Kabbalists . . . regard . . . language as something more precious than an inadequate instrument for contact between human beings. To them Hebrew, the holy tongue, is not simply a means of expressing certain thoughts, born out of a certain convention and having a purely conventional character, in accordance with the theory of language dominant in the Middle Ages. Language in its purest form, that is, Hebrew, according to the Kabbalists, reflects the fundamental spiritual nature of the world; in other words, it has a mystical value. Speech reaches God because it comes from God. All creation – and this is an important principle of most Kabbalists – is, from the point of view of God, nothing but an expression of His hidden self that begins and ends by giving itself a name, the holy name of God, the perpetual act of creation. All that lives is an expression of God's language – and what is it that Revelation can reveal in the last resort if not the name of God?

As in conventional Judaism, then, the notions of language and the Torah can scarcely be disentangled: but

> Torah does not so much mean anything specific, though it in fact means many different things on many different levels, as it articulates a universe of being ... The true essence of the Torah ... is defined in the Kabbalah according to three basic principles: the Torah is the complete mystical name of God; the Torah is a living organism; and the divine speech is infinitely significant, and no finite human speech can ever exhaust it.[176]

This vastly enriched spiritual potentiality of the Torah is released by the introduction of a new dimension, constructed out of the midrashic (i.e. exegetical) imagery of the 'fiery law'[177] received by Israel at Sinai as having consisted of a document 'written' in black fire on white.[178] Out of this conceit is drawn the idea that the text of the Torah, as we know it, is merely the result of the pre-created[179] quality of the Torah having been rendered, so to speak, 'corporeal' at the time of Adam's sin. Prior to that, the sequence of letters in the Torah (the principle of the primeval 'immutability' of which had to be safeguarded) had been quite otherwise, so that, for example, the prohibitions now to be found in it were quite different in import. In the messianic age it will once again cast off its garments, and become spiritually renovated and deepened.[180]

The mystical profundity of this metaphysical scheme was rendered yet more profound by the extremely daring notion of the 'missing letter' of the Hebrew alphabet. This idea is quoted by David ibn Abi Zimra ('*RaDbaZ*'), 1479–1593, one of the Spanish exiles in 1492, in his book *Maghen Dawid*,[181] a work the ideas in which go back to the same cabbalistic circles that produced the *Sefer ha-temunah*[182] in Catalonia around 1250. This twenty-third letter of the alphabet was present in the Torah during the previous cosmic cycle and will re-appear there in the next. Because of its being obscured in the Torah of our own experience, there are to be found therein the positive and negative ordinances, every prohibition being connected with the fact that this letter is temporarily missing.[183] The cabbalistic technique of meditation on the permutations and combinations of letters is here to be observed utilizing material that is essentially, integrally, and indeed idiosyncratically Jewish in order to find a means of enunciating a sublimity of truth in the way that other great creative artists have found the idiom of their self-expression in music.

4.8 Renaissance illusions: Haskalah and Aufklärung

The beginning of the modern period of Jewish history is marked by the impact on entrepreneurial capitalism in Europe, from the seventeenth century, of Jewish emigrants from the Iberian peninsula. It is marked, too, by the cultural consequences of progressive Jewish social integration in Holland and, in the later eighteenth century, in Germany, which percolated through a broader – though still numerically small – segment of north European Jewry. Such is the background to the emergence of the *haskalah* ('enlightenment'), at first in Germany in the wake of *Aufklärung*, to spread early in the nineteenth century to the demographically far stronger Jewish communities of Russia and Poland. The attitude towards Hebrew of the *maskilim*, as the devotees of *haskalah* were called, was very much that of the European Renaissance towards classical Latin, with similar assumptions as to linguistic purity as a panacæa for social and other ills: and it is not fanciful to compare its leading exponents – Moses Mendelssohn, N. H. Wessely, and their associates – with Pico della Mirandola, Erasmus and More. Their motivation was educative; and they were concerned, while promoting the cultivation of Hebrew, also to breach the popular Jewish siege mentality in regard to German culture. Although their moderate iconoclasm with respect to Jewish institutions was anything but anti-nomian, it evoked opposition from the rabbinical establishment which sensed – correctly – that the movement was pregnant with the seeds of religious reform. Its secular Hebrew products were, as the parallel with classicism would suggest, biblicizing (and consequently somewhat stilted) in language, while in form and content they imitated contemporary European models. It is in this period that the Hebrew novel makes its first appearance,[184] but of greater significance is the foundation in 1783 of the literary Hebrew periodical *Ha-me'assef* ('the Rearguard').[185] Journalism is of crucial importance, since in the nineteenth century there emerged – partly under the tutelage of the Yiddish press – a significant number of Hebrew newspapers whose interests were not confined to intellectual and literary matters, and whose contributors, representing more authentically than did the *maskilim* the voice of the Yiddish-speaking masses of eastern Europe, were not animated by ideals of classicism in Hebrew, but were concerned rather to carry forward, through the medium of both journalism and literature, the down-to-earth awareness in the Talmud and rabbinic Jewish culture generally of the importance of the daily round in Jewish life. This does not (as yet) amount to a tension with *haskalah*, since there is no particular interest here in language *per se*, but rather the traditional Jewish awareness of language as a dimension of ethnicity[186] is taken for granted.

4.9 The handmaiden of nineteenth-century nationalism

The subsuming – or rather transformation – of these attitudes into a frankly nationalist approach to Hebrew is, of course, the achievement of Zionism over the last hundred years – Leon Pinsker's (German) *Auto-emancipation* appeared in 1882. Although Zionism is a phenomenon *sui generis*, its study may be usefully approached by viewing it as a mutation of the nationalist movements that emerged in Europe in the nineteenth century. Of the factors which fused, making it possible to convert the perennial Jewish awareness of love of Zion, as being one of the mainsprings of Judaism, into a political force, several are closely linked to language and its evaluation.[187] These may be summarily reviewed.

Of the emergent nationalisms within the Austro-Hungarian empire and its Turkish flank, several found in their ethnical language a major focus of their identity. The case of Greece affords an instructive parallel to the containment, noticed above, of the purism of Hebrew *haskalah* by traditional idiom, that is the organic continuation of the rabbinic form of the language known from late antiquity: a language fully capable of developing its own neologisms and of extending its vocabulary by adoption and adaptation of loan-words, but not yet thinking of itself as 'modernizing'. Greek aspirations towards national independence coincided with the movement to promote 'purist' Greek (*katharevousa*)[188] – an artificial revival, thinking of itself as the prolongation of the late classical Greek of the period following Alexander the Great that had been maintained in the Byzantine empire. The early *katharevousa* abounded in false archaisms, hyper-corrections, and so on, and its doctrinaire classicism rendered it self-defeating as a vernacular, particularly since the role of the Peloponnese in the Greek war of independence had elevated the demotic Peloponnesian dialects into the basis of a national language. After the middle of the nineteenth century a somewhat modified *katharevousa* continued in official publications and for certain other purposes, while also being taught as 'correct' in schools, but from 1917 demotic was taught in the lower forms. Subsequent political upheavals have restored and dethroned *katharevousa*, while already before 1917 a compromise form of the language (*mik*[*h*]*te*) had been developing in which demotic is the dominant partner. The result is that *katharevousa*, *mikte*, and *demotike* co-exist in different registers of the written language, and newspapers (at any rate up to 1967) would evince all three forms in different sections of the same issue. The important point of comparison with the reactions within Jewry to *haskalah* Hebrew is that the protagonists of Greek liberation found their real inspiration in the Greek life and literature of which Byzantine Christianity under the Turk had been the focus (the counterpart, on the Jewish side, of the Talmud and institutions of rabbinic Judaism); and they judged it unnecessary to disillusion Byron and the western philhellenes, who had convinced themselves that the cause which their heroes had espoused was animated by the spirit of Periclean Athens.[189]

Nor can the latest phases of Jewish history – and consequently also of Jewish 'philosophy' of the Hebrew language – be understood without reference to the French Revolution, which brought political emancipation to French Jews and gave a fillip to the agitation for political emancipation of Jews in other countries of western Europe, in some of which (e.g. England) pragmatic, social emancipation was already far advanced. Jewish acknowledgement – explicit in the proceedings of the 'Sanhedrin' convened by Napoleon in 1806 – was implicit in the extension of the franchise to Jews by the countries of their domicile, that they renounced pretensions to any Jewish nationality, or at any rate were prepared to consign its realization to the conveniently remote and misty vistas of a messianic *dénouement*: with the corollary that they should, without prejudice to their religious observances, integrate culturally into their host environment, not least in the matter of accepting the standard form of its vernacular and the use of that, rather than Yiddish, and so on, as the medium of Jewish education. Such an abdication of 'national' identity would not have been acceptable to the Yiddish-speaking masses of eastern Europe, and in any case it was not seriously on offer to them in Russia even under Alexander II. The result of the pogroms in Russia in the 1880s, combined with the effect of Jewish over-population there, was to set myriads of Jews migrating westwards, to affect with their own attitude in this matter significant sectors of the emancipated Jewries in Western Europe and the United States of America among whom they found refuge. It was as the representative of their outlook that the humane Zionist thinker Ahad Ha'am (Asher Ginzberg, 1856–1927), who settled in London and finally in Palestine, wrote in 1891 that abdication of realistic Jewish aspirations to national sovereignty in exchange for political emancipation on western lines was not a price that the Jewish people as a whole were prepared to pay.[190] This background meant that the incipient efforts of Ben-Yehuda and his devotees to 'modernize' (in effect, to westernize the syntax and word-order of Hebrew) fell on fertile ground, to be taken seriously right across the Jewish world, instead of being ridiculed as the fond endeavour of a band of well-meaning but harmless enthusiasts.

What were the internal Jewish forces that rendered the enterprise of modernizing Hebrew so much more successful (judged on its own premises) than other nationalistically motivated language-revivals, notably Irish Gaelic? Fundamental, of course, was the traditional *Sehnsucht* for Zion which had hitherto found expression, since Roman times, in religious terms and messianic dreams only. But an eschatology that envisages divine intervention at the climax of history which will rebuild the temple and re-gather the exiles can easily enough take in its stride the assumption that those ultimately to be gathered in would find themselves miraculously speaking Hebrew with mutual intelligibility. However, messianism apart, there were also significant demographic factors at work under contemporary eyes. The Ladino-speaking Sephardi settlements in Jerusalem, Safed, and so on, which dated back to the early sixteenth century, were being reinforced by a steadily increasing trickle of elderly Ashkenazim intent on passing their last years in study at Jerusalem as their Benares, and, towards the end of the century, of young pioneer colonists, mainly from Russia, whose mother-tongue was Yiddish; and, not surprisingly, it was to Hebrew rather than to Arabic that Sephardim and Ashkenazim turned for mutual communication. Hebrew as a spoken language thus had a pre-history that ante-dates Ben-Yehuda;[191] and as Jewish colonization sponsored by western Jewish philanthropy increased, the language revival enjoyed the support and enthusiastic approbation of the *Ḥobhebhey Ṣiyyon* ('Lovers of Zion')[192] – an international forerunner of the Zionist movement, overtaken and displaced by the latter before 1914. Literary history falls outside the scope of this survey: but alongside the vibrating life of the progressively more self-confident and politically more self-aware Jewish settlements in Palestine, the output of Hebrew writers in Russia and elsewhere (particularly in Odessa) was a most powerful factor in the revival of Hebrew. The poetry of the traditionally-minded Ḥayyim Naḥman Bialik (1873–1934), who left Russia to settle in Palestine and to be acclaimed as the 'national poet' of modern Hebrew; that of the violently iconoclastic Saul Tchernichowsky (1875–1943), who emigrated to Palestine in 1931; the philosophical essayist Ahad Ha'am already referred to; the writings of the journalist and Zionist publicist Nahum Sokolow (1859–1936), and such influential Hebrew periodicals as *Ha-shiloaḥ* ('Siloam')[193] – items such as these cannot be left out of account in this context. As the dates show, all of those listed here were active well into the final phase of Zionist history which, preceding the declaration of independent Israeli statehood in 1948, had long been thoroughly politicized in its aims and its attitude towards the language; but because of their historical *Sitz im Leben*, they constitute a bridge between old and new.

The latest stages – in which the *crescendo* of enthusiasm for Hebrew, and the greatly increased number of those who can speak and read it, are due to factors mainly external to Jewry – may be briefly summarized. Eliezer Ben-Yehuda's single-minded campaign to turn Hebrew into a self-reliant and comprehensive Jewish vernacular marches alongside endeavours both cultural and political. The idea of a Jewish university at Jerusalem had been mooted as early as 1884, and serious planning for what proclaimed itself, in the unmistakeable terms of a manifesto, 'the Hebrew University', began in 1913. When, in 1923, Albert Einstein delivered the first lecture under its auspices, he himself managed to introduce it with a few sentences spoken in Hebrew. With the rapid growth of the university and the Haifa Technion, especially after 1948, and the distinction of many of the scholars and scientists on the academic staff, the importance of the university as a contributing factor to the extension of the modern Hebrew vocabulary has been generally recognized. The political efforts of Herzl and his associates (whose *lingua franca* was mainly German), from the first Zionist congress in 1897, via its successors and the Balfour Declaration of the British government in 1917 that viewed with favour the establishment of a Jewish national home in Palestine, reached a landmark with the setting up in 1920 of the British mandatory government. The previous year A. M. Ussishkin had insisted, when addressing the Paris peace conference as a Jewish delegate, on speaking Hebrew. An already increased flow of colonists (*ḥaluṣim*, 'pioneers') from eastern Europe was henceforth substantially swollen by others, also inspired by Zionist ideals, including immigrants from western countries where they had received secondary and in some cases also university education; and after Hitler's accession to power in Germany in 1933 this became a flood, temporarily checked by British sensitivity to Arab opposition and then starkly interrupted by the Second World War, to be followed by the convergence on Palestine (from 1948 the independent State of Israel) of the pitiful remnant of European Jewries that Hitler had sought to exterminate.

4.10 The dethronement of tradition

The significance of this great wave of demographic change lies, for our purposes, in the circumstance that the approach of those who constituted it to Hebrew and the evaluation of its history was much more heterogeneous than that of those who had emigrated to Palestine before the early 1930s. It could be presumed that most of the earlier immigrants had received a significant amount of Jewish education or background, and that (at any rate in the case of the men) they possessed some degree of familiarity with liturgical Hebrew, even if some of them adopted a negative stance *vis-à-vis* Jewish traditional institutions and values. Of the later arrivals, both those impelled by Zionist idealism and those merely seeking a refuge from persecution, a large proportion possessed no such background; and indeed, a substantial number were not particularly concerned to come to terms with an institutional system integrally linked with religious values, which they were in some instances actively concerned to repudiate or erode. The primary demand of this wave of immigration was to acquire a knowledge of Hebrew on the same terms that they might, as immigrants, have needed to master English, French, or Spanish; and the effect of their needs was to intensify the (already well advanced) process of the westernization of Hebrew syntax, and so on. For those with psychological links and residual loyalties to Jewish tradition and the organically developed Hebrew that had nurtured it, this process of westernization – and consequent secularization – was the more easily dissembled from themselves because of the tenacity of modern Hebrew in the matter of vocabulary; the old lexical *thesaurus* was used as a base on which to build neologisms as far as possible, comparably to the principles of *katharevousa* Greek, and this circumstance would take the spotlight off syntactical nonchalance for all except a tiny minority sensitive to philological niceties. This *tendenz* was reinforced, naturally enough, by the linguistic by-products of technological development, immigrant absorption, and defence, as well as by the general awareness on the part of the population of Hebrew as a substantive dimension of the national existence, and of the importance of fostering the growth of a modern Israeli literature and scientific language of a kind that should put minimal obstacles in the path of those wishing to translate them into Western languages: facilitation of mutual intelligibility with speakers of Arabic has not stood high on the scale of priorities. All this explains the extent of the influence exercised by the *Wa'adh ha-lashon* (Academy of the Hebrew Language),[194] founded originally in 1890, refounded in 1903, and established as the 'supreme institute' for the Hebrew language by an act of the *keneseth* (Israeli parliament) in 1953. Operating through specialist committees for terminological coinages, as propounder of approved neologisms and as the decisive voice in such matters as simplified orthography, the Academy has been accorded by the Israeli public a self-disciplined response that has invested it with an authority surpassing anything ever exercised by the *Académie Française*. The result of the confluence of all these factors is that the small minority, both within and beyond the State of Israel, who insist on preserving an unmodernized Hebrew that is syntactically efficient while retaining its organic bond with the fibres of the traditional language, are regarded by the Hebrew-speaking majority – whether with amused indulgence, or with impatience – as no more than fossilized curiosities.

There is, however, one voice which the massed bands that accompany the linguistic flag-wavers have not succeeded in drowning out. Franz Rosenzweig (1886–1929), who had been born into a family only nominally Jewish, and who had contemplated conversion to Christianity, discovered his essential Jewish being while preparing to take that step and abandoned the plan, thereafter devoting his life to the exploration and exposition of Judaism at a theologically sensitive level, informed by all that was best in pre-1914 German liberal education. Best known for his *Der Stern der Erlösung*,[195] begun on post-cards written from the front during the First World War, and for his collaboration with Martin Buber in producing a new German translation of the Hebrew Bible, Rosenzweig had to struggle during his last eight years with progressive paralysis: and the pathos of his own heroic determination to continue writing, combined with his influence on a remarkable band of associates in a Jewish educational endeavour in Frankfurt am Main in the 1920s, are in part responsible for the fulfilment of his prophecy, 'only posthumously shall I wholly speak out'.[196] Himself a very sensitive translator, who had rendered poems by Judah Hallevi (see above, p. 126) into German, Rosenzweig felt himself existentially confronted by language as a human phenomenon, and also challenged by the impossibility and the ineluctable obligation of translating.[197] His understanding of what ought to be implied by a culturally and Jewishly responsible endeavour to expand, and thereby to modernize Hebrew was infinitely more sophisticated than that characteristic of those who addressed themselves to the task being themselves impelled by political considerations. In 1926 Rosenzweig used the occasion of reviewing Jacob Klatzkin's Hebrew translation of Spinoza's *Ethics*[198] to indicate some of his misgivings about the way things were going. The following extracts may be usefully rehearsed here:[199]

> Within Zionist theory, Klatzkin is the leading representative of what he himself calls a 'formal nationalism', i.e. a nationalism that denies the Jewish heritage any claim whatsoever on the new generation about to assume it. He does not expect national rebirth to spring from anything but the future – from the miraculous powers of race, soil, and, above all, language. But thus presented, these three factors become so 'purely formal', so utterly devoid of substance, that the modern rationalist's

belief in miracles must needs surpass that which tradition demanded of the Jews of old . . . Klatzkin tends to deprecate his choice of medieval Jewish terminology [in his own translation], which is solely responsible for bringing these fruits within his reach . . . Yet in his second appendix, equally interesting from the viewpoint of language and of philosophy, he gives the lie to his cool hypothesis . . . The truth that Hebrew is the holy language of the holy people, and the untruth that it is the spoken language of a people like all other peoples, seem irreconcilable. But Jewish reality makes both the truth and the untruth dependent upon each other . . . The holiness of the Hebrew language never signified holiness in the original sense of 'seclusion' . . . The holy language, the language of God, has always drawn strength for renewal from the spoken language, from the spoken languages of man; . . . Hebrew . . . always stayed alive. The Hebrew of the Torah . . . the pious sobriety of Maimonides . . . the historicism of the *Haskalah* in the historical nineteenth century – all this is Hebrew . . . By the fabric of language so wrought, the Holy of Holies of this sacerdotal people is both veiled from and indicated to the eyes of the world. The difference between its vitality and the vitality of a profane language is that nothing once received into it can ever be lost. The . . . other languages must obey the law of a continual and at times critical self-purification . . . But the life of the eternal language unfolds exactly like that of the people. It does not proceed in a sequence of deaths and resurrections . . . It endures because it cannot, it will not, and may not, die. Nothing that has become an integral part of it is ever discarded . . . one cannot read Klatzkin's *Spinoza*, or even a Hebrew newspaper, without deriving something that would help to understand Ibn Ezra's commentaries, or talmudic argumentations, or the original text of the Bible. To read Hebrew implies a readiness to assume the total heritage of the language. Reading German, English, or Latin, one merely harvests the crop raised by a single generation on the acre of language. The holy language . . . lacks the true characteristic of a sacred language, that is, separation from the colloquial, and so it never degenerated into anything like the magic sacredness of church Latin . . . Moreover, the languages spoken by the Jewish people in their everyday life lack the essential characteristic of profane vitality: complete dedication to the present moment. They swarm with quotations . . . If the new Hebrew, the Hebrew spoken in Palestine, should set out to evade this law of Jewish destiny, it might indeed achieve its purpose theoretically, but it would have to bear the consequences. Nor would these consequences be merely what some of our young and old radicals actually desire: that the new Hebrew should no longer be the language of the old Jewish people . . . The point is that one cannot simply speak Hebrew as one would like to; one must speak it as it is. And it is tied up with the past. It does have obligations to the rest of the world, even when spoken by the youngest child in the most recently founded settlement . . . a circle is indeed drawn around its centre, but in terms of construction the centre does not in the least determine the area the circle will occupy, whilst the smallest arc of its

> periphery indicates the centre quite unambiguously. Thus a spiritual centre such as we have in mind in regard to Palestine can be seen at a great distance and so become representative for all Jewry. But if it is to be a real centre, it must depend on the periphery and the laws governing it . . . These general observations are especially applicable to language, which is the core of all national life. Language cannot develop as it wants to but as it must. And for the Hebrew language, this 'must' does not lie within itself, as in every normal national language but from something beyond its 'spokenness', that is, from the heritage of the past, and the connection maintained with those whose Jewishness is essentially that of the heir. But the more apparent the abnormality of this twofold dependency becomes, the more it tends to cast off the shackles of 'normalcy'.

While it would be difficult to refute the substance of this remonstrance without asserting that, as the price of political normalization, all traditional values are if need be dispensable, we may take note that a defence of westernizing modernity in Hebrew was advanced by Leon Roth (1896–1963), professor of philosophy at Jerusalem and himself imbued with a mature appreciation of Jewish values no less discerning than was Rosenzweig's.[200] Thus writing of Ahad Ha'am – generally considered a model of modern Hebrew prose – Roth could say[201] 'here is a man . . . who talks sense; and he talks sense sensibly . . . His prose is prose, not pastiche'. Roth's advocacy is the more significant in that it was written when, feeling disillusioned with the extent to which his own humane Zionist ideals were finding implementation in Israel, he had left the country.

4.11 Master and servant

A talmudic adage,[202] prompted by the many restrictions that, in rabbinic law, hem in the Jewish owner of a Jewish (as opposed to a gentile) slave, ironically observes that 'whoever acquires a Hebrew slave thereby acquires a master'. Identification of the roles of master and servant as between Hebrew, with its theological or ideological overspill, and those who speak it, will be determined (and not necessarily correctly) by the *parti pris* considerations of the individual or collective body that presumes to pronounce on such a subject from within. Balaam, the gentile prophet hired to curse Israel but who found himself blessing it *malgré soi*,[203] observed that 'it is a people dwelling apart, not reckoning itself among the nations'.[204] Latter-day Israel, in its concern to make political capital of its language as a means of rebutting that judgement, may persuade itself that Balaam was not inspired, but fundamentally mistaken: whether it will invariably convince the outsider, is a different question.

Notes

* Conventions used in the transcriptions: the *h* following a consonant is not pronounced; *h* [h], *ḥ* [ħ], *ṣ* [sˠ], *ṭ* [tˠ], ᶜ[ʕ], ʾ [ʔ], *q* [q], *w* [w], *y* [j].

1. Ben-Yehuda (1879); Mandel (1981).
2. Baron (1952, vol. 1, 168f., 370f., nn. 5, 7) estimates the population of Herod's Palestine at 2,500,000 of which half a million were not ethnically Jewish; and that Syria, Egypt, Babylonia and Asia Minor probably each included a million Jews, apart from settlements further west.
3. Ep. 71, ii, 4; Goldbacher (1895, 252), Migne (1844–64), *P.L.* 33, 242. Further references in the index to Augustine, *P.L.* 46, 602, *s.v. Septuaginta*; R. Loewe (1969, 107, n. 2).
4. Cf. Judah Hallevi, *Kuzari*, ii, 72, 'oral communication is better than writing'; Baneth (1977, 81), Hirschfeld (1931, 110).
5. Ex. 20, 1.
6. *Mekhilta, Ba-ḥodesh* 6, Weiss (1865, f. 74b, 11. 8f.), Lauterbach (1933–35, vol. 2, 238).
7. Gen. 27, 33, Num. 23, 20.
8. Gen. 32, 28f., 35, 10.
9. Gen. 2, 19.
10. Homer, *Odyssey* 17, 1. 292f.
11. Greek text (II), 6, 2; Hanhart (1983, 108); Simpson (1913, 217).
12. *Pesaḥim* 6b; *Soncino Talmud*, p. 25. Elsewhere attributed to Rabbi Me'ir (second century).
13. See below, p. 120.
14. The whole subject, which (as far as I am aware) has not yet been approached in a way that would take comprehensive account of rabbinic and medieval Judaism and the effect of integration in the modern west from the seventeenth century onwards, cannot be pursued here in depth. As a starting-point, see Barr (1962); R. Loewe (1949).
15. Gen. 11, 6f., 10, 30; cf. *Esther* 1, 22, 8, 9. *Mekhilta*, *Beshallaḥ* 1, on Ex. 14, 5, 'every people and tongue that has ever had dominion over Israel, etc.', Weiss (1865, f. 31b foot), Lauterbach (1933–5, vol 1, 196).
16. Gen. 10. In v. 6 Canaan, despite its semitic speech, is placed alongside Egypt as a 'son' of Ham.
17. *Genesis Rabbah* 38, 11, on Gen. 12, 2; Theodor (1903–16, 323); *Midrash Rabbah*, vol. 1, 319.
18. *Sanhedrin* 17a; *Soncino Talmud*, vol. 1, 87. Further references in L. Ginzberg (1913–38, 5, 194, n. 72).
19. *Genesis Rabbah* 3, 2, Theodor (1903–16, 19), *Midrash Rabbah*, vol. 1,

20. The world was created by ten utterances (in Gen. 1 there are ten occurrences of the formula 'God said'). *Mishnah, 'Abhoth* 5, 1, Danby (1933, 455). The formula 'He who spake and the world came into existence' (*mi she-'amar we-hayah ha-'olam*) is a frequent surrogate for the divine name: Marmorstein (1927, 89); cf. above, pp. 98f.

20. Gen. 10, 21, 25, Jubilees 12, 25–6, Charles, ed. (1913, vol. 2, 32). Rab (i.e. 'Abba 'Arekha) found in alleged aramaisms in Ps. 139, 17 a hint that Adam spoke Aramaic: *Sanhedrin* 38b, *Soncino Talmud*, vol. 1, 243. Rab was a Babylonian, and his exegesis, if not merely a learned joke, may be apologetically motivated to justify the Jewish use in Babylonia of Aramaic as a vernacular. See below, pp. 103f.

21. Jubilees 3, 28, Charles, ed. (1913, vol. 2, 17); Josephus, *Antiquities* I. i, 4 (41), Whiston (1906, 2). L. Ginzberg (1913–38, 5, 94, n. 58).

22. *Leqaḥ Ṭobh* on Gen. 3, 1, Buber (1880, f. 12b).

23. *Zephaniah* 3, 9. According to Rabbi Simeon b. Eleazar in *Berakhoth*, 57b, *Soncino Talmud*, 358, this verse refers to the future conversion of the gentiles, which in itself implies their liturgical use of Hebrew, and presumably also their adoption of it as a vernacular alongside an Israel restored to the pristine state of Adam in paradise.

24. Katz (1981), and (1982), ch. 2: 'Babel Revers'd: the Search for a Universal Language and the Glorification of Hebrew', pp. 43–88.

25. *Genesis Rabbah* 31, 8, Theodor (1903–16, 281 1. 6), *Midrash Rabbah*, vol. 1, 242. Although the Torah was written down in Hebrew and, effectively, promulgated in that language, its universal availability and import are enunciated in the legend that as each of the ten commandments was uttered by God (*sc.* in Hebrew), it was 'divided into the seventy languages' of the world: *Shabbath* 88b, *Soncino Talmud*, vol. 2, 420; L. Ginzberg (1913–38, 3, 97).

26. *Genesis Rabbah* 1, 1, Theodor (1903–16, 2), *Midrash Rabbah*, vol. 1, 1.

27. *Pesaḥim* 54a, *Soncino Talmud*, 265.

28. *Genesis Rabbah* 28, 4, Theodor (1903–16, 263), *Midrash Rabbah*, vol. 1, 225f.; derived from the reference in *Ps.* 105, 8 to the 'word' (taken as = Torah) which God commanded 'for a thousand generations' – Moses being the 26th generation after Adam. Other versions view the period of the Torah's pre-existence as 1000 years: L. Ginzberg (1913–38, 5, 5f., n. 5).

29. *Esther* 8, 9.

30. *Sanhedrin* 22a, *Soncino Talmud*, vol. 1, 120; 'some nations have their own language but not script, some *vice versa*, and some neither – unlike Israel, which has both'.

31. See articles on the *Genizah* in *Encyclopaedia Judaica*, 7, 404f., and 16 (supplementary entries), 1333–42.

32. Six MS fragments of the Hebrew Bible in Arabic characters (British Library, Orient. 2539–47) were published in facsimile by Hoerning (1889). On Karaism, a biblicizing movement which rejected the Talmudic overlay, see Nemoy (1971–2). But it should be noted that G. Khan has now revealed, from documents in the *Genizah* collection at

Cambridge (which emanated from a Rabbinic Jewish community) evidence for wider use of the Arabic script by Rabbinic Jews.

33. See e.g. 2 Kings 18, 26 = Isaiah 36, 11. It seems to me likely that the confidence of the Judaean leadership that the common folk on the walls could not follow Aramaic rests on the circumstance that the Assyrian officer was haranguing an open-air meeting. In closer contact some, at least, of the populace would presumably have been able to understand Aramaic no less easily than their masters could.
34. E.g. on Proverbs 7, 7, *petha'im* ('simpletons') Rabbi Levi observed that 'in Arabia they call a stripling *patya*' (i.e. Arabic *fatay*); *Genesis Rabbah*, 87, 1, Theodor (1903–16, 1061), *Midrash Rabbah*, vol. 2, 806. (The *New English Bible*, *in loc.* renders 'simple youths').
35. M. Terentius Varro (116–27 BCE) adduces many Greek 'etymologies' for Latin in his *De Lingua Latina*, e.g. at vi. X. 96, Kent (1938, vol. 1, 262). He notes (vi. V. 40, Kent, vol. 1, 210) that the origin of the Latin words for time are obscure, in part because they are not cognate with Greek (*verborum quae tempora adsignificant ideo locus difficillimus ἔτυμα, quod neque his fere societas cum Graeca lingua, neque vernacula ea quorum in partu[m] memoria adfuerit nostra*). Varro's teacher Tyrannion supposed that Latin was derived from the Aeolic dialect of Greek, Sandys (1921, 844); for the general lack of Roman interest in such matters, see Momigliano (1975, 7, 9, 18, 38f., 54, 55, 81, 149).
36. See Hirschfeld (1926); *Encyclopaedia Judaica* 11, 323f. In particular, the comparative approach of Abraham ibn Ezra (died 1164) should be noted; *Encyclopaedia Judaica*, 8, 1168. Barr (1971–2), in a comprehensive article, lists relevant Jewish works from 900 CE to the sixteenth century. See pp. 113f.
37. See above, n. 20.
38. *Shabbath* 12b, *Soncino Talmud*, vol. 1, 48, = *Soṭah* 33a, *Soncino Talmud*, 162.
39. *Berakhoth* 13a, *Soncino Talmud*, 76, *Tosefta Soṭah* 7, 7. Despite the insistence of Rabbi Judah the Patriarch that the *Shema'* must be recited in Hebrew, the majority view was that any language intelligible to the praying individual was legitimate. Maimonides, *Mishneh Torah, Hilkhoth Qeri 'ath shema'* 2, 10, Hyamson (1949, f. 95b).
40. The basic document is the Greek so-called *Letter of Aristeas*, see Andrews (1913). The kernel of the legend of the origin of the 'Septuagint' is preserved in Hebrew in *Megillah* 9af., *Soncino Talmud*, 49f.
41. *Soferim* 1, 7, Müller (1878, ii, 12); Cohen (1965, vol. 1, 212f.).
42. *Megillath Ta'anith*, final chapter, Grossberg (1905, 78).
43. Jerusalem Talmud, *Megillah* 1, 9, Schwab (1871–89, vol. 6, 213), cf. *Megillah* 9a, *Soncino Talmud*, 49.
44. *Genesis Rabbah* 36, 8, Theodor (1903–16, 342), *Midrash Rabbah*, vol. 1, 294, Lieberman (1950, 18), Mussies (1976).
45. Jerusalem Talmud, *loc. cit.* (n. 43), Schwab (1871–89, vol. 6, 212), cf. *Soṭah* 7, 2, Schwab (1871–89, vol. 7, 299), *Esther Rabbathi* on *Est.* 1, 22, *Midrash Rabbah*, vol. 9, 64.

46. See p. 101.
47. *Midrash Psalms* 31, 7, Buber (1891, f. 120v), Braude (1959, vol. 1, 398).
48. See Buber's note 26 *in loc.*
49. Jonah 1, 9; Exodus 2, 6.
50. *Sanhedrin* 21b, *Soncino Talmud*, vol. 1, 119. See Naveh (1971–2).
51. Of the pre-medieval examples of *'ibhri*, *'ibhrith* assembled by Ben-Yehuda (1910, vol. 9, 4295f.), the only one apart from those considered here and other parallels is the *dictum* of Rabbi Judah Ha-levi b. Shalom that 'in Hebrew wine is called *yayin*, in Aramaic *ḥamra*'. *Tanḥuma, Shemini* 7, Buber (1913), *Bemidbar* f. 13b, Bietenhard (1980–2, vol. 2, 44).
52. 2 Kings 26, 28.
53. Nehemiah 13, 24. Most modern scholars consider that 'Ashdodite' in this context means [Nabataean] Aramaic, rather than a non-semitic language surviving from the age of the Philistines. Rudolph (1949, 208), Batten (1913, 299), referring to Neubauer (1885, 230).
54. Isaiah 19, 8.
55. *Sifre, Naso'*, *in loc.*, Horovitz (1917, 42); Kuhn (1933–7, 120), Levertoff (1926, 28). *Mishnah, Soṭah* 7, 2, Danby (1933, 300).
56. Stern (1870), p. 7 (of 3rd pagination). The introduction of the word *'ibhrith* is here conditioned by the rhyme.
57. *Genesis Rabbah* 18, 3. Theodor (1903–16, 164), *Midrash Rabbah*, vol. 1, 143.
58. Rashi on Ex. 18, 23, and on *Megillah* 3a.
59. Other medieval instances of *'ibhri(th)* = *language* noted by Ben-Yehuda (1879) (see n. 51) are (possibly) Eliezer b. Samuel of Metz (1566, no. 102, f. 49b, l.14), and Judah ibn Tibbon's *Sefer Hariqmah*, xi (i.e. the translation of Ibn Janaḥ, Neubauer (1875), Goldberg (1856, xi) (but the reference here is to 'the tongue of the Hebrews').
60. Ladino dictionaries compiled on scholarly principles are only now in the course of production. Oral enquiries have proved entirely negative; notably Rabbi Dr Solomon Gaon, born in Travnik (Bosnia) in 1912 into a Ladino-speaking community, is emphatic that *hebreo* (meaning *language*) was regarded as Spanish and not as Ladino. C. Crews (1935, 16), reporting on her investigation of Balkan Ladino in 1930, writes of children learning 'à traduire *l'hébreu, le lašon ha kodeš* ou "langue sacrée", en ladino'. Nehama and Cantera (1977) in translating *ebréo* by *langue hébraïque* are guilty of historical anachronism.
61. See Mohrmann (1955; 1958). For the Jewish counterpart and its relevance for the emergence of the Romance languages, see Blondheim (1925).
62. See H. Loewe (1911); S. A. Birnbaum (1971–2).
63. Ben-Yehuda (1910, introduction, vol. 1, 27), explained that he admitted as Aramaic loan-words in Hebrew those only which occur embedded in a purely Hebrew context. His own antipathy to the Aramaic 'virus' is clear from the end of his introduction, 253f.; Rabin (1976).

64. See n. 31, and Steinschneider (1893; 1902).
65. Description, with Hebrew text and bibliography, in Cantera and Millas (1956, 171f.).
66. See Weinreich (1971–2, 800–801); Yiddish glosses are found from at least the twelfth century, and manuscripts of Yiddish texts are extant from the fourteenth.
67. Weitzmann (1949, vol. 1, 27).
68. Ben-Yehuda (1879); see n. 1.
69. Originally published in *Ha-Shiloaḥ*, 22, 2; reprinted in Ahad Ha'am (1921, iv, 116f.). English translation by L. Simon (1946, 222f.).
70. p. 103, n. 36.
71. See Dotan (1971–2).
72. See note (? by N. Ṭur-Sinai) in Ben-Yehuda (1910–59), 4, p. 3113, col. ii; Dotan (1971–2), 1418.
73. These were collated by Kennicott (1776–80) and by de Rossi (1784–8).
74. See Morag (1962); J. Segal (1953), pp. 7f.
75. See Kahle (1913, 1927–30, 1928, 1947); Saenz Badillos (1988), p. 120, etc.
76. Kittel and Kahle (1937).
77. See Dotan (1971–2), 1413; Loewe (1964), pp. 168f.
78. By Elijah Levita (see below, p. 118); Medan (1971–2b).
79. See Smalley (1941), pp. 180f. (3rd edn, pp. 221f.).
80. By Kittel and Kahle (1937); see Kahle (1947), pp. 73f. (2nd edn, pp. 132f.).
81. See Halkin (1971–2a), 552; Hirschfeld (1926), pp. 35f.
82. See Skoss (1936–45).
83. Edited by Filipowski (1854).
84. See Rabin (1971–2).
85. See Allony (1971–2); Hirschfeld (1926), pp. 35f.
86. See Tene (1971–2); Hirschfeld (1926), pp. 40f.
87. Edited by Bacher (1896); the original Arabic by Neubauer (1875).
88. For this see Hirschfeld (1926).
89. See Talmage (1971–2); Hirschfeld (1926), pp. 83f.
90. See *Encyclopaedia Britannica*, eleventh edition, Cambridge, 1911, 21, p. 584; Wirszubski (1971–2).
91. See Robertson Smith (1911); Silverman (1971–2b).
92. Reuchlin (1506).
93. *Leshon torah le-ʿaṣmah u-leshon ḥakhamim le-ʿaṣmam*, 'the language of the Torah and rabbinic Hebrew each has its respective conventions', Babylonian Talmud, *Ḥullin*, 137b, *Soncino Talmud*, Kashdan (1948), 2, p. 790.
94. See David (1971–2).
95. Edited by Kohut (1878–92).
96. See Loewe (1974), pp. 139f., n. 7.
97. See Medan (1971–2b).
98. See Signorelli (1929); Loewe (1971–2a).
99. See *Encyclopaedia Judaica*, 6, 1136.

100. See Silverman (1971–2a).
101. J. Buxtorf *Senior* (1607); *Senior* and *Junior* (1640).
102. See Suler (1971–2); Levy (1867–8), (1876–89).
103. See Rotschild and Riemer (1971–2); Jastrow (1886–1903).
104. See Klausner (1971–2).
105. Ben-Yehuda (1910–59).
106. See *Encyclopaedia Judaica*, 15, 1465.
107. 'Even-Shoshan (1947–58).
108. 'Alcalay (1959–61).
109. For a survey see Hirschfeld (1926) and Barr (1971–2). Barr's important article includes, 1379f., short summaries concerning the individual grammarians and their work (including what is known of lost works) from 900 to 1342, contributed by D. Tene.
110. See Hirschfeld (1926), pp. 17f.; Allony (1971–2).
111. Edited by Bargès and Goldberg (1857).
112. Hirschfeld (1926), pp. 35f.; edited by Jastrow (1897).
113. Edited by Nutt (1870); Abraham ibn Ezra's translation was edited by Dukes (1844).
114. Hirschfeld (1926), pp. 40f.; edited by J. and H. Derenbourg (1880).
115. Arabic text edited by J. Derenbourg (1886); French translation by Metzger (1889).
116. *Sepher ha-riqmah*, edited by Goldberg (1856), Vilenski (1963–4).
117. See *Encyclopaedia Judaica*, 8, 1163f., especially 1168; Bacher (1882b); Hirschfeld (1926), pp. 71f.; Targarona Borrás (1990).
118. Edited by Lippmann (1827); selections in Levin (1985).
119. Edited by Höchheim[er] (1793), and many earlier editions, English translation by Chomsky (1952), criticism of whom by McFall (1982), pp. 7f., should be noted.
120. See Daiches (1941), pp. 91 etc. (index, p. 223); Loewe (1961), p. 139.
121. Steinschneider (1852–60), 634f., no. 4020; Hirschfeld (1926), pp. 83f.; for an alternative attribution see Tene, in Barr (1971–2), 1386, no. 47.
122. 'Know that all human speech is divided into three parts (*ḥalaqim*), past, future, and present'. This is the only quotation of this type given by Ben-Yehuda (1910–59), 2, p. 1055, col. i. However, Judah ibn Tibbon, David Qimḥi's senior by about 40 years, uses *ᶜathid* to render the Arabic *istiqbal*, e.g. Goldberg (1856), p. 82 = J. Derenbourg (1886), p. 145, l. 9, Metzger (1889), p. 136, Vilenski (1963–4), p. 168, l. 23. See also below, p. 122, n. 141.
123. See Brown, *et al.* (1906), p. 473, **2. c.**
124. von Arnim (1903), p. 6, II. 18f. See Matthews (1994) pp. 4, 34f., 44.
125. Edited by Uhlig (1910); translated by Householder (1981). For treatment of conditional sentences see III, 123f., Uhlig, pp. 374f., Householder, pp. 200f. For Apollonius Dyscolus see Matthews (1994), p. 80ff.
126. Edited by Hertz (1855–9); for conditional sentences see XVIII 81f., Hertz, 2, pp. 241f. For Priscian see Matthews (1994), p. 78ff.
127. Edited by H. Derenbourg (1881–9); translation by Jahn (1895–1900). For Sībawayhi see Fleisch (1994), p. 172.
128. Fleisch (1994), p. 173.

129. Efros and Kaufman (1929) explain the meaning of *syntax* without offering a one-word translation (*torath ha-mishpaṭ* [*ḥeleq ha-diqduq ha-dan be-harkabhath ha-mishpaṭ*], 'the rule[s] for sentence[-construction], *sc.* the department of grammar governing sentence-composition').
130. I am grateful to Dr Gabriel Birnbaum, academic secretary of the Academy, who informs me that the earliest occurrence that he can trace is in an article listing grammatical concepts in *Leshonenu*, 7, 1936, where the word appears as a sub-title, glossed *syntax*, alongside other headings such as *torath ha-ṣuroth* (i.e. morphology); he surmises that the neologism may well have emanated from the Academy's own grammar committee, and further states that it is included in Judah Goor's Hebrew-Hebrew dictionary which appeared in the same year. Professor E. Ullendorff informs me that he recalls that the word was coined by N. H. Torczyner (Ṭur-Sinai, see above, note 106) at the time co-president of the Academy.
131. So frequently; quoted by Ben-Yehuda (1910–59), 4, p. 3411, col. i, from his *Ṣaḥoth*, f. 22b (of *editio princeps*, 1545/6).
132. Chap. 33(32), J. Derenbourg (1886), p. 342, Metzger (1889), p. 339, Goldberg (1856), p. 212, Vilenski (1963–4), p. 359. Geoffrey Khan points out to me that ibn Janaḥ also discusses *apposition* (ch. 9(8), Derenbourg, p. 99, Metzger, p. 92, Goldberg, p. 52, Vilenski, p. 119); *ellipse* (ch. 25(24), Derenbourg, p. 249, Metzger, p. 241, Goldberg, p. 150, Vilenski, p. 263); *emphatic redundancy* (ch. 26(25), Derenbourg, p. 278, Metzger, p. 269, Goldberg, p. 168, Vilenski, p. 293); *repetition* (ch. 27(26), Derenbourg, p. 290, Metzger, p. 281, Goldberg, p. 175, Vilenski, p. 304), and *transposition of consonants* (ch. 32(31), Derenbourg, p. 337, Metzger, p. 334, Goldberg, p. 207, Vilenski, p. 352). But nearly all of this material falls within the department of rhetoric rather than that of syntax.
133. See Blau (1971–2a).
134. Edited by Kokovcov (1916).
135. See Kaddari (1971–2). Ben-Ze'ev's *Talmud leshon 'ibhri* appeared at Breslau, 1796.
136. Steinschneider (1852–60), 795, no. 4573, 2; Luzzatto (1836), p. 64.
137. For Ben-Ze'ev's treatment of conditional sentences see V iii 343 (1818), f. 154f. For 'syntax' he uses the term *ḥibbur ha-mishpaṭim* – conjunction of sentences. *Ḥibbur* is formed from the same stem as the modern *taḥbir* discussed above, and may indeed have prompted the latter (Ben-Ze'ev, IV i 364, 1796, ff. 182rf.).
138. See n. 145. The section on syntax begins on sig. 14, iv, verso.
139. See McFall (1982), pp. 12, 17. For the background in the gentile oriental scholarship of the West, see the note in Ben-Yehuda (1910–59), 2, p. 1255.
140. See *Encyclopaedia Judaica*, 9, 1286.
141. Quoted by McFall (1982), pp. 2f.
142. See Filipowski (1854), p. 75, *s.v. kebhar wa-'asher li-heyoth.*
143. Ed. Fürth (1793), ff. 54b. 55a.

144. Section 347, Ben-Ze'ev (1818), f. 156a.
145. It occurs in Abraham de Balmes' grammar *Miqneh 'abhram* (1523), sig. 10 i verso. On de Balmes (c. 1440–1523) see J. Heller (1971–2).
146. See Ben-Yehuda (1910–59), 2, p. 1141. A factor may have been the circumstance that one of the only two attested meanings of the form *haphikhah* refers to a deprecated sexual practice.
147. M. Segal (1927), (1936).
148. Rabin (1948); Goshen-Gottstein (1951); 'Avinery (1956); Glinert (1990).
149. Ornan (1971–2).
150. See Garbell (1971–2).
151. For the best account see Scholem (1971–2) and (1955, 75f.). For German translation of the text, see Goldschmidt (1894). P. Hayman (1986) has recently shown that the purpose of the author was to transfer to Hebrew the total symbolic structure earlier identified in the dimensions of the Temple.
152. See Landauer (1880), Kafiḥ (1970), Rosenblatt (1948, English translation).
153. i, 3, Landauer (1880, 43f.), Rosenblatt (1948, 53); vi, 5, Landauer (1880, 202), Rosenblatt (1948, 252).
154. Landauer (1880, 8) (. . . *allaḏi huwa al-ḥuruf al-22*), Rosenblatt (1948, 11). Elsewhere (Landauer (1880, 167), Rosenblatt (1948, 208), Sa'adyah distinguishes between sound and its representation by graphical device. See Vajda (1959–60, 26, n. 2 (of reprint)).
155. See Lambert (1891), Vajda (1959–60), Sirat (1983, 36f.).
156. iii, 2, Lambert (1891, 58 (Arabic), 81 (French)), Vajda (1959–60), 8, 22, 24, 30 (of reprint).
157. The earliest quotation in Ben-Yehuda (1910, vol 2, 883), is from this work of ibn Gabirol, 21, Wise (1901, 12, l. 17 (Arabic), 44 (English)). *Medhabbereth* in the Hebrew translation by Judah ibn Tibbon (c. 1120–c. 1190) here renders *nāṭiqat*, i.e. *articulate*. Other Hebrew terms for the rational soul are *maskeleth* (= *intelligent*), and *ḥakhamah* (= *wise*), etc. Klatzkin (1928–30, vol. 3, 58f.). For *medhabberim* = *humans*, rendering Arabic *nāṭiqin* = *articulate ones*, see Sa'adyah's exordium, Landauer (1880, 1), Rosenblatt (1948, 3).
158. See Brockelmann (1943, 330f., 376f. for Spain); Nicholson (1953, 285). For the stimulus to Jewish literary criticism see Allony (1975).
159. On Hebrew translation from Arabic the fundamental study is Steinschneider (1893). For a bird's eye view of the body of literature, see Halkin (1963).
160. i, 49, Baneth (1977, 14f.), Hirschfeld (1931, 44f.).
161. i, 53f., Baneth (1977, 15f.), Hirschfeld (1931, 45).
162. ii, 66f., Baneth (1977, 79f.), Hirschfeld (1931, 109f.).
163. ii, 74, Baneth (1977, 82), Hirschfeld (1931, 111). Cf. above, p. 106, n. 56.
164. By S. I. Kaempf (1845).
165. For the virtual indispensability of recourse to quotation and allusion for genuinely organic Hebrew writing, compare F. Rosenzweig's remarks cited below, p. 141.

166. Gen. 24, 10–27, 42f.
167. Lagarde (1883, 4f.), Kaempf (1845, 67f.).
168. i.e. Al-Ḥarizi's translation of Qasim ibn 'Ali al-Ḥariri, *Maḥberoth 'Ithi'el*, ed. by I. Peres (*Maḥbaroth le-sifruth*), Tel Aviv, 1961.
169. Cf. above, pp. 99, 126. *Guide*, ii, 30; Pines and Strauss (1963, 357f.); Friedländer (1910, 217f.) in his annotated (1885) translation, vol. 2, 157, n. 3, thought that Maimonides is here criticizing Judah Hallevi (*Kuzari* iv, 26, Baneth (1977, 184), Hirschfeld (1931, 211)). But that passage, which deals with the *Sefer Yeṣirah* (see above, pp. 124f.) concerns the instantaneity of creation, with no immediate bearing on the origin of language; and Judah Hallevi himself shared the view that languages are conventional (see above, p. 126, n. 161).
170. iii, 8; Pines and Strauss (1963, 435f.).
171. e.g. 'One should not utter a gross expression', *Pesaḥim* 3a (*Soncino Talmud*, 7f.), *Genesis Rabbah*, 86, end, Theodor (1903–16, 1059), *Midrash Rabbah*, vol. 2, 805 (on Gen. 39, 6).
172. *Hilkhoth Tefillah* i, 4, Hyamson (1949, f. 98b).
173. Ex. 30, 13.
174. Gen. 1, 5, 8, etc.
175. Scholem (1955, 17).
176. Scholem, *Encyclopaedia Judaica* (1971–2), 10, 620 f. (article 'Kabalah').
177. cf. Deut. 33, 2.
178. Jerusalem Talmud, *Soṭah* 8, 22d, Schwab (1871–89, v, 303), *Midrash Psalms* 90, Buber (1891, f. 196a), Braude (1959, vol. 2, 94).
179. See above, p. 101, n. 27.
180. Scholem, *Encyclopaedia Judaica* (1971–2), 10, 624; Scholem (1960, 101f. = English translation, 74f.).
181. f. 47b.
182. Printed Lemberg, 1892.
183. Scholem (1960, 105f., 110 = English translation, 78f., 81).
184. See Patterson (1964), and Slutsky (1971–2) (with bibliography).
185. See Tsamriyon (1971–2).
186. See above, pp. 101f., n. 30.
187. See the comparison between the Hebrew and the Slovak revivals of T. V. Parfitt and M. Torčanova (1981).
188. See Browning (1969, ch. 6, 'The development of the national language', 103f., 107, 111f.).
189. Browning (1969, 110); Talmon (1967, 110f.).
190. '*Abhduth be-thokh ḥeruth* ('Slavery in Freedom'), originally published in *Ha-Meliṣ*, 1892; Ahad Ha'am (1921, vol. 1, 123); translated by L. Simon (1912, 170f., 193).
191. See Parfitt (1972) and (1984).
192. See Kressel (1971–2a) and Ettinger (1971–2).
193. See Kressel (1971–2b).
194. See Medan (1971–2a).
195. Originally published in 1921; English translation by Hallo (1971) from the second edition, 1930.

196. In a letter written from the trenches, 1 May 1917; Glatzer (1953, 54).
197. See Glatzer (1953), index, *s.v.* 'language' and 'translation', 391, 399.
198. Published in 1924. Rosenzweig's review appeared in *Der Morgen*, 2 (1926) 105–109, and was reprinted in Rosenzweig (1937, 220–27).
199. English translation by Glatzer (1953, 263–7).
200. Roth (1959).
201. Roth (1960, 35).
202. *Qiddushin* 20a, *Soncino Talmud*, 92.
203. Numbers 22, 5–6; Deut. 23, 5–6.
204. Numbers 23, 10.

Bibliography

ABRAMSON, S. (1975) *Sheloshah sepharim shel rabh yehudah ben bal'am, maqor we-thargum*, Qiryath Sepher, Jerusalem.

AHAD HA'AM (pseud. Asher Ginsberg) (1921) *'Al Parashath Derakhim*,[2] 4 vols, Jüdischer Verlag, Berlin. For transl., see Simon, L. (1912; 1946).

'ALCALAY, R. (1959–61) *The Complete English-Hebrew Dictionary*, Massadah, Tel Aviv/Jerusalem.

ALLONY, N. (1968–9) *Ha-'agron, kitab usul al-shi'r al-'ibrani me-'eth rabh sa'adyah ga'on*, Ha-'aqademiyah la-lashon ha-'ibhrith, Jerusalem.

ALLONY, N. (1971–2) Ḥayyuj, Judah ben David, in *Encyclopaedia Judaica*, 7, 1513f.

ALLONY, N. (1975) The Reaction of Moses ibn Ezra to "Arabiyya', *Bulletin of the Institute of Jewish Studies* (London), 3, 19–40.

ANDREWS, H. T. (1913) *The Letter of Aristeas* (English transl.), see Charles (ed.) (1913, 2, 83–122).

Aristeas, Letter of, see Andrews (1913).

ARNIM, H. VON, see von Arnim.

AUGUSTINE, ST, see Goldbacher (1895); Migne (1844–64).

'AVINERY, Y. (1956) *Heykhal Rashi*, 3, 15f. (*Diqduqey Rashi*), Tel Aviv (revised edition Mosadh Ha-rabh Kook, Jerusalem 2, 1985, 4f. of Hebrew pagination).

Babylonian Talmud, see *Soncino Talmud*.

BACHER, W. (1882a) *Die grammatische Terminologie des Jehûdâ b. Dâwîd (Abu Zakarjâ ibn Dâud) Ḥajjûĝ*, Kaiserliche Akademie der Wissenschaften (Carl Gerold's Sohn), Wien.

BACHER, W. (1882b) *Abraham ibn Ezra als Grammatiker*, Trübner, Strassburg.

BACHER, W. (1895) *Die Anfänge der hebräischen Grammatik*, Brockhaus, Leipzig. (=*Zeitschrift der deutschen morgenländischen Gesellschaft*, 49, 1895, 1f., 335f.) Repr. Benjamins, Amsterdam, 1975.

BACHER, W. (1896) *Sepher haschoraschim . . . von Abulwalid Merwan ibn Ganah*, M'kize Nirdamim, Berlin. Repr. Philo, Amsterdam, 1969.

BALMES, ABRAHAM DE (1523) *Miqneh 'abhram*, D. Bomberg, Venice.

BANETH, D. H. (1977) *Kitāb . . . Al-khazāri ta'lif R. Yehudah Ha-Lewi*, Magnes Press, Jerusalem. For transl. see Hirschfeld (1931).

BARGÈS, J. and D. (B.) GOLDBERG (1857) *R. Judah ben Koreisch Epistola de studii Targum utilitate*, Duprat-Maisonneuve, Paris.

BARON, S. W. (1952–) *A Social and Religious History of the Jews*, second edition, vols i–xviii-, Jewish Publication Society of America, Philadelphia.

BARR, J. (1962) *Biblical Words for Time* (Studies in Biblical Theology), 33, SCM Press, London.

BARR, J. (1971–2) Linguistic Literature, Hebrew, in *Encyclopaedia Judaica*, 16, 1352–1401 (includes a section on grammarians by D. Tene).

BATTEN, L. W. (1913) *The Books of Ezra and Nehemiah* (International Critical Commentary), T . and T. Clark, Edinburgh, Repr. 1949.

BEN-YEHUDA, E. (1879) She'elah nikhbadhah, *Ha-Shaḥar*, Nisan 5639 (= March–April 1879).

BEN-YEHUDA, E. (1910–59) *Millon ha-lashon ha-'ibhrith (A Comprehensive Dictionary of Ancient and Modern Hebrew)*, Jerusalem[–Berlin]. Repr. 8 vols, Thomas Yoseloff, New York/London, 1959.

BEN ZIMRA, D., see Ibn Abi Zimra (1713).

BEN-ZE'EV (BEN-SEEV, BENSEW), J. (1796) *Talmud leshon 'ibhri*, fourth edition (1818) Breslau, Vienna.

BIETENHARD, H. (1980–2) *Midrasch Tanḥuma B* (German transl.) (Judaica et Christiana, 5–6), Peter Lang, Bern.

BIRNBAUM, S. A. (1971–2) Jewish Languages, in *Encyclopaedia Judaica*, 10, 66–9.

BLAU, Y. (1971–2a) Ibn Bal'am, Judah, in *Encyclopaedia Judaica*, 8, 1156f.

BLAU, Y. (1971–2b) Ibn Kuraysh, Judah, in *Encyclopaedia Judaica*, 8, 1192f.

BLONDHEIM, D. S. (1925) *Les Parlers judéo-romans et la Vetus Latina*, Champion, Paris.

BRAUDE, W. G. (1959) *The Midrash on Psalms. Transl. . . .*, 2 vols (Yale Judaica Series, 13), Yale University Press, New Haven.

BROCKELMANN, C. (1943) *Geschichte der arabischen Litteratur*, second edition, 3 vols, Brill, Leiden.

BROWN, F., DRIVER, S. R. and BRIGGS, C. A. (1906) *Hebrew and English Lexicon of the Old Testament*, Clarendon Press, Oxford; Houghton, Mifflin, Boston.

BROWNING, R. (1969) *Mediaeval and Modern Greek*, Hutchinson, London.

BUBER, S. (1880) *Midhrash leqaḥ ṭobh . . . yesadho R. ṭobhiyyah b. 'eli'ezer*, Romm, Vilna.

BUBER, S. (1891) *Midhrash Tehillim*, Romm, Vilna.

BUBER, S. (1913) *Midhrash Tanḥuma*, Romm, Vilna.

BUXTORF, J. the Elder (1607) *Epitome radicum hebraicarum et chaldaicarum*, C. Waldkirch, Basel.

BUXTORF, J. the Elder (1640) (with J. Buxtorf the Younger) *Lexicon chaldaicum talmudicum*, L. König, Basel.

CSEL = *Corpus Scriptorum Ecclesiasticorum Latinorum*, Kaiserliche Akademie der Wissenschaften, Wien.

CANTERA, F., and MILLAS, J. M. [VALLICROSA] (1956) *Las inscripciones hebráicas de España*, Consejo Superior de Investigaciones Científicas, Madrid.

CHARLES, R. H. (ed.) (1913) *The Apocrypha and Pseudepigrapha of the Old Testament in English*, 2 vols, *Tobit*, vol. 1, 174-241 *Jubilees*, vol. 2, 1–82, Oxford University Press, Oxford.

CHOMSKY, W. (1952) *David Ḳimḥi's Hebrew Grammar (Mikhlol)*, Bloch, New York.

COHEN, A. (1936), see *Soncino Talmud.*

COHEN, A. (1965) *The Minor Tractates of the Talmud . . . transl. into English*, 2 vols, Soncino Press, London.

CREWS, C. M. (1935) *Recherches sur le judéo-español dans les pays balcaniques* (Société de publications romanes et françaises, 16), Droz, Paris.

CRYSTAL, D. (1965) *Linguistics, Language and Religion* (Faith and Facts Books, 131), Burns and Dales, London.

DAICHES, D. (1941) *The King James Version of the English Bible*, Chicago University Press, Chicago. Reprinted (1983) by Shoe String Press, Hamden.

DANBY, H. (1933) *The Mishnah* (English transl.), Oxford University Press, Oxford.

DAVID, A. (1971–2) Nathan ben Yehiel, in *Encyclopaedia Judaica*, 12, 859f.

DERENBOURG, H. (1881–9) *Le Livre de Sibawaihi. Traité de Grammaire Arabe*, Imprimerie Nationale, Paris.

DERENBOURG, J. (1886) *Le Livre des parterres fleuris. Grammaire hébraïque en arabe d'Abou'l-Walid Merwan ibn Djanah de Cordoue* (Bibliothèque de l'École des Hautes Études, Sciences philologiques et historiques, 66), Vieweg, Paris.

DERENBOURG, J. and DERENBOURG, H. (1880) *Opuscules et traités d'Abou'l-Walid Merwan ibn Djanah . . .*, Imprimerie Nationale, Paris (*Kitab al-mustalḥaq*, p. 1f.).

DE ROSSI, G. B. (1784–8) *Variae Lectiones Veteris Testamenti*, Ex Regio Typographeo, Parma.

DOTAN, A. (1971–2) Masorah, in *Encyclopaedia Judaica*, 16, 1401f.

DRIVER, S. R., SANDAY, W., WORDSWORTH, J. (eds) (1885) *Studia Biblica et Ecclesiastica. Essays in Biblical Archaeology and Criticism and Kindred Subjects*, vol. 1, Oxford University Press, Oxford.

DUKES, L. (1844) *Literatur-historische Mittheilungen über die ältester hebräische Exegeten, Grammatiker und Lexikographen* (Beiträge der ältesten Auslegung und Schrifterklärung des Alten Testaments, 2, 3), Krabbe, Stuttgart.

EBAN, A. S. (ed.) (1939) L. Pinsker, *Auto-Emancipation* (English transl.), Federation of Zionist Youth, London.

EFROS, I. (1929) *English-Hebrew Dictionary*, ed. by J. Kaufman, Dvir, Tel Aviv.

ELIEZER B. SAMUEL OF METZ (1566) *Sepher Yere'im*, ed. Benjamin b. Abraham, G. de Cavalli, Venezia.

Encyclopaedia Judaica (1971–2) [in English], 16 vols, Keter Publishing House, Jerusalem.

EPSTEIN, I. (1935), see *Soncino Talmud.*

ETTINGER, S. (1971–2) [Zionism] Ḥibbat Zion, in *Encyclopaedia Judaica*, 16, 1037f.

ʾEVEN-SHOSHAN, A. (1947–58) *Millon ḥadash*, Qiryat Sefer, Jerusalem.

FILIPOWSKI, H. (1854) *The First Hebrew and Chaldaic Lexicon to the Old Testament . . . by Menahem ibn Saruk* (Hebrew Antiquarian Society), J. Madden, London and K. F. Köhler, Leipzig.

FLEISCH, H. (1994) *Arabic Linguistics*, in Lepschy (ed.) (1994, vol. 1, 164–184).

FREEDMAN, H. (1938) see *Soncino Talmud.*

FREEDMAN, H. (1939) see *Midrash Rabbah.*

FRIEDLÄNDER, M. (1910) Maimonides, *The Guide for the Perplexed* (English transl.), second edition Routledge, London. (First edition Trübner, London, 1885.)

GARBELL, I. (1971–2) Gesenius, Heinrich, in *Encyclopaedia Judaica*, 7, 524.

Genesis Rabbah, see *Midrash Rabbah*; Theodor (1903–16).

GINSBERG, A., see Ahad Haʿam (1921).

GINZBERG, L. (1913–38) *The Legends of the Jews*, 7 vols, Jewish Publication Society of America, Philadelphia.

GLATZER, N. (1953) *Franz Rosenzweig: His Life and Thought*, Jewish Publication Society of America, Philadelphia.

GLINERT, L. (1990) The Unknown Grammar of Abraham ibn Ezra. Syntactic Features of *Yesod Diqduq*, in F. Díaz Esteban (ed.) *Abraham ibn Ezra y su tiempo*, Asociación española de orientalistas, Madrid, 129f.

GOLDBACHER, A. (ed.) (1895) *S. Aurelii Augustini . . . Epistulae* (CSEL, 34), Kaiserliche Akademie der Wissenschaften, Wien.

GOLDBERG, B. (1856) *Sepher Harikma. Grammaire hébraïque de Jona ben Gannach . . . Traduite par Jehuda Ibn Tabbon.* Revue par R. Raphael Kirschheim, Frankfurt am Main. See also Bargès and Goldberg (1857).

GOLDSCHMIDT, L. (1894) *Das Buch der Schöpfung* (German transl. of *Sepher Yeṣirah*), J. Kauffmann, Frankfurt am Main.

GOSHEN-GOTTSTEIN, M. (1951) *Taḥbirah u-milonah shel . . . ʿibhrith she-bithehum hashpaʿathah shel ʿarabith*, Jerusalem PhD thesis, cyclostyled, Waʿad ha-lashon haʿibhrith, Jerusalem/Tel Aviv/Haifa.

GROSSBERG, M. (1905) *Meghillath Taʿanith*, E. Salat, Lemberg.

HABERMANN, A. M. (1971–2) Genizah, in *Encyclopaedia Judaica*, 7, 404f.

HALKIN, A. S. (1963) The Medieval Jewish Attitude Towards Hebrew, in *Biblical and Other Studies*, ed. by A. A. Altman (Studies and Texts, 1), Harvard University Press, Cambridge, Mass., 233–48.

HALKIN, A. S. (1971–2a) Saʿadyah Gaʾon [as grammarian], in *Encyclopaedia Judaica*, 14, 552.

HALKIN, A. S. (1971–2b) Translation and Translators, in *Encyclopaedia Judaica*, 15, 1318f.

HALLO, W. W. (1971) *The Star of Redemption* (English transl. of Franz Rosenzweig, *Der Stern der Erlösung*, second edition 1930), Routledge and Kegan Paul, London.

HANHART, R. (1983) *Tobit* (Septuaginta, 8/5), Vandenhoeck and Ruprecht, Göttingen.

ḤARIZI, JUDAH, see Kaempf (1845); Lagarde (1883).

HAYMAN, P. (1986) Some Observations on Sefer Yesira (2) The Temple at the Centre of the Universe, *Journal of Jewish Studies*, 37, 176–82.

HELLER, J. (1971–2) Balmes, Abraham Ben Meir de, in *Encyclopaedia Judaica*, 4, 140f.

HERTZ, M. (1855–9) *Prisciani . . . Institutionum grammaticarum libri*, see Keil (1855–9).

HIRSCHFELD, H. (1926) *Literary History of Hebrew Grammarians and Lexicographers* (Jews' College Publications, 9), Oxford University Press, Oxford.

HIRSCHFELD, H. (1931) *Judah Hallevi's Kitab al Khazari* transl. from the Arabic, second edition M. L. Cailingold, London.

HÖCHHEIM[ER], M. (1793) *Sepher mikhlol . . . rabbi dawid qimḥi*, Fürth.

HOERNING, R. (1889) *Six Karaite Manuscripts of the Hebrew Bible in Arabic Characters*, Williams and Norgate, London.

HOROVITZ, H. S. (1917) *Siphre d'be Rab ad Numeros*, Gustav Fock, Leipzig.

HOUSEHOLDER, F. W. (1981) *The Syntax of Apollonius Dyscolus* (Studies in the Theory and History of Linguistic Science, III, 23), Benjamins, Amsterdam.

HYAMSON, M. (1949) *The Mishneh Torah by Maimonides. Book II* (with English transl.), Bloch Publishing Co., New York.

IBN ABI ZIMRA, D. (1713) *Maghen Dawid*, Asher Anschel, Amsterdam.

IBN GABIROL, S., see Wise (1901).

IBN JANAḤ, J., see Goldberg (1856); Neubauer (1875).

IBN-SHOSHAN, A., see 'Even-Shoshan, A.

IBN TIBBON, J., see Goldberg (1856).

JAHN, G. (1895–1900) *Sibawaihi's Buch über die Grammatik*, Reuther und Reichard, Berlin.

JASTROW, MARCUS (1886–1903) *Dictionary of the Targumim, the Talmud . . . and . . . Midrashic Literature*, Trübner, London and Putnam, New York.

JASTROW, MORRIS (1897) *The Weak and Geminative Verbs in Hebrew by . . . Hayyug*, Brill, Leiden (*Abu Zakarijjâ Jaḥjâ Dâwud Ḥajjuğ und seine zwei grammatischen Schriften über die Verben mit schwachen Buchstaben und die Verben mit Doppelbuchstaben*, Keller, Giessen = *Zeitschrift für die alttestamentlische Wissenschaft*, 5, 1885, 193f.).

Jerusalem Talmud, see Schwab (1871–89).

JOSEPHUS, see Whiston (1906).

Jubilees, see Charles (ed.) (1913).

JUDAH HALLEVI, see Baneth (1977); Hirschfeld (1931).

KADDARI, M. (1971–2) Ben-Zeev, J., in *Encyclopaedia Judaica*, 4, 573.

KAEMPF, S. I. (1845) *Die ersten Makamen aus dem Tachkemoni . . . des Charisi . . . in's Deutschen übertragen*, Alexander Duncker, Berlin.

KAFIḤ, Y. (1970) *Sepher ha-nibhḥar ba-'emunoth ubha-de'oth* (Hebrew transl. of Sa'adya), Sura, Jerusalem.

KAHLE, P. (1913) *Masoreten des Ostens; die ältesten punktierten Handschriften des Alten Testaments . . .*, Hinrichs, Leipzig. Repr. Olms, Hildesheim, 1966.

KAHLE, P. (1927–30) *Masoreten des Westens*, Kohlhammer, Stuttgart, Repr. Olms, Hildesheim, 1967.

KAHLE, P. (1928) *Die hebräischen Bibelhandschriften aus Babylonien*, Topelmann, Giessen.

KAHLE, P. (1937), see Kittel and Kahle (1937).

KAHLE, P. (1947) *The Cairo Geniza* (Schweich Lectures of the British Academy, 1941), London (Oxford). Second edition, Blackwell, Oxford, 1959.

KATZ, D. D. (1981) The Language of Adam in Seventeenth-Century England, in H. Lloyd-Jones *et al.* (eds) (1981, 132–45).

KATZ, D. D. (1982) *Philo-semitism and the Readmission of the Jews to England*, Clarendon Press, Oxford.

KAUFMAN, J., see Efros (1929).

KEIL, H. (ed.) (1855–9) *Grammatici Latini*, 2–3, Teubner, Leipzig. Repr. Olms, Hildesheim, 1961.

KENNICOTT, B. (1776–80) *Vetus Testamentum hebraicum cum variis lectionibus*, E Typographeo Clarendoniano, Oxford.

KENT, R. G. (ed.) (1938) M. Terentius Varro, *De Lingua latina* (with English transl.), 2 vols (Loeb Classical Library), Harvard University Press, Cambridge, Mass. W. Heinemann, London.

KIMḤI, DAVID, see Höchheim[er] (1793).

KITTEL, R. and KAHLE, P. (1937) *Biblia Hebraica*, third edition, Würtemburgische Bibelanstalt, Stuttgart (previously publ. in parts).

KLATZKIN, J. (1924) *Torath ha-middoth me-'eth barukh spinoza* (Hebrew transl. of Spinoza's *Ethics*), Joseph Stiebel, Leipzig.

KLATZKIN, J. and ZOBEL, M. (1928–30, 1968) *'Oṣar munaḥim ha-philosofiyyim. Thesaurus Philosophicus Linguae Hebraeae*, 4 vols, Eshkol, Berlin, and, for vol. 4, Philip Feldheim, New York.

KLAUSNER, J. (1971–2) Ben-Yehuda, Eliezer, in *Encyclopaedia Judaica*, 4, 564f.

KOHUT, A. (1878–92) *Aruch Completum ('Arukh ha-shalem)*, Vienna. Repr. Menorah, Vienna/Berlin 1926.

KOKOVCOV, P. (1916) *K istorii srednevekovoj evrejskoj filologii i evrejsko-arabskoj literatury*, 2. *Novye materialy dlja kharakteristiki Jekhūdy Khajjūdža, Samuila Nagīda i nekotorykh drugikh predstavitelej evrejskoj filologičeskoj nauki v X, XI, i XII vek*, Tipografija Imperatorskoj Akademii Nauk, Petrograd.

KRESSEL, G. (1971–2a) Ḥibbat Zion, in *Encyclopaedia Judaica*, 8, 463.

KRESSEL, G. (1971–2b) Ha-Shiloaḥ, in *Encyclopaedia Judaica*, 7, 1368f.

KUHN, K. G. (1933–7) *Sifre zu Numeri* (with German trans.), W. Kohlhammer, Stuttgart. Second edition, 1959.

LAGARDE, P. DE (1883) *Iudae Harizii Macamae*, Dieterich, Göttigen.

LAMBERT, M. (1891) *Commentaire sur le Séfer Yesira ... par Saadya ... traduit* [*en français*] (Bibliothèque de l'École Pratique des Hautes Études, Sciences philosophiques et historiques, 85), É. Bouillon, Paris.

LAMPE, G. W. H. (ed.) (1969) *The Cambridge History of the Bible*, vol. 2, Cambridge University Press, Cambridge.

LANDAUER, S. (1880) *Kitâb al-Amânât wa'l-I'tiqâdât von Sa'adja*, Brill, Leiden.

LAUTERBACH, J. Z. (1933–5) *Mekilta de-Rabbi Ishmael* (with English

transl.), 3 vols, Jewish Publication Society of America, Philadelphia.
LEPSCHY, G. (ed.) (1994) *History of Linguistics*, vols I, II, Longman, London.
Leqaḥ Ṭobh, see Buber (1880).
LEVERTOFF, P. P. (1926) *Midrash Sifre on Numbers* (English transl.), Society for Promoting Christian Knowledge, London.
LEVIN, I. (1985) *Abhraham ibn Ezra Reader (Yalquṭ 'abraham ibn 'ezra)*, Matz and Kiev Foundation, New York/Tel Aviv.
LEVY, J. (1867–8) *Chaldäisches Wörterbuch über die Targumim*, Baumgartner, Leipzig.
LEVY, J. (1876–89) *Neuhebräisches und chaldäisches Wörterbuch über die Talmudim und Midraschim*, Brockhaus, Leipzig.
LIEBERMAN, S. (1942) *Greek in Jewish Palestine*, Jewish Theological Seminary of America, New York.
LIEBERMAN, S. (1950) *Hellenism in Jewish Palestine*, Jewish Theological Seminary of America, New York.
LIPPMANN, G. (1827) *Sepher ṣaḥoth . . . 'abhraham ibn 'ezra*, Fürth.
LLOYD JONES, H., PEARL, V. and WORDEN, B. (eds) (1981) *History and Imagination. Essays in Honour of H. R. Trevor-Roper*, Duckworth, London.
LOEWE, H. (1911) *Die Sprachen der Juden*, Jüdische Verlag, Köln.
LOEWE, R. (1949) Jerome's Rendering of 'Olam, *Hebrew Union College Annual*, 22, 265–306, 432.
LOEWE, R. (1961) Jewish Scholarship in England, in V. D. Lipman (ed.) *Three Centuries of Anglo-Jewish History*, Jewish Historical Society of England, London, 125f.
LOEWE, R. (1964) The 'Plain' Meaning of Scripture in Early Jewish Exegesis, in J. G. Weiss (ed.) *Papers of the Institute of Jewish Studies* [*London*], 1, 140–85, Magnes Press, Jerusalem. Repr. University Press of America, Lanham, 1989.
LOEWE, R. (1969) The Medieval History of the Latin Vulgate, see Lampe (ed.) (1969, 102–54).
LOEWE, R. (1971–2a) Egidio da Viterbo, in *Encyclopaedia Judaica*, 6, 475.
LOEWE, R. (1971–2b) Hebraists, Christian (1100–1890), in *Encyclopaedia Judaica*, 8, 9–71.
LOEWE, R. (1974) Rabbi Joshua ben Ḥananiah: Ll.D. or D.Litt.?, in B. S. Jackson (ed.) *Studies in Jewish Legal History. Essays in Honour of David Daube*, Jewish Chronicle, London, 137f. (= *Journal of Jewish Studies*, 25, 137f.)
LUZZATTO, S. D. (1836) *Prolegomeni ad una grammatica ragionata della lingua ebraica*, Cartellier, Padova. English transl. by Sabato Morais, New York, 1897 = 5th Biennial Report of the Convention of the Jewish Theological Seminary [New York], 1896.
MCFALL, L. (1982) *The Enigma of the Hebrew Verbal System: Solutions from Ewald to the Present Day* (Historic Texts and Interpreters in Biblical Scholarship, 2), Almond Press, Sheffield.
MAIMONIDES, *Mishneh Torah*, see Hyamson (1949).
MAIMONIDES, *Guide for the Perplexed*, see Friedländer (1910); Munk (1856–66); Pines (1963).

MANDEL, G. (1981) *Sheelah Nikhbadah* and the Revival of Hebrew, see Silberschlag (ed.) (1981, 25–39).

MANHEIM, R. (1965), see Scholem (1960).

MARGOLIOUTH, D. S. (1906), see Whiston (1906).

MARMORSTEIN, A. (1927) *The Old Rabbinic Doctrine of God, I, the Names and Attributes of God* (Jew's College Publications, 10), Oxford University Press, London.

MATTHEWS, P. H. (1994) Greek and Latin Linguistics, in Lepschy (ed.) (1994, vol. 2, 1–133).

MEDAN, M. (1971–2a) Academy of the Hebrew Language, in *Encyclopaedia Judaica*, 2, 205–8.

MEDAN, M. (1971–2b) Levita, Elijah, in *Encyclopaedia Judaica*, 1, 132f.

Meghillath Ta'anith, see Grossberg (1905).

Mekhilta, see Lauterbach (1933–5); Weiss (1865).

MENAHEM IBN SARUQ, see Filipowski (1854).

METZGER, M. (1889) *Le Livre de parterres fleuris; grammaire hébraïque en arabe d'Abou'l Walid Merwan ibn Djanah de Cordoue* [French trans.], Vieweg, Paris.

Midrash Psalms, see Braude (1959); Buber (1891).

Midrash Rabbah (1939) English transl., H. Freedman and M. Simon, 10 vols, *Genesis*, The Soncino Press, London. For *Genesis Rabbah*, see Theodor (1903–16).

Midhrash Tanḥuma, see Bietenhard (1980–2); Buber (1913).

MIGNE, J. P. (1844–64) *Patrologiae Cursus Completus. Series Latina*, J. P. Migne, Paris.

Mishnah, see Danby (1933).

MILLAS VALLICROSA, J. M., see Cantera (1956).

MOHRMANN, C. (1955) *Latin vulgaire, latin des Chrétiens, latin médiéval*, Klincksieck, Paris.

MOHRMANN, C. (1958) *Études sur le latin des Chrétiens*, Edizioni di Storia e Letteratura, Roma.

MOMIGLIANO, A. (1975) *Alien Wisdom. The Limits of Hellenization*, Cambridge University Press, Cambridge.

MORAG, S. (1962) *The Vocalization System of Arabic, Hebrew and Aramaic*, Mouton, The Hague.

MUNK, S. (1856–66) *Le Guide des égarés . . . accompagné d'une traduction française*, 3 vols, A. Franck, Paris.

MÜLLER, J. (1878) *Masechet Soferim* (with German transl.), J. C. Hinrichs, Leipzig.

MUSSIES, G. (1976) *Greek in Palestine and the Diaspora*, see Safrai and Stern (1976), ch. 22, 1040–64.

NAVEH, J. (1971–2) Alphabet, Hebrew, in *Encyclopaedia Judaica*, 2, 674–89.

NEHAMA, J. and CANTERA, J. (1977) *Dictionnaire du judéo-espagnol*, CSIC, Inst. Benito Arias Montano, Madrid.

NEMOY, L. (1971–2) Karaites, in *Encyclopaedia Judaica*, 10, 761f.

NEUBAUER, A. (1875) *The Book of Hebrew Roots by . . . Ibn Janâḥ*, Clarendon Press (Macmillan), Oxford. Repr. Philo Press, Amsterdam, 1968.

NEUBAUER, A. (1885) On Some Newly-Discovered Temanite and Nabataean Inscriptions, in Driver *et al.* (eds) (1885, 209–32).

NICHOLSON, R. A. (1907, repr. 1953) *A Literary History of the Arabs*, Fisher Unwin, London.

NUTT, J. (1870) *Two Treatises on Verbs Containing Feeble ... Letters Translated ... from Arabic by R. Moses Gikatilla ... Treatise on Punctuation by the Same ... Translated by Aben Ezra ... with an English Translation*, Asher, London.

ORNAN, U. (1971–2) Hebrew Grammar, in *Encyclopaedia Judaica*, 8, 77f.

PARFITT, T. V. (1972) The Use of Hebrew in Palestine 1800–1882, *Journal of Semitic Studies*, 17, 237–52.

PARFITT, T. V. (1984) The Contribution of the Old *Yishuv* to the Revival of Hebrew, *Journal of Semitic Studies*, 29, 255–65.

PARFITT, T. V. and TORČANOVA, M. (1981) Language Revival: A Comparison of the Work of Eliezer Ben-Yehuda and L'udovit Stur [on the Slovak Revival], in Silberschlag (ed.) (1981, 40–53).

Patrologia Latina, see Migne (1844–64).

PATTERSON, D. (1964) *The Hebrew Novel in Czarist Russia* (Edinburgh University Publications: Language and Literature, 13), Edinburgh University Press, Edinburgh.

PHILIPOWSKI, H., see Filipowski, H.

PINES, S. and STRAUSS, L. (translators) (1963) *The Guide of the Perplexed.* University of Chicago Press, Chicago.

PINSKER, L. (1882) *'Autoemancipation!'*, W. Issleib, Berlin. For English transl., see Eban (1939).

QIMḤI, DAVID, see Höchheim[er], M. (1793).

RABIN, CH. (1948) *The Development of the Syntax of Post-biblical Hebrew*, Oxford D.Phil. thesis (apparently unpublished).

RABIN, CH. (1971–2) Dunash ben Labrat, in *Encyclopaedia Judaica*, 6, 270f.

RABIN, CH. (1976) Hebrew and Aramaic in the First Century, in Safrai and Stern (eds) (1976), ch. 21. 1007–39.

REUCHLIN, J. (1506) *De Rudimentis Hebraicis* (including a *Dictionarium Hebraicum*), T. Anshelm, Pforzheim.

ROBERTSON SMITH, W. (1911) Reuchlin, Johann, in *Encyclopaedia Britannica*, eleventh edition, 23, 204f.

ROSEN, H. (1956) *Ha-ʿibhrith shellanu*, ʿAm Obed, Tel Aviv.

ROSENBLATT, S. (1948) *Saadia Gaon. The Book of Beliefs and Opinions. Translated* ... (Yale Judaica Series, 1), Yale University Press, New Haven.

ROSENZWEIG, F. (1921) *Der Stern der Erlösung*, J. Kauffmann, Frankfurt am Main. For English transl. see Hallo (1971).

ROSENZWEIG, F. (1937) *Kleinere Schriften*, Schocken, Berlin.

ROTH, L. (1959) The Resurgence of Hebrew, *Jewish Journal of Sociology*, 1, 177–86.

ROTH, L. (1960) Back to, Forward from, Ahad Haʿam?, *Addresses*, 13th Conference of Anglo-Jewish Preachers, Narod Press, London, 35–47.

ROTSCHILD, Y. and RIEMER, J. (1971–2) Jastrow, Marcus, in *Encyclopaedia Judaica*, 9, 1296f.

RUDOLPH, W. (1949) *Esra und Nehemia* (Handbuch zum alten Testament, 1, Reihe 20), J. C. B. Mohr «Paul Siebeck», Tübingen.

SA'ADYAH, see Kafiḥ (1970); Landauer (1880); Rosenblatt (1948); Vajda (1959–60).

SAENZ BADILLOS, A. (1988) *Historia de la lengua hebrea* (Colección: Estudios orientales, 2) AUSA, Sabadell, Barcelona. English trans. *A History of the Hebrew Language*, transl. by J. Elwolde, Cambridge University Press, Cambridge, 1993.

SAFRAI, S. and STERN, M. (eds) (1976) *The Jewish People in the First Century*, vol. 2, Van Gorcum, Assen / Amsterdam.

SANDYS, J. E. (1921) *A Companion to Latin Studies*, third edition, Cambridge University Press, Cambridge.

SCHACHTER, J., see *Soncino Talmud.*

SCHNEIDER, R. and UHLIG, G. (eds) (1910) *Apollonii Dyscoli Quae Supersunt* (Grammatici Graeci, 2), Teubner, Leipzig.

SCHOLEM, G. G. (1955) *Major Trends in Jewish Mysticism*, Thames and Hudson, London.

SCHOLEM, G. G. (1960) *Zur Kabbala und ihrer Symbolik*, Rhein-Verlag, Zürich. English transl. *On the Kabbalah and its Symbolism*, transl. by R. Manheim, Routledge and Kegan Paul, London.

SCHOLEM, G. G. (1971–2) Yeẓirah, Sefer, in *Encyclopaedia Judaica*, 16, 782f.

SCHOLEM, G. G. (1974) *Kabbalah*, Keter Publishing House, Jerusalem [A collection of Scholem's articles on *Kabbalah* and kindred subjects in *Encyclopaedia Judaica.*]

SCHWAB, M. (1871–89) *Le Talmud de Jérusalem traduit*..., 11 vols, Maisonneuve, Paris.

Sefer ha-temunah, Lemberg, 1892.

Sefer yere'im, see Eliezer b. Samuel of Metz (1566).

SEGAL, J. B. (1953) *The Diacritical Point and the Accent in Syriac*, Oxford University Press, Oxford.

SEGAL, M. (1927) *Grammar of Mishnaic Hebrew*, Clarendon Press, Oxford.

SEGAL, M. (1936) *Diqduq leshon ha-mishnah*, Dvir, Tel Aviv.

Sifre, Numbers, see Horovitz (1917); Kuhn (1933–7); Levertoff (1926).

SIGNORELLI, G. (1929) *Il Cardinale Egidio da Viterbo*, Libreria della SAI, Firenze.

SILBERSCHLAG, E. (ed.) (1981) *Eliezer Ben-Yehuda. A Symposium in Oxford*, Oxford Centre for Postgraduate Hebrew Studies, Oxford.

SILVERMAN, G. (1971–2a) Muenster, Sebastian, in *Encyclopaedia Judaica*, 12, 505.

SILVERMAN, G. (1971–2b) Reuchlin, Johann, in *Encyclopaedia Judaica*, 14, 108f.

SIMON, L. (1912) *Selected Essays by Ahad Ha-'am*, Jewish Publication Society of America, Philadelphia.

SIMON, L. (1946) *Ahad Ha-Am: Essays, Letters, Memoirs*, East and West Library, Oxford.

SIMON, M., see *Midrash Rabbah* (1939); *Soncino Talmud* (1935–).

SIMPSON, D. C. (1913) *Tobit* (English transl.), in Charles (1913), vol. 1, 174–241.

SIRAT, C. (1981) *La Lettre hébraïque et sa signification* (Études de paléographie hébraïque), Centre National de la Recherche Scientifique, Paris; Israel Museum, Jerusalem.

SIRAT, C. (1983) *La Philosophie juive au moyen Âge selon les Textes manuscrits et imprimés*, Centre National de la Recherche Scientifique, Paris. English transl. *A History of Jewish Philosophy in the Middle Ages*, Cambridge University Press, Cambridge, 1985.

SKOSS, S. L. (1936–45) *Hebrew-Arabic Dictionary of the Bible of David Abraham Alfasi*, Yale University Press, New Haven.

SLUTSKY, Y. (1971–2) Haskalah, in *Encyclopaedia Judaica*, 7, 1433–52.

SMALLEY, B. (1941) *The Study of the Bible in the Middle Ages*, Clarendon Press, Oxford. Third edition, Blackwell, Oxford, 1983.

Soferim, see Cohen (1965); Müller (1878).

Soncino Talmud (1935–) *The Babylonian Talmud Translated into English*, ed. by I. Epstein, Soncino Press, London.

Berakhoth (*Zera'im* vol. 1) M. Simon 1948.
Shabbath (*Mo'edh* vol. 1) H. Freedman 1938.
Pesaḥim (*Mo'edh* vol. 4) H. Freedman 1938.
Meghillah (*Mo'edh* vol. 8) M. Simon 1938.
Soṭah (*Nashim* vol. 6) A. Cohen 1936.
Qiddushin (*Nashim* vol. 8) H. Freedman 1936.
Sanhedrin (*Neziqin* vol. 5) J. Schachter and H. Freedman 1935.
Ḥullin (*Qodashim* 2 vols) E. Kashdan 1948.

STEINSCHNEIDER, M. (1852–60) *Catalogus Librorum Hebraeorum in Bibliotheca Bodleiana*, A. Friedlander, Berolini. Repr. G. Olms, Hildesheim 1964.

STEINSCHNEIDER, M. (1893) *Die hebräischen Übersetzungen des Mittelalters und die Juden als Dolmetscher*, Kommissionsverlag des Bibliographischen Verlags, Berlin. Repr. Akademische Druck- und Verlagsanstalt, Graz 1956.

STEINSCHNEIDER, M. (1902) *Die arabische Literatur der Juden*, J. Kauffman, Frankfurt am Main.

STERN, M., see Safrai (1976).

STERN, S. G. (1870) *Sefer Teshubhoth . . . talmidhey Menaḥem ibn Saruq . . .*, Ad. della Torre, Wien.

STRAUSS, L., see Pines (1963).

Studia Biblica et Ecclesiastica, see Driver *et al.* (1885).

SULER, B. (1971–2) Levy, Jacob, in *Encyclopaedia Judaica*, 11, 158.

TALMAGE, F. (1971–2) Kimḥi, David, in *Encyclopaedia Judaica*, 10, 1001f.

TALMON, J. L. (1967) *Romanticism and Revolt. Europe 1815–1848*, Thames and Hudson, London.

Talmud: Babylonian Talmud, see *Soncino Talmud*. *Jerusalem Talmud*, see Schwab (1871–89).

TARGARONA BORRÁS, J. (1990) Conceptos gramaticales en el Sefer moznayim de Abraham ibn Ezra, in F. Díaz Esteban (ed.) *Abraham ibn Ezra y su tiempo*. Asociación española de orientalistas, Madrid, 345f.

TENE, D. (1971–2) Ibn Janaḥ, Jonah, in *Encyclopaedia Judaica*, 8, 1181f.

TENE, D., see Barr (1971–2); Vilenski (1963–4).

THEODOR, J. (1903–16) *Bereschit Rabba*, H. Itzkowski, Berlin. For transl. see *Midrash Rabbah*.

ṬOBHIYYAH B. ELIEZER, see Buber (1880).

Tobit, see Hanhart (1983); Simpson (1913).
TORČANOVA, M., see Parfitt (1981).
Tosefta, see Zuckermandel (1881).
TSAMRIYON, TS. (1971–2) Me'assef, in *Encyclopaedia Judaica*, 11, 1161f.
UHLIG, see Schneider (1910).
VAJDA, G. (1959–60) Sa'adyā Commentateur du 'Livre de la Création', *École Pratique des Hautes Études. Section des Sciences religieuses. Annuaire* 1959–60, Paris.
VALLICROSA, J. M. MILLAS, see Cantera (1956).
VILENSKI, M. (1963–4) *Sepher ha-riqmah . . . le-r' yonah ibn janaḥ be-thargum shel r' yehudhah ibn tibbon*, second edition, D. Tene (ed.) Ha-aqademiyah la-lashon ha-'ibhrith, Jerusalem.
VON ARNIM, H. (ed.) (1903) *Stoicorum veterum fragmenta*, 2, Teubner, Leipzig.
WEINREICH, U. (1971–2) Yiddish Language, in *Encyclopaedia Judaica*, 16, 789, 795f.
WEISS, I. H. (1865) *Mekhilta*, J. Schlossberg, Wien.
WEITZMANN, CH. (1949) *Trial and Error*, 2 vols, Jewish Publication Society of America, Philadelphia.
WHISTON, W., transl. (1906) Josephus . . . *The Works*. Translated . . . and Newly Edited by D. S. Margoliouth, Routledge, London.
WILENSKI, M., see Vilenski, M.
WIRSZUBSKI, C. (1971–2) Pico della Mirandola, in *Encyclopaedia Judaica*, 13, 500.
WISE, S. S. (1901) *The Improvement of Moral Qualities . . . by Solomon ibn Gabirol . . . Arabic . . . with a Translation* (Columbia University Oriental Studies, 1), Columbia University Press, New York.
ZOBEL, M., see Klatzkin (1928–30, 1968).
ZUCKERMANDEL, M. (1881) *Tosefta*, Fr. Lintz, Trier, Pasewalk.

5

Arabic linguistics

H. Fleisch

5.1 Introduction*

Arabic is the language of the Bedouins who led a nomadic life in the Arab desert (camel herders) or on its northern edges (sheep herders), especially in the fifth and sixth centuries AD. Arabic is a Semitic language, and therefore one should begin by placing it in context among other Semitic languages.

Semitic is divided into two large branches: East and West Semitic. East Semitic is the language of ancient Assyria and Babylonia, and was written in cuneiform characters; Western Semitic, after a period in which there were only dialects – Ugaritic, Amorite and, very probably, Eblaitic, when we shall know more about it – also divided into two branches: North-West Semitic, subdivided into Canaanite (Hebrew, Phoenician) and Aramaic (imperial Aramaic, Biblical Aramaic, Syriac, etc.), and South-West Semitic, subdivided into North Arabic – the language we shall be dealing with – and South Arabic, represented particularly by ancient Ethiopian (Geez).

On the divisons of Semitic see Fleisch (1947), table on p. 19, and Marcel Cohen, *Sémitique*, in the section 'Chamito-sémitique' by Cohen (1952, 98–148), or the concise table set out by B. Pottier (1973, 229).

The most ancient texts in Arabic writing are three graffiti on the wall of the temple of Ramm in the Sinai, which have been dated to about 300 AD (see Savignac and Horsfield 1935, 270 and Grimme 1936, 90–5 and the other references under the heading *'Arabiyya* in *E.I.* (1954–86), vol. I, 582). Other rare and brief inscriptions can be found later (see *ibid.*).

* See beginning of Notes.

This Arabic language arises, if we may put it like that, in the desert, particularly in the sixth century AD. It appears among the Arabs as a language of poetry, and it is a mature language. The poetry it expresses has its traditions, which seem to be well established. There was abundant production of poetry: one could mention the names of more than 80 pre-Islamic poets, by whom we have at least a few verses, scattered in various works in books on Adab (manners or etiquette) or in books of lexicography (see Nallino 1950, 37).

5.1.1 Poetry

The poet was a very important man in the tribe: he was its spokesman in the defense of honour, in praise and in satire. Praise: extolling the tribe, its chiefs, its ancestors, their recent and ancient deeds, their warlike qualities, their hospitality, their generosity. Satire: satire (*al-hiğā'*) of the tribe or of enemy tribes, in order to diminish and humiliate them by mentioning, in the most biting, most cutting terms, anything that could tarnish or destroy the enemy's honour, including even the most base insults. One must also consider the special character attributed to the poet: a man of special, extraordinary knowledge (he is the *šāʿir* 'the sage') in contact with the world of invisible powers, through a familiar genius who inspires him. Thus, the poet was a precious man for his tribe.

Poetry could be said to have been the Archive of the desert Arabs: 'it was a great register where their customs, their beliefs, their proverbs, their deeds were entered' (Nallino 1950, 63–4). The poet had a real social role in the tribe and among the Arabs. He was the journalist of his day, because every event, great or small, passed into poetry, and this was still happening in the Omayyad (661–750) period, for example among the K̲āriğite poets, who worked to exalt their sect (see Nallino 1950, 182–85).

5.1.2 Preservation of poetry

The poet, particularly a great poet, was surrounded by a small court of men who specialized in memorizing his compositions: these were *ruwāt* (sing. *rāwī*) 'reciters'. They repeated the poems in the camps, and ensured the poems would spread. The whole of Arab desert culture was oral, based on memorization, and even Muḥammad originally entrusted his Koran to his companions' memory. As for Arabic poetry, in later years Muslim philologists went to the tribes to collect *Dawāwīn* (collections of poetry) by famous ancient poets from the reciters; this is what Abū Saʿīd ʿAbd al-Malik al-Aṣmaʿi (who died in 216/831)[1] did in the collection called *al-Aṣmaʿiyyāt*.

Life was very hard for the Arabs in Arabia, a vast desert country of about three million square kilometres (Britain is only 230,000 square kilometres), where, with the exception of Yemen which benefits from the rains of the Indian monsoons, rainfall reaches a maximum of 100 mm of rain a year. Temperatures are high: summer averages are above 25°C everywhere, and can reach beyond 30°C and 35°C. In a country with such severe natural conditions, population density was very low and the Bedouins rarely managed to satisfy their hunger; they were undernourished,[2] infant mortality was very high and only strong children survived.

It is useful to place the Arabs in their natural context in the pre-Islamic age. Thus we shall better understand that we cannot expect a linguistic doctrine on its language from this people which was so intent on the reality of everyday survival. Naturally, they could tell the difference between a good poet and a mediocre one, or a bad one, but this was because of their simple linguistic feeling. There was as yet no theory of Arabic metrics; one knew what was or was not traditional only through usage.[3]

5.2 Classical Arabic

In order to derive vocabulary one does not proceed as one does in English, using a base and prefixes and suffixes, for example the base *work* from which one gets *work-er*, *work-able*, *un-work-able*, and so on. Classical Arabic is a triliteral language, that is the base of a word is a root consisting of three consonants, which has a general meaning. Words are formed by introducing vowels into this root. In this way, from the root *K t b*, by using the three Arabic long and short vowels *a*, *ā*, *i*, *ī*, *u*, *ū* (leaving aside the final vowel *a*: on this, see below, p. 174) one gets:

Katab-a 'has written' active verb with *a-a*
Kātab-a 'has written to someone' with *ā-a*
Kutib-a 'was written' so-called passive verb (but see Fleisch 1979, 239–49) with *u-i*
Kūtib-a passive of *Kātab-a*, with *ū-i* (see note above)
Kātib 'scribe' with *ā-i*
Kitāb 'book' with *i-ā*

Such a root does not exist in itself; it is a part of words that differ from each other, and its existence is shown by analysis; it has a true linguistic reality, a 'signifier', that is a given group of consonants, and a 'signified', the general idea connected to this group of consonants. Moreover, the speaker is aware of this linguistic reality, although it is not an explicit awareness. The Arab learned men identified the reality of the root very early: as we find in the *Kitāb al-ʿAyn* by al-K̲alīl b. Aḥmad, where the root is used to classify words.

5.2.1 The Koran

A very important event took place in Arabia in the seventh century: the preaching of Muḥammad, Prophet of the Arabs. This is not the place to describe how he managed to make his influence felt and to leave a holy Book, the Koran, to his followers for their instruction;[4] what we are interested to know is how the Muslim considered the Koran. 'From the beginning the *Ḳur'ān* had been considered as a sign (*'āyah*) or proof (*burhān*) of the prophecies of Muḥammad' (*EI* 1954–86, vol. V, 420). This is based on several verses of the Koran in which Muḥammad challenges his rivals to produce at least one sura like the one he was reciting, such as II, 23; V, 38; XI, 13; XVII, 88.[5] But since it is Allāh who speaks in the Koran, it was natural for Muslims to think that the Koran was the actual word of Allāh, as is said in sura IX, verse 6, a word as eternal as Allāh himself. Muslim thought on this point developed into two areas of thought: theology and philology.

5.2.2 Theology

Under the influence of Greek philosophy, which the Arabs had come to know, the theory of a Koran that was not eternal but created developed among the so-called Muʿtazilites (followers of the theological school which created the speculative dogmatics of Islam: see the entry *Muʿtazila* in *EI* 1908–38, vol. III, 787–93). It became the official doctrine when the ʿAbbāsid caliph al-Ma'mūn (786–833) imposed it as an article of faith. Its opponents were persecuted. Al-Ma'mūn's third successor, al-Mutawakkil, returned to the doctrine of orthodox theologians: the Koran is not created (see Massé (1930, 168–71), the entry *Ḳur'an* in *EI* (1954–86),[6] and also D. and J. Sourdel (1968, 75–6)).

5.2.3 Philology

H. Loucel (1963; 1964) studied the origin of language according to Arab grammarians. According to him, the Arab grammarians were not concerned with this problem before the fourth century of the Hegira (the beginning of the Muslim era, from the migration of the Prophet from Mecca to Medina in 622), when they reached the end of a slow evolution in thought. We can find an explicit doctrine in the works of Ibn Fāris:[7] the Koran, *Kalām Allāh*, 'Word of Allāh', was revealed in Arabic; however, the revelation did not take place all at once. The text is very clear on this point (Ibn Fāris 1963, 6, ll. 7–13; 1328/1919, 33, ll. 7–15). The English translation is as follows; for the Arabic text we refer the reader to our article in *Oriens* (Fleisch 1963, 135–6).

> Someone may think perhaps that the language which we have shown to be *tawqīf*[8] came uniquely in a single totality, on one occasion. Now it is not so; but Allāh (He is powerful and great) let Adam (salvation be upon him) know what He was pleased to teach him of things he needed to know in his days, and of these some spread according to the will of Allāh. After Adam (salvation be upon him), among the Arabs of the Prophets (the blessings of Allāh upon them), He taught, Prophet after Prophet, what He wished to teach, until his choice fell on our prophet Muḥammad (on him and on his family be the blessing and the salvation of Allāh) and Allāh (He is powerful and great) gave him entirely what He had given to no-one before him, more than he well (knew) of the earlier language, and so it ended. We have no knowledge of any language coming after him, and if someone nowadays tried to investigate this matter, he would find critics of Science who would tell him no and would contradict him.

In this way, therefore, the revelation of the Arab language reached perfection and its final limit with the Prophet Muḥammad. This is why we give *tawqīf*, in the complete expression *waḥy wa-tawqīf* which sums up doctrine, the meaning of 'limit', and translate this expression as 'closed revelation'.[9] On his part, Loucel (1963, 254) translates *tawqīf* as 'revealed definitiveness', and also (1963, 255–7) gives a full translation of chapter I of *Ṣāḥibī*, where Ibn Fāris explains the origin of the Arabic language by divine revelation; he also added the translation of chapter II on Arabic writing (1963, 257–69). Ibn Fāris claims that it is also *tawqīf*, that it was given to mankind by divine revelation. We shall not dwell on this point, but readers may see Loucel (1963, 259–61) if they wish.

Tawāḍuʿ wa-i ṣṭilāḥ, 'institution and convention'[10] are set against *waḥy wa-tawqīf*. These terms seem to appear suddenly with Ibn Fāris, but nevertheless he handles them easily, and does not seem to doubt that they are understandable. They had already become established in Arabic vocabulary, but since when? There is no answer to this question. This means that he had opponents who maintained that language (and likewise the Arabic language) did not come from divine revelation, but had a human origin.

There is clear evidence of opponents to the *tawqīf* in a work by Ibn Ǧinnī,[11] the *K̲aṣā'iṣ*.[12] This is a treatise on grammar of a particular kind, where one finds a constant concern to prove that, in the Arabic language, everything can be explained and has valid in the Arabic language, everything can be explained and has valid reasons. Therefore, this text goes beyond simple grammatical descriptions: it tackles the nature of language and of the Arabic tongue in vol. I, ch. VI, 40–7. The arguments of the two positions, *tawqīf* and *iṣṭilāḥ*, are set out and criticized: the first position is based mainly on a verse of the Koran (sura II, verse 31: 'And He gave Adam knowledge of all names'). Ibn Ǧinnī was strongly attracted by the second theory, and this may have caused confusion:[13] in actual fact he never took a decided stance (see I, 47, 14–16).

However, it must be noted that all these discussions between grammarians on the origin of language remained academic.[14] All the famous grammarians whose texts have been preserved worked in the belief that their Arabic language was due to divine revelation. Even in the grammatical works by Ibn Ǧinnī[15] there is no trace of the above-mentioned uncertainties.

5.3 The holy Book

We have examined Muslim ideas on the origin of language, or rather of the Arabic language, because they were interested only in this language, which came about through divine revelation. Why did they study their own language? In order to satisfy pressing needs, that is: (a) reciting their holy Book correctly; (b) understanding its text precisely; (c) being able to teach it to converts who were not Arabs.

First of all we must outline, even if only in brief, the situation of the Arabs after the conquests: they had an immense empire where people spoke different languages, and initially they behaved like an occupying force, restricting themselves to maintaining order and collecting taxes. Later, however, much of this empire underwent a process of Arabization, and a large number of 'Arabized' people had to learn their conqueror's language.

In this empire the Arabs created cities where they could live among themselves and find the tribal structure they were used to, such as Baṣrah, Kūfah in Mesopotamia, Fusṭāṭ in Egypt, then Qayrawān in Tunisia (and later Fās in Morocco).

Very soon these cities became centres for Arabic studies and for the spread of Arab culture, but they were soon enriched by foreign contributions as well.[16]

5.3.1 Reciting the Koran correctly

In the beginning the Book was preserved above all thanks to the fact that the faithful knew it by heart, then thanks to the reciters, the *Qurrā'*, who, despite everything, could not escape the influence of their own dialect. The vulgate attributed to the third Caliph, ʿUṯmān, ensured the preservation and the spread of the text. However, its still incomplete writing was to be completed with the living elements in the *Qurrā'*'s memory. It was not possible to eliminate a number of small variants in the reading of the text. Finally, the solution was found of accepting the reading according to the system of each of the Seven Readers who were recognized as orthodox, representing the authentic text.[17]

5.3.2 Understanding the text precisely

Before being able to teach the Koran to the converts, it was necessary first that the Arabs themselves should understand the text well, not just for the intellectual satisfaction of the individual, but also in order to codify religious doctrine, that is what should be believed, and to develop a legal code, that is all the rules that regulate the believer's religious, moral, civil and political life, since the Koran is the main source of the law.

5.3.3 Being able to teach the Koranic text and the Arab language correctly

It was necessary to teach the converts this book of Allāh, but it was also necessary to teach them to speak Arabic, and to speak it correctly. Thanks to the contacts with the Bedouins who lived in the empire, the majority of non-Arabs (whether converted to Islam or not) learned Arabic; but which Arabic? One can assume that if it was not true *ʿarabiyyah*, it was at least these Bedouins' dialect. But this was an Arabic which had lost the *'iʿrāb*, the desinential inflection.[18] Therefore, it was already a vernacular Arabic (on this subject, see Fleisch 1974, 21–3). So, very soon, in the cities, even those founded by the Arabs for themselves, the Arabized people were speaking an Arabic without *'iʿrāb*, an Arabic that was taking shape outside the *'iʿrāb* system. Some facts reported about Baṣrah and Kūfah by some authors of *Ahbār an-naḥwiyyīn* (al Marzubānī, as-Sīrafī, see Fleisch 1974, 23–4), are very illuminating about the linguistic situation in two great Arab cities.

The Arabs' general situation after settling the conquered territories forced them to study their own language in order to create a grammar; it was a vital necessity, both for understanding their Book and reciting it correctly, and for teaching the converts a correct Arabic, thus allowing them to become integrated into the culture which came from the desert, based on the Bedouins' Arabic, especially on their poetry. When one is driven by such a necessity, one finds the necessary means. Very soon a new kind of man, a technician of the Arabic language, the 'grammarian' (*an-Naḥwī*), was to emerge from the ranks of the men of the *Qirā'ah* (the *Qurrā'*).

5.4 The 'Grammarians'

The first 'grammarian' we know of, and also the oldest grammarian mentioned in the *Kitāb* (Book) by Sībawayhi, is ʿAbd Allāh b. Abī Isḥāq (d. 117/535–6). In his work we can see grammar becoming detached from the Koranic sciences and establishing itself as an autonomous discipline, with a method of its own. We do not know of any predecessors on this subject. It seems that he must be considered to be the creator of this science. He was a grammarian through and through, who attacked the poet al-Farazdaq, accusing him of not respecting *qiyās* (analogy), his grammarian's *qiyās*.[19] He died in very old age, when he was 88, which puts his birth about the year 30 of the Hegira. He was a *mawlā*, an Arabized man.

As a representative of the second generation of grammarians we can mention ʿĪsā b. ʿUmar at-Taqafī (d. 149/766). He, too, was a *mawlā*. It seems he was the first to produce a written version, though we must not forget Abū ʿAmr ibn al-ʿAlā', a man of immense knowledge, one of the Seven Readers, but a man who had more knowledge of vocabulary and poetry than of grammar. He was an Arab born in Meccah around the year 70, and died in 154/770.

The third generation included three first class grammarians: al-Kalīl (d. 175/791), an Arab from ʿUmān, the Iranian Sībawayhi (d. 177/793) and the *mawlā* Yūnus b. Ḥabīb (d. in 182/798). The result was the *Kitāb* by Sībawayhi. He had the great merit of producing a written version, which includes an important personal contribution, but his work depends on the work of many generations, especially his own, which was enlivened by al-Kalīl's strong personality. On the other hand, if one finds the early date of this *Kitāb* a little strange, one must remember the pressing need that drove the Arab world to give itself a grammar.

Grammarians were city-dwellers. Among all the ones we have mentioned, only Abū ʿAmr ibn al-ʿAlā and al-Kalīl were Arabs for whom *'iʿrāb* was spontaneous. The others were *mawālī*, Arabized men, who had learned vernacular Arabic and *'iʿrāb* as children, from masters in some *madrasah* (school, mainly for teaching the Koran). One should not be surprised at the fact that for them it was an addition to the spoken word. On the other hand, it is important to point out the Arabized *mawālī*'s important role in the creation of grammar.

The efforts of three earlier generations of grammarians were crowned by success: out of them emerged Sībawayhi's *Kitāb*. All the essential elements of the Arabic grammar are already codified in it. Sībawayhi died before he could use it in teaching; the book was taken up by al-Akfaš. Very soon the *Kitāb* had an increasing importance among the grammarians. With al-Mubarrad (d. 216/831) it became the starting point for every grammatical dispute. He made the *Kitāb* the base of the grammatical tradition in Baṣrah. After him, in Baghdad, the *Kitāb* was the object of such veneration that people came to call it *Qur'ān an-naḥw* (see Fleisch 1961, 34) 'The Koran of grammar'. Sībawayhi's *Kitāb* therefore had an enormous importance in the field of grammar, and it is the system of this book which the Arab world is still teaching today, though without naming it.

It is important to examine this *Kitāb* closely. The grammarian's task was to teach Arabic to those who did not know it or who did not know it well. We should not expect the *Kitāb* to be a 'historical' grammar. The Arabs did not have, and could not have, any notion of a work of this kind; grammatical facts are set out on the same static, rigid plane. The *Kitāb* is not a 'descriptive' grammar either, one which describes the way people actually speak, because this would have entailed describing the various different dialects or idioms spoken in Arabia, among the Arabs. This is not what the Muslim world was expecting. It needed a book to guide it, to explain the rules of correct language, in short, a 'normative' grammar. The *Kitāb* was precisely that book: it shows 'how one should speak'.[20] The result was a normalization of the Arabic language, which was so successful that it provided the Muslim world with a new instrument, a common cultural language in which a vast literature would be expressed: 'regular' Arabic, 'literary' Arabic, or 'classical' Arabic.

This normalization did not form a break with the past, but, on the contrary, made use of the best the past had to offer, the beautiful language of the Arabs, the artistic language which had been the means of expressing the poetry of the desert and the prose of the Koran. In the same way it provided a tool for studying, not only the Book of Islam, but also that ancient poetry which would continue to embody the ideal of culture in the Arabic-speaking world, and which would continue to be intensively practiced. It is possible, however, to reproach the grammarians for bringing about a too-rigid normalization, to the detriment of the flexibility of the old desert *'arabiyyah*. At any rate, this formalization produced a common cultural language, a written language learned in school; for everyday use there was a dialect. This written language was the means of expression of a vast literature in the Middle Ages, and at the present time, after several centuries of lethargy, the Arab countries are endeavouring to bring it back to its full vitality. A modern classical Arabic exists. Monteil (1960) has described its status, and Wehr (1961) has compiled its dictionary, translated into English, from the German third edition, by Milton Cowan.

We must now see 'how' these grammarians worked, and how they thought of their Arabic language.

5.5 Linguistic analyses of the grammarians

In the course of reflecting on their language, the grammarians divided the grammatical sciences into four main branches: *al-Luġah*, *at-Taṣrīf*, *an-Naḥw*, *al-Ištiqāq*.

Al-Luġah (lexicon) concerns vocabulary as such. It includes collecting the vocabulary, communicating it (*naql*), explaining it and registering it in lexicographical works.

At-Taṣrīf (morphology): the purpose of *tasrīf* is determining the 'Form' of the word (given by *luġah*), or, in Arabic terms, its *wazn* or *binā'* or *sīga*.[21]

Naḥw (syntax)[22] implies texts, or at least some Arabic language expressed in sentences; it studies *al-'i'rāb*, that is the variation of the different *ḥarakāt* (vowels) at the end of certain words (noun-adjectives and verb imperfect). In other words it studies the use of cases for noun-adjectives, and the use of moods for (imperfect) verbs; it is actually very similar to syntax. But *an-naḥw* presupposes a knowledge of all the final vowels of words, both the ones which are part of *'i'crāb* and those that are excluded (*al-binā'*), and therefore the knowledge of the system of *'i'rāb* (on *'i'rāb* see our article *I'rāb* in *EI* 1954–86).

Al-Ištiqāq (derivation) returns to examining the word as such, but approaches it from the point of view of its origin, in its *wazn*: '*uk̲id̲a min* . . .' 'derives from . . .' (see our article *Is̲h̲tiḳāḳ* in *EI* 1954–86).

For Arab grammarians therefore, grammatical research consisted of making the facts of language fit into the general structure of *taṣrīf* and *naḥw*.

Everything was considered from the point of view of *Taṣrīf*: vocabulary in the strict sense of the word, but also morphological formulations, including the verb: perfect, imperfect, imperative; each form of verb conjugation was dealt with in isolation, by itself, in order to draw the *mit̲āl* (morphological pattern) from it and thus make known its *ziyādah* (extra-radical elements). When saying 'everything' we except elements which are not included in the *taṣrīf*, namely: pronouns (personal, demonstrative and relative), which are outside the triliteral structure, with no readily analysable *miṯāl* and, moreover, *mabnī* (not subject to *'i'rāb* variation); *hurūf* 'particles' belonging to *binā'*, included in the exposition of *Naḥw*, and clearly everything which relates to *'i'rāb* and which is dealt with in *naḥw*. We must also mention that the Arab grammarians have set out two basic principles:

1. The *'i'rāb* system resides in the variability of word terminations betwen the vowels *-u*, *-a*, *-i* and zero-vowel. These four states are termed respectively *raf'*, *naṣb*, *ğarr*, and *ğazm*; a word in one of these states is *marfū'*, *manṣūb*, *mağrūr*, or *mağzūm*; the factor which determines the use of the appropriate state is a *rāfi'*, *nāṣib*, *ğarr* or *ğāzim*.[23] *Raf'* and *naṣb* can occur in both nouns and imperfect verbs; *ğarr* is proper only to nouns, and *ğazm* only to imperfect verbs.

2. *Binā'* is the antithesis of *'i'rāb*, and means that the termination of the word (whether that be one of the three vowels or zero-vowel) is not subject to any variability at all; this is typical of the perfect verb and of particles. A noun of this kind is *mabnī*, and it can be further categorized as *mabnī 'alā ḍ-ḍamm* (terminating in *-u*), *'alā l-fatḥ* (-*a*), *'alā l-kasr* (-*i*), or *'alā s-sukūn* (no vowel).

Phonetic units, on the other hand, were considered by Arab grammarians to belong to a single class: the *ḥarf* (pl. *ḥurūf*).[24] The Arabic alphabet comprises only *ḥurūf*. *Ḥarakāt* are not *ḥurūf*.[25] *Ḥurūf almadd* 'letters of prolongation' show the continuation of the sound *a* for *'alif layyina* (soft *'alif*),[26] of the sound *i* for *yā'*, of the sound *u* for *wāw*. *Ḥarakāt*, vowels, are essentially deficient: they cannot stand by themselves, they need the support of a *ḥarf*. And a *ḥarf* must also be immediately preceded, or followed, by a *ḥarakah* in order to be able to exist: thus an initial consonant group is not acceptable in Arabic, one must put a vowel in front of it: one says *'Ifranğ* for Frank, *'Aflatūn* for Plato. For more details on the concept of *ḥarakah* see Fleisch (1961, 204–5, 231–3). The concept of a vowel in isolation is unknown to Arab grammarians.[27]

In their analyses the Arab grammarians had only this notion of *ḥarakah* to designate what modern phonetics calls 'vowel'. They did not recognize the length of vowels.[28] They built a whole system of metrics which, for a language like Arabic, is based on quantity, with no mention of either long or short sounds. They analysed the metres of desert poetry taking into account the succession of *ḥarakāt* and *sukūn* (silence, absence of *ḥarakah*). It is a complicated but effective system, which was invented by the philologist al-Ḵalīl (see note 3).

As for the verb, the second fundamental principle the grammarians formulated was opposed to its *'i'rāb*. The difficulty about the imperfect was avoided by resorting to another principle, which is important in the Arab grammarians' procedure: similarity allows one word to act like the one it resembles and within the extent of the similarity.[29] This principle is well applied here: the Arab grammarians have postulated the existence of close similarity between the imperfect and the agent noun *fā'il*.[30] The imperfect, *qua* verb, has no right to have *'i'rāb*, but gains it as *far'*, 'branch', thanks to its similarity and by reason of this similarity. This is why it has been called *muḍāri'*, 'that which is similar' (to *ism fā'il* an 'agent noun').

We now have the elements for examining the work of Arab grammarians in the way they applied the *taṣrīf* to the Arabic language. The purpose of *taṣrīf*, as we have said, is to determine the form of a word. In practice this meant essentially distinguishing, for all words which could be analysed, the *ḥurūf 'uṣūl* (what we call the root), their *ḥarakāt* and their *sukūn* and anything else that could be added, indicated by the word *az-ziyādah*, 'addition', to effect a representation of the whole (*tamṯīl*, the process of determining the *miṯāl* – see above), by means of *ḥurūf* of the root *f.'.l* (meaning 'do'), which take the place of *ḥurūf uṣūl*, and so form its *miṯāl*.[31]

We mentioned earlier the analysis of the verb. Here is what we can say:

5.5.1 The perfect tense: *al-māḍī*

In forming the various *amṯila* (sing. *miṯāl*) of the first and second person, the Arab grammarians recognized among their suffixes the addition of a *ḍamīr* (personal pronoun) (az-Zamaḵšarī 1879, § 161), and we agree with them.

In the case of the third person also they saw a *ḍamīr* in the perfect tense suffixes: *tā'* for the f. sing. of *fa'ala-t*, *wāw* for the m. pl. of *fa'al-ū*, *nūn* for the f. pl. of *fa'alna*, *'alif* for the two duals *fa'al-ā* and *fa'alat-ā* (az-Zamaḵšarī 1879, § 161). These are really marks of gender and number. As for the third person m. sing. *fa'al-a* the Arab grammarians in Baṣrah considered it *mabnī 'alā l'fatḥ* (Sībawayhi 1881, 2, l. 22–3; az-Zamaḵšarī 1879, § 403; Ibn Ya'īš 1882–6, 914, p. 3 ff.; Ibn Mālik 1888, verse 19; Ibn 'Aqīl 1951, I, 34, l. 6–7). The *fatḥ* it receives is the only result of the lack of similarity of the *māḍi* to the noun. As for *ḍamīr*: whether one says *qāma* 'he has got up' or *qāma Zaydun* 'Zeid has got up', no *ḍamīr* is expressed, but the third person m. sing. is implied (*mustatir*, 'veiled', 'intentional') in the verbal form *qāma* (az-Zamak̲šarī 1879, § 160).

5.5.2 The imperfect: *al-muḍāri'*

The imperfect is full of complications in the analysis of the Arab grammarians:

'a-f'al-u	1st sing.	:	*ziyādah* of *'alif*
na-f'al-u	1st pl.	:	*ziyādah* of *nūn*
ta-f'al'u	2nd m. sing.	:	*ziyādah* of *tā'*
ya-f'al-u	3rd m. sing.	:	*ziyādah* of *yā'*

The final vowel *-u* belongs to the *'i'rāb*. As for the prefixes (*'alif*, *nūn*, *tā'*, *yā'*) 'they are called the four *zawā'id*' (non radical consonants) (az-Zamak̲šarī 1879, § 404). They are ancient elements in the grammatical tradition: they are found already in the *Kitāb* by Sībawayhi (1881, 2, l. 5); they are considered a peculiarity of the *muḍāri*, which receives them in the initial position.[32] Their use is stated later, modelled on this formal analysis (az-Zamak̲šarī 1879, § 404).[33]

ta-f'al-ī-na	2nd f. sing.	*ta-f'al-ū-na*	2nd m. pl.
ta-f'al-ā-ni	2nd dual	*ya-f'al-ū-na*	3rd m. pl
ya-f'al-ā-ni	3rd m. dual	*ta-f'al-āni*	3rd f. dual

Tā' and *yā'* prefixes are, as above, two of the four *zawā'id*. But they are not *ziyādah* for the suffixes *-ī-*, *-ū-*, *-ā-*, as they are for *fa'al-ū* and *fa'al-ā* of the *māḍī*. Though the Arab grammarians have seen *ḍamā'ir* (pl. of *ḍamīr*), personal pronouns, in these suffixes (az-Zamak̲šarī 1879, § 406), they are actually *also* marks of gender or number (in the perfect they are *only* this). This wrong interpretation is an idea that still survives, and is still widespread in the field of teaching in the present Arab world, both for *māḍī* and for *muḍāri*; see, for example, R. aš-Šartūnī (1961, § 225).

5.5.3 The energetic mood

The so-called energetic mood (which would better be called 'emphatic') is formed on the imperfect, but it has been seen by the Arab grammarians as a particle, a *ḥarf*, the *nūn at-tawkīd* (*n* of emphasis) (Ibn Ya'īš 1882–6, 919, p. 19). For this reason they tackle the energetic mood in the section concerning the particles, like az-Zamakšarī (1879) in *Mufaṣṣal*, part 3, 'On the *ḥurūf*' (§§ 610–14). In Sībawayhi's *Kitāb* (1881–9) it is found in ch. 402–7.

In front of this *nūn* (which may be *kafīfa* 'light' (*-n*), or *taqīla* 'heavy' (*-nna*)), the verb is *mabnī 'alā l-fatḥ*: *mabnī* describes a word having no *'i'rāb*, syntactically determined variants; but it will of course then end in an invariable *-a, -u, -i* or a consonant, and is said to be *mabnī 'alā l-fatḥ/l-ḍamm/l-kasr/s-sukun* (Sībawayhi 1881, 5, l. 6). For example: *hal taḍriba-n, hal taḍriba-nna* 'do you really knock?'. This *binā'* (quality of being *mabnī*) holds true when this *nūn* is added directly onto the *muḍāri'*, but if the dual's *alif* (*hal taḍribā-nni*), the plural's *wāw* (*hal taḍribū-nna*), or the feminine singular's *yā* (*hal taḍribī-nna*) intervene, then there will be *'i'rāb* (Ibn 'Aqīl 1951, I, 35 end, and 36, for verses 19–20 of the *Alfiyya*: see also Ibn Mālik 1967, 216, l. 11 ff.).

5.5.4 The imperative: *al-'amr*

The imperative *if'al, if'il, uf'ul* is *mabnī'alā s-sukūn*. This is the doctrine of the grammarians in Baṣrah, as opposed to that of the grammarians in Kūfah, who considered it *mu'rab mağzūm*, subjected to the *ğazm* variety of *'i'rāb* (see the seventy-second question debated in the *K. al-Inṣāf* by Ibn al Anbārī 1913). Grammarians in Baṣrah argued from the following two fundamental principles (*ibid.*, 217, l. 14–15). 'The base (*al-'aṣl*), in verbs is that they should be *mabniyyah*'. 'The base (*al-'aṣl*), in the *binā'* is that it should be *'alā s-sukūn*'. Now, one can find no similarity between imperative and noun, such as to confer any *'i'rāb* on it. Therefore, it must remain on its base (*'aṣl*), as a verb, i.e. it must remain *mabnī* and on the *'aṣl fī l-binā'*, i.e. *mabnī 'alā s-sukūn* (*ibid.*, 217, l. 15–16, see also 220, l. 1–2 and 10–11).

Grammarians in Baṣrah defended the imperative's autonomy (*ibid.*, 224, l. 19) as against grammarians from Kūfah. The latter basically presented the imperative *if'al* as a reduction, due to frequency of use, of a base form *li-taf'al*[34] with the *lām al'amr wa-ldu'ā'*, the *li-* which is prefixed to a command or exortation or aspiration, and the *tā'*, second person imperfect prefix (*ibid.*, 214, l. 21–3 and 215, l. 1). The imperative, therefore, is not thought to be an original form, but one that is only separated from the *muḍāri'* by accident.

The imperative (which is *mabnī 'alā s-sukūn*) is specific to the second person m. sing.: *if'al, if'il, uf'ul*. The other persons, second f. sing., f. pl., dual, receive a suffix, respectively: *-ī, -na, -ū, -ā*, which the Arab grammarians also saw as a *ḍamīr*, a personal pronoun, as earlier in the case of *yā* in *taf 'al-ī-nu*, *nūn* in *fa'al-na*, *yaf ʿal-na*, *wāw* in *faʿal-ū*, *yaf-ʿal'-ū-na*, *tafʿal-ū-na* and it is appropriate to view it from the Arab point of view, as before: *binā'* of the verb before *nūn* (*-na*), *'iʿrāb* with the other three: *-ī-*, *-ū-*, *-ā-*.

After this presentation of the analysis of the verb according to the Arab grammarians, it is easy to understand why they did not speak of conjugations, voices, or moods. These terms are absent from their grammatical terminology. Their interest lay elsewhere: they had no other purpose than to apply to each verbal form, taken in isolation, the procedures of *taṣrīf* and to integrate its result in their system of *'iʿrāb*. The result could only be fundamentally inorganic.

This purely formal analysis, without any other unity than that bestowed by the very loose structures of *taṣrīf* (*ḥurūf 'uṣūl* + *ziyādah*), loaded down with all the problems (which in such a situation are inevitable) of *'iʿrāb* and of *binā'*, not to mention the introduction of all these *ḍamā'ir*, is distracting and tiring for a mind formed in the European tradition. But one should not criticize the Arab grammarians for what they were not; one should judge them in the context of what they wished to be. When considered on its own terms, their analysis proves to be a model study, diligent, conscientious, thorough in its smallest detail, concerned with justifying any statement that could be contested. This analysis shows a mentality, a way of considering grammar, which still deeply imbues ideas in the Arab world today.

The *naḥw* deals with the *ʿawāmil* (governing elements) determining the *'iʿrāb* in the variation of *ḥarakāt* at the end of words. But what kind of action do these *ʿawāmil* take, that they should place these final elements in the state of *marfūʿ* (*manṣūb*, *mağrūr*) for the noun only, and of *marfūʿ* (*manṣūb*, *mağzūm*) for the verb? The mere presence of a certain governing *ʿāmil* (pl. *ʿawāmil*) before a noun or before a *muḍāriʿ* is enough to make it a *ʿāmil lafẓī* ('formal'). This one looks for material contacts between words, and these contacts are the *ʿilal* ('the causes') of the variation of *ḥarakāt*. The following is a typical example: *'an in-nāṣibah*, '*'an* which puts into *naṣb*'. When this *'an* is found before a *muḍāriʿ*, this is *manṣūb*, simply because it is immediately preceded by *'an*. Another example shows clearly the intentions of the Arab grammarian towards *fāʿil* 'the agent' which is *marfūʿ*. Why is it *marfūʿ* (i.e. provided with *-u*)? az-Zamak̲šarī (1879, § 20) answers: 'what is proper to it, is the *rafʿ*, and its *rāfiʿ* is what leans on it'. The *rāfiʿ* is what puts into *rafʿ*, and the *ʿāmil* (*regens*) that is sought is the governor of the *marfūʿ*. This governor is the verb, which leans on the *marfūʿ* noun. It is hence often said that the form of the noun is occasioned by the simple fact of the *isnād*, the 'leaning' of the verb on it.

5.6 Greek influences

Throughout this process there is nothing to remind us of Greek thought. Nevertheless, people maintained that there was some Greek influence on the Arabs in the study of their own language. To begin with, Merx (1889, ch. IV) believed that the Arabs had received some elements of Aristotelian logic: their tripartite division of 'parts of speech (*ism*, noun, *fiʿl*, verb, *ḥarf*, particle); the distinction of the genders into masculine and feminine; the concept of *ḥāl* 'state'; the temporal notions of present, past, future; the notions of *fāʿil*, *fiʿl*, *mafʿūl* –all, according to Merx, developed under the influence of this Greek logic. These are general categories which existed in contemporary thought, and we have seen how the Arab grammarians worked within these general categories.

Versteegh (1977) has returned to the question of Greek influence on the Arab grammarians; he states that Greek grammar was used as a model and as a starting point for the Arab grammarians (A 15, l. 27). We can reply that Versteegh has neglected the first Arab grammarian, ʿAbd Allāh b. Abī Isḥāq. He died in 117 of the Hegira, i.e. sixty years before Sībawayhi (d. 177). His date of birth therefore can be placed between 30 and 40 of the Hegira. He lived a long time, even if we are not obliged to accept the eighty years al-Qifṭī (1950–5, II, 107, l. 12) attributes to him. He was a true grammarian, who already had a terminology and a *qiyās* (system of arguing from analogy): see references in Fleisch (1979, 506). Sībawayhi quotes him seven times (see *ibid.*).

During the reign of ʿAbd al-Malik (66–87 of the Hegira), ʿAbd Allāh was, therefore, in his mature years. The Arabs were engaged in the great sweep of conquest. Their concern was to occupy the conquered areas, to keep them, enlarge them and, above all, to ensure the collection of taxes. There was no question of acculturation. How is it possible to conceive in such a political and social context 'the direct, personal contact with living Greek education and with grammar, in the recently conquered Hellenistic countries' (VIII, l. 16–18)? On the other hand, how can Versteegh see a clear resemblance between Arabic and Greek grammar in their categorization, when we can see that Arabic grammar adopts a tripartite division (*ism*, *fiʿl*, *ḥarf*) and that the Greek grammarians recognized those other parts of speech which have come to us through the Latin grammarians?

However, one must recognize that very soon the Arabs started to take an interest in the Greek sciences: arithmetic, geometry, medicine. The name of K̲ālid b. Yazīd is mentioned, but his importance has been overestimated: see the study by Manfred Ullmann (1978) which restores him to just proportions.

The Arabs were interested in those Greek sciences because they did not impinge on the Arabs' own cultural heritage. They had an instinctive repugnance for the Greek approach in those that did impinge. They knew Aristotle's *Poetics*, in translation, but they remained attached to the desert lyric, which belonged to their tradition. In the days of Hārūn ar-Rašīd modern poetry with, for example, Abū Nuwās and some others, introduced new themes, but the Arabs were not faithful to such themes, and returned to the models of Bedouin poetry. They knew Aristotle's *Rhetoric* in translation; they created a rhetoric in Arabic (the art of *Bayān*), but this developed on rather different lines.

As we have seen the Koran was the word of Allāh. Grammar was a sacred science. How could the Arabs ask outsiders to Islam, *kuffār* (impious people), to provide the means for studying their own language? The general concepts mentioned above were able to be adopted and used because they had lost their foreign character and were available to everyone. On the other hand, we can see how vain it is to look in the works of Arab grammarians for any anticipation of modern linguistics, structuralism or the like, which were all completely outside the scope of their ideas.

Notes

* The English translation was prepared after the death of the author. I am grateful to Professor A. F. L. Beeston who generously provided me with suggestions for emendations and clarifications, which I have incorporated into the text and added in the form of notes within square brackets marked 'Ed.'. The conventions used in the transcriptions are as follows: underlinings for fricatives: *ṯ* [*θ*], *ḏ* [*ð*], *ḵ* [*x*]; subscript points for velarized sounds: *ṭ* [t^{γ}], *ḍ* [d^{γ}], *ṣ* [s^{γ}], *ẓ* [z^{γ}]; but *ḥ* is a voiceless fricative pharyngeal [ħ], and ʿ its voiced counterpart [ʕ]; *g* is a voiced velar fricative [*γ*]; ʾ is a glottal stop [ʔ]; *q* is a voiceless uvular plosive [q].

1. The double dates give the year of the Christian era and the year of the Muslim era. The latter begins from AD 622 and has lunar years of 354 and 355 days. Abū Saʿid ʿAbd al-Malik al-Aṣmaʿi was born in Baṣrah, of Arab origin, he taught in Baṣrah; he was called to Baghdad by the Caliph Hārūn ar-Rašīd as tutor for his son, the future Caliph al-Amīn.
2. See Marçais (1961, 6) on hunger among the Bedouins in Arabia and the consequences he attributes to it.
3. This theory of Arabic metrics was developed much later by al-Ḵalīl b. Aḥmad al-Farahīdī, a learned philologist of Arab origin (from ʿUmān), who lived in Baṣrah, where he died in 176/791.
4. More details can be easily found in Massé (1930, 4, 7, 30), or in Sourdel and Sourdel (1968, 34–8).
5. This was the starting point of the doctrine of *Iʿǧaz* 'inimitability (of

the Koran)'. We cannot examine this aspect of Muslim thought here, see in *EI* (1954–86) the entry *Iʿdjāz*.

6. *Al-Kuran*, in *EI* (1954–86), vol. V, 400–29, by A. T. Welch. This article provides information on everything concerning the Koran. As far as our theme is concerned, see section H 'The Koran in Moslem life and thought' (428–9), with ample bibliography; or see the critical bibliography by Sourdel and Sourdel (1968, 637–8), which is shorter but more practical.
7. Ibn Fāris was an Iranian lexicographer. He lived in Hamadān, where he taught with great success. He was Mağd ad-Dawlah Ibn Buwayh's tutor, and according to the generally accepted date, he died in Rayy in 395/1004. See the entry *Ibn Fāris* in *EI* (1954–86).
8. [There is an untranslatable wordplay in *tawqīf*. It is (a) the noun of the verb which in the next sentence is used about God 'teaching' Adam, and it is more likely that this lies behind the binomial expression 'inspiration' (*waḥy*) and *tawqīf* = 'divinely inspired teaching', than that it should there have its other sense, (b) 'bringing to a stop', i.e. definitiveness, discussed below. Ed.]
9. See our article in *Oriens* (Fleisch 1963, 37) where the meaning of the *tawqīf* is discussed.
10. See the explanation of these two terms provided by Loucel (1963, 254–5).
11. Abū l-Fatḥ ʿUṯmān Ibn Ğinnī, philologist, born in Mosul in 330/941, the son of a Byzantine slave. He taught in Baghdad, where he became very famous, and died there in 392/1002.
12. *al-Kaṣāʾis*, new ed. (Ibn Ğinnī, 1952–6). H. Loucel used the old edition, which is incomplete and carelessly edited, Cairo 1330/1912.
13. See H. Fleisch (1961, 32, n. 2).
14. Unlike what happened among theologians. See what has been said above.
15. Both in *al-Munṣif* (1954) and in *Mukṯaṣar at-taṣrīf al-mulūkī*, published in Leipzig with a Latin translation (1885).
16. On the situation in Baṣrah see Pellat (1953, 21–42) and Fück (1955, 12–14); on Kūfah, *ibid.*, 14–15.
17. These are: Nāfiʿ, Ibn Kaṯīr, Abū ʿAmr Ibn al-ʿAlāʾ, Ibn ʿĀmir, ʿĀṣim ibn Abī n-Nağūd, Ḥamzah ibn Ḥabīb, al-Kisāʾī. On these men, see Blachère (1959, 118–21). The edition of the Koran published in Cairo in 1342/1923 under the patronage of the King of Egypt Fuad I follows the reading in ʿĀṣim (see *ibid.*, 134–5).
18. [The system of vowels (mostly short, but in a few cases long) at the end of a word, which vary according to the syntactic position of the word in the sentence. Ed.]
19. To shut him up, al-Farazdaq composed a satirical text against him outside the tradition of *qiyās*, which is preserved in the grammatical tradition (see Fleisch 1961, 27).
20. This has been set out very clearly by Reuschel (1959, 15).
21. [The grammarians use *bināʾ* in two very different senses, (a) as here, overall morphological pattern of a word; (b) as appears later, p.

174, it is also the quality of being without *'i'rāb* (syntactically determined variation in the termination of a word; *wazn* is used in prosody, alluding to the 'metrical value' of a word; *sīġah* 'mould' is also used, but not so frequently as *binā'*. Ed.]

22. [In ordinary non-technical language, this means 'a direction', but no plausible explanation has ever been produced for how it came to be used as a grammatical term for something very similar to 'syntax'. Ed.]
23. [*Ğazm* 'cutting off' is easily understandable as a formal description of absence of vowel; *ğarr* 'trailing' is a functional term due to the fact that the *mağrūr* is mostly a dependent genitive; but nobody has yet produced a convincing explanation for the other two terms. Ed.]
24. [The term *ḥarf* has two distinct meanings. Up to here it has been used for the word class of particles. In the present, phonological, context, it is a consonant. Ed.]
25. [*ḥarakāt* are graphically expressed by marks placed above or below the alphabetic (consonantal) letters. Ed.]
26. [The alphabetic letter *alif* serves two functions, (a) as here, a 'continuant' of the vowel *a*, (b) as a graphic 'support' (*'imād*) for a symbol noting the consonantal glottal stop. Ed.]
27. *marfū'* noun of the patient of the verb *rafa'a* 'to put into *raf'*', state of the noun or of the *muḍāri'* (imperfect) whose graphic sign is the *ḍammah* (final *-u*); *manṣūb* noun of the patient of the verb *naṣaba* 'to put into *naṣb*', state of the noun or of the *muḍāri'* (imperfect) whose graphic sign is the *fatḥaḥ* (final *-a*).
28. [In fact, they analysed what we call a 'long vowel' as a short vowel plus a phoneme of length, graphically noted by one of the 'letters of prolongation', as explained above. Ed.]
29. This principle was applied to *wāw* and *yā*; *mutaḥarrikah* 'provided with a *ḥarakah*', see Fleisch (1961, s. 42, 205).
30. See Fleisch (1961, 6, note 2), on the way in which Arab grammarians considered the elements of this similarity.
31. The Arab grammarians spoke of *miṯāl*, in the practice of *Taṣrīf*, when they sought a representation of the word by means of *ḥurūf* of *fa'ala*.
32. And that is what the name *ḥurūf al-muḍāra'ah* derives from.
33. *'af'alu*, for *al-mutakallim* (first person); *naf'alu*, for *al-mutakallim* if one or more others are with him; *taf'alu*, for *al-mukāṭab* (second person) and *al-ġā'ibah* (third person, feminine); *yaf'alu*, for *al-ġā'ib* (third person masculine).
34. [*li-taf'al*, if understood as a second person (and not as a third person feminine) should probably be starred as a hypothetical form. The strictly classical language requires positive commands to be phrased exclusively by the imperative (*'if'al*, 'Do!'). But modern writers employ the form as an optative, as in *li-taḏhab 'ilā ğahannam*, 'May you go to hell!' on the analogy of the third person *li-yaḏhab*, 'May he go', and beside the imperative *'iḏhab 'ilā ğahannam*, 'Go to hell!' Ed.]

Bibliography

BLACHÈRE, R. (1959) *Introduction au Coran*, 3 vols, Adrien-Maisonneuve, Paris.

COHEN, M. (1952) *Les langues du monde*, new edition, Champion, Paris.

EI (1908–38) *The Encyclopedia of Islām*, Brill, Leiden/Luzac, London.

EI (1954–86) *The Encyclopedia of Islam, New Edition*, Brill, Leiden/Luzac, London.

FLEISCH, H. (1947) *Introduction à l'étude des langues sémitiques*, Adrien-Maisonneuve, Paris.

FLEISCH, H. (1961) *Traité de philologie arabe*, vol. I, Imprimerie catholique, Beyrouth.

FLEISCH, H. (1963) Observations sur les études philologiques en arabe classique, *Oriens*, 16, 134–44.

FLEISCH, H. (1974) *Études d'arabe dialectal*, Dār El-Machreq, Beyrouth.

FLEISCH, H. (1979) *Traité de philologie arabe*, vol. II, Dār El-Machreq, Beyrouth.

FÜCK, J. W. (1955) *ʿArabīya. Recherches sur l'histoire de la langue et du style arabe*, French trans. by Cl. Denizeau, 2 vols, Didier, Paris.

GRIMME, H. (1936) À propos de quelques graffites du temple de Ramm, *Revue Biblique*, 45, 90–5.

IBN AL-ANBĀRĪ (1913) Abū-l-Barakāt ʿAbd ar-Raḥmān b. Muḥ. b. Abī Saʿīd, *Kitāb al-Inṣāf fī masāʾil al-hilāf bayna an-naḥawiyyīn al baṣriyyīn wa l-kūfiyyīn*, ed. by G. Weil, Brill, Leiden.

IBN ʿAQĪL (1951) Bahāʾ ad-Dīn ʿAbdallāh, *Šarḥ Ibn ʿAqīl ʿalā Alfiyyat Ibn Mālik*, sixth edition by Muḥ. Muḥyī d-Dīn ʿAbd al Ḥamīd, Cairo, 1370/1951.

IBN FĀRIS (1963) Abū-l-Ḥusayn Aḥmad, *aṣ-Ṣāhibī fī fiqh al-luġa wa-sunan al-ʿarab fī kalāmihā*, ed. by Muṣṭafā aš-Šuwaymī, Badran, Bayrut, 1382/1963 (Cairo ed. 1328/1919).

IBN ĞINNĪ (1952–6) Abū-l-Fatḥ ʿUṯmān, *al-Ḵaṣāʾis*, ed. by Muḥammad ʿAlī an-Naǧǧār, Maṭba ʿat Dār al-Kutub al-Miṣriyya [Cairo], vol. I, 1371/1952; vol. II 1374/1955; vol. III 1376/1956.

IBN ĞINNĪ (1885) *Muḵtaṣar at-taṣrīf al-mulūkī*, ed. by G. Hoberg, with Latin Trans., Brockhaus, Leipzig.

IBN ĞINNĪ (1954) *al-Munṣif, Šarḥ li-Kitāb at-Taṣrīf*, by Abū ʿUṯmān al-Māzinī, ed. by Ibrāhīm Muṣṭafā and ʿAbdallāh Amīn, vols I–III, Muṣṭafā al-Bābī al-Ḥalabī, bi Miṣr [Cairo].

IBN MĀLIK (1888) Abū ʿAbdallāh Muḥammad aṭ-Ṭāʾī al-Ğayyānī, *al-Alfiyya*, French trans. and ed. by A. Goguyer, *La Alfiyya d'Ibnu-Mālik*, Imprimerie des Belles Lettres, Beyrouth.

IBN MĀLIK (1967) *Tashīl al-Fawāʾid wa takmīl al-maqāṣid*, ed. by Muḥ. Kāmil Barakāt, Dār al-Kātib al-ʿArabī li-ṭ-Ṭibāʿah wa-n-Našr, Cairo, 1387/1967.

IBN YAʿĪŠ (1882–6) Abū-l-Baqāʾ Muwaffaq ad-Dīn, *Kitāb Šarḥ al-Mufaṣṣal li-l-Zamaḵšarī*, ed. by G. Jahn, Brockhaus, Leipzig, vol. I, 1882, vol. II, 1886.

KORAN (1923) Edition published in Cairo in 1342/1923 under the patronage of King Fuad I, Maktabah wa maṭba'at al-Šīmī, Cairo.

LOUCEL, H. (1963; 1964) L'origine du langage d'après les grammairiens arabes, *Arabica*, 10 (1963), 188–208 and 253–81; 11 (1964), 57–72 and 151–87.

MARÇAIS, W. (1961) *Articles et conférences*, postumous edition by Georges Marçais, Adrien-Maisonneuve, Paris.

MASSÉ, H. (1930) *L'Islam* (Collection Armand Colin), Colin, Paris.

MERX, A. (1889) *Historia artis grammaticae apud Syros* (Abhandlungen für die Kunde des Morgenlandes), Brockhaus, Leipzig.

MONTEIL, V. (1960) *L'arabe moderne*, Klincksieck, Paris.

NALLINO, C. A. (1950) *La littérature arabe des origines à l'époque de la dynastie umayyade*, Adrien-Maisonneuve, Paris.

PELLAT, C. (1953) *Le milieu basrien dans la formation d'al-Ǧāḥiẓ*, Adrien-Maisonneuve, Paris.

POTTIER, B. (ed.) (1973) *Le langage* (Dictionnaires du savoir moderne), Centre d'étude et de promotion de la lecture, Paris.

AL-QIFṬĪ (1950–5) *Inbāh ar-ruwāt 'alā anbāh an-nuḥāt*, ed. by Muḥ Abūl-Faḍl Ibrāhīm, 4 vols, Maṭba'at Dār al-Kutub al-miṣriyya, Cairo.

REUSCHEL, W. (1959) *Al-Ḫalīl Ibn Aḥmad der Lehrer Sībawaihs, als Grammatiker*, Akademie-Verlag, Berlin.

SAVIGNAC, M.-R., HORSFIELD, G. (1935) Le temple de Ramma, *Revue Biblique*, 44, 245–78.

AŠ-ŠARTŪNĪ (1961) *Mabadi' al-'arabiyya*, IV, 9th edition, Al-maṭba'ah al-Kāṯūlikiyyah, Bayrut.

SĪBAWAYHI (1881–9) Abū Bišr 'Amr b. 'Uṯmān, *al-Kitāb*, ed. by H. Derenbourg, Imprimerie nationale, Paris, I 1881, II 1889.

SOURDEL, D. and SOURDEL, J. (1968) *La civilisation de l'Islam classique*, Arthaud, Paris.

ULLMANN, M. (1978) Ḫālid ibn Yazīd und die Alchimie: eine Legende, *Der Islam*, 55, 181–218.

VERSTEEGH, C. H. J. (1977) *Greek Elements in Arabic Linguistic Thinking*, Brill, Leiden.

WEHR, H. (1961) *A Dictionary of Modern Written Arabic*, ed. by. J. Milton Cowan, Harrassowitz, Wiesbaden.

AZ-ZAMAKŠARĪ (1879) Abū-l-Qāsim Maḥmūd b. 'Umar, *Kitāb al-Mufaṣṣal fīn-naḥw*, ed. by J. P. Broch, Libraria P. T. Mallingii, Christiania.

Index